The
British
Psychological
Society

British Journal of **Educational Psychology**
Monograph Series II: Psychological Aspects of Education - Current Trends

Number 6

Teaching and Learning Writing

Edited by
Vincent Connelly (Oxford Brookes University, UK)
Anna L. Barnett (Oxford Brookes University, UK)
Julie E. Dockrell (Institute of Education, UK)
Andrew Tolmie (Institute of Education, UK)

British Journal of Educational Psychology

'Psychological Aspects of Education – Current Trends'
Monograph Series

The *British Journal of Educational Psychology* hosts a series of annual conferences in the UK on psychological aspects of education where world-leading researchers provide inputs on the latest cutting-edge advances within their fields. The conferences are free of charge and the papers are published in a corresponding series of edited monographs.

No.1- **Learning and Teaching Reading**

No.2- **Development and Motivation – Joint Perspectives**

No.3- **Pedagogy – Teaching for Learning**

No.4- **Student Learning and University Teaching**

No.5- **Learning through Digital Technologies**

No.6- **Learning and Teaching Writing**

Cost: £15 (£40 for libraries/institutions)
To order, please contact the Commercial Sales Department, The British Psychological Society, St Andrews House, 48 Princess Road East, Leicester, LE1 7DR. Tel: +44 (0)116 252 9551, Fax: +44 (0)116 247 0787, email: sales@bps.org.uk or order online: www.bps.org.uk/bjepmonographs.

FORTHCOMING MONOGRAPH
Understanding Number Development
2010

Published in 2009 by The British Psychological Society, St Andrews House, 48 Princess Road East, Leicester LE1 7DR, UK.

ISSN 1476-9808 Monograph Series II: Psychological Aspects of Education - Current Trends
ISBN: 978-1-85433-490-9 Learning and Teaching Writing

www.bps.org.uk
Typeset by Alden Prepress Services, India
Printed in Great Britain by Cambrian Printers, Aberystwyth

Contents

The British Psychological Society

www.bpsjournals.co.uk

ingenta *connect*

Submit a paper: http://bjep.edmgr.com
View online articles: http://www.ingentaconnect.com/content/bpsoc/bjep
For more information, visit http://www.bpsjournals.co.uk/bjep

The
British
Psychological
Society

www.bpsjournals.co.uk

Series preface

This is the sixth volume in this series of BJEP monographs. In the original preface to the series, written in 2002 by the then Editor, Peter Tomlinson, it was noted that the motivation for the monographs, and the annual conferences from which they derive, lay in 'a striking but lamentable paradox'. On the one hand, psychological work of direct relevance to educators and education had increased in both its range and the extent of the insights it offered with respect to the processes of learning, the characteristics of learners, the nature of effective learning environments, and the role of teachers within these. At the same time, however, initial teacher education, particularly within the UK, had steadily lost psychological input from qualified staff for a variety of reasons, meaning that access to these burgeoning insights was typically limited or even absent.

The object of the annual conferences and monographs – made possible by the independent funds that accompanied the journal on its transfer to the British Psychological Society in 1995 – was to attempt to play some part in ameliorating this situation. Each year, world-leading researchers in a specific area of psychology of education would be invited to a two-day conference to present overviews of their own and related work in a manner accessible to educators, as well as fellow researchers. Access to these reports, particularly for practitioners, would be maximised by making these conferences free of charge, and by publishing the papers as a corresponding series of monographs, under the rubric *British Journal of Educational Psychology Monograph Series II: Psychological Aspects of Education – Current Trends* (Series II because BJEP had published an earlier series of edited monographs in the 1980s).

Seven years on, both the conferences and the monographs have bedded down into a consistent and highly successful format. The conferences are well-attended events, attracting an audience of researchers, postgraduate students, and practitioners from a range of sectors, and generating genuinely incisive exchanges of views between these groupings. Critically, these debates have meant that the events have gone beyond simply providing practitioners with a point of access to research, to the creation of a forum in which both current and future researchers are brought into direct contact with the issues that concern practitioners, and with the insights that they have gleaned, helping to reinvigorate and reshape the research agenda. The monographs provide an opportunity not just to publish the original papers, but to do so taking these debates into account. They have therefore become a sought-after resource for those with interests in the areas covered, as much for the agenda that they set as for the overview that they present – and perhaps for this reason, even the earliest volumes still attract eager readers.

DOI:10.1348/000709909X452447

The aspirations expressed in the original preface, 'to hold events and publish monographs in some major areas and aspects of educational interest', and to 'offer useful resources to the international community of those concerned with psychological aspects of education' have therefore been amply met. Moreover, if anything the enterprise seems to be gathering momentum. At the time of writing, the seventh conference, Understanding Number Development and Number Difficulty, has taken place, and the preparation of the accompanying monograph is well advanced. The eighth conference, on anti-social behaviour in schools, will take place later in 2009, and a ninth is in planning for 2010. As yet, at least, there has been no shortage of suitably significant topics, nor of willing hosts and contributors.

How far the series has itself gone towards addressing the paradox that was the original source of concern is harder to gauge, but it has certainly coincided with a returning and increasing interest in psychological perspectives on the part of trainee teachers, to the extent that psychological input to qualifying courses is not just sought, but often heavily subscribed to when available. Even if BJEP cannot claim credit for this shift, the Editorial Board can reasonably hope that the monographs will play a significant role in resourcing this renewed thirst, and that the conferences will continue to develop as a major point of contact between researchers and practitioners. If anything, these are in fact rather less modest ambitions than those with which the series commenced; it is a sign of the success achieved to date that they also seem rather less speculative.

ANDREW TOLMIE (Institute of Education, London, UK)

Teaching and Learning Writing, 1–4
BJEP Monograph Series II, 6
© 2009 The British Psychological Society

The
British
Psychological
Society

www.bpsjournals.co.uk

Introduction

Teaching and learning writing

V. Connelly* and A. L. Barnett

Department of Psychology, Oxford Brookes University, Oxford, UK

In the majority of societies across the world competence in writing is demanded in many aspects of day-to-day life (Swedlow, 1999). Thus it is important that children become competent writers and writing is, therefore, a major concern of educators. While the definition of a competent writer may be fluid, and a point for debate, there does appear to be a consensus that we need to pay more attention to the teaching and learning of writing (for example, see National Commission on Writing, 2005, in the USA, the 'every child a writer' proposal in the UK, DCSF, 2007, and a cross psychology review by Rijlaarsdam *et al.*, 2005). These reviews all point out that more needs to be done in the school to support the teaching of writing through new and innovative teaching methods built on the latest research.

However, writing is a complex skill and can be studied in many different ways. Psychology is but one of many disciplines contributing to research on the teaching and learning of writing. The purpose of this monograph is to highlight recent national and international psychological research on the teaching and learning of writing to inform educational psychologists and education professionals alike. The contributions are derived from the proceedings of the *Psychological Aspects of Education: Current Trends* conference funded by the *British Journal of Educational Psychology* and held at Oxford Brookes University in July 2007.

The studies in this monograph fall into two broad and overlapping areas of interest. The first is concerned with charting performance and development in writing skills in typical and in special populations (Galbraith, Myhill, Dockrell, & Connelly; Fayol, Zorman, & Lété, pp. 63–75; Berninger *et al.*, pp. 77–95). The second area is concerned directly with assessment, assistance and instruction in writing (Graham & Harris, pp. 97–113; Harris & Graham pp. 115–137; Barnett, Henderson, Scheib, & Schulz, pp. 139–159; MacArthur, pp. 161–177).

Part 1: Modelling performance and charting development in writing skill

In order to best inform educational practice it is necessary to have a full picture of the writing process and how writing skills develop in children. Considerable advances have

Correspondence should be addressed to Dr Vincent Connelly, Department of Psychology, Oxford Brookes University, Headington Campus, Gipsy Lane, Oxford OX3 0BP, UK (e-mail: vconnelly@brookes.ac.uk).

DOI:10.1348/978185409X421110

been made in understanding the cognitive processes underlying reading development, and this has led to effective interventions. In contrast, our understanding of the cognitive processes underpinning writing and writing development is less advanced (Graham, 2008). The field of reading research has been propelled forward by the many recent models of reading development examining the complexities of the processes involved. These models were developed once researchers began questioning in detail the assumptions about how the many aspects of the reading process actually worked together. Writing researchers have tended to be more cautious in developing those kinds of models but now there is a more firm basis of research evidence more models are being proposed (Levy & Marek, 1999; McCutchen, 2000; Torrance & Galbraith, 2006). We can also see that the papers in this section are linked by their open questioning of previously common assumptions about the relationships between variables involved in the development of writing.

For example, the paper by Galbraith (pp. 5–26) sets out to argue that the role of implicit text production processes has been overlooked and the role of explicit thought in writing has been overemphasized. Galbraith makes the point that language production for writing is not a simple translation process of thoughts into words as is commonly assumed. He proposes a dual process model of writing based on a convincing series of experiments highlighting differences between knowledge retrieval and knowledge constituting processes.

Myhill (pp. 27–44) also points out in her paper that writing is not simply translating thoughts in your head. In a detailed and well illustrated paper she examines the writing of secondary school students from a linguistic theory approach. She clearly demonstrates that children need to develop a linguistic repertoire for writing that is different from that for talking. The poorer writers in her study were those children who wrote more the way they actually talked.

Language as a limiting factor is also the theme of the paper from Dockrell and Connelly, pp. 45–61. Here a review is presented showing that children with specific language impairment (SLI) struggle with writing throughout their school career. Although in the general population many children have difficulty with the production of written text (Hooper, Swartz, Wakely, de Kruif, & Montgomery, 2002; McArthur & Graham, 1987), writing is particularly poor in this special population. The importance of competent oral language skill as a baseline for writing development would seem obvious (Shanahan, 2006). However, what is not so clear is how oral language actually impacts on the different writing processes. The text production skills of children with language difficulties seem particularly hard hit with both vocabulary deficits and spelling problems contributing heavily to poor performance.

Spelling is also dealt with in the paper by Fayol, Zorman, and Lete, pp. 63–75. Here the authors questioned the frequently reported? strong correlation between reading and spelling. As with language, reading is assumed to be a prerequisite for writing by many authors, although the amount of studies investigating links between aspects of reading and aspects of writing is rather small and has shown a mixed bag of results (Shanahan, 2006). By testing both reading and spelling in one large population, Fayol and colleagues demonstrate in their paper that there can be a dissociation between these skills in some writers. The fact that this is associated with phonological deficits and processing speed makes for an interesting educational point.

Berninger and colleagues take the idea of testing skills to identify patterns in populations one step further by studying idea generation (prior to a writing task) and the associated brain activation patterns identified by MRI scanning. Here they show that good and poor writers could be differentiated in their idea generation skills by different patterns of response in the brain. The areas that were highlighted provided further evidence that good writers had better working memory and were thus more efficient at idea generation, further illuminating connections between complex cognitive skills.

Part 2: Assessment, assistance and instruction in writing

The papers in this section focus directly on the educational demands of writing in the school environment. In particular, Graham and Harris, in their joint chapters, reflect the research focus in the USA on specific educational implications for writing instruction (See the recent COST Action IS0703: The European Research Network on Learning to Write Effectively, 2007, proposal for more detail on the divergence between the USA and European research directions in writing research). The papers here allow us to integrate lessons and research from the USA on these issues.

Graham and Harris expand on the recent highly acclaimed 'Writing next' report (Graham & Perin, 2007) and other meta-analyses and meta-syntheses to detail a number of explicit recommendations for the teaching of writing in their article. The authors are quick to point out that these are recommendations based on the available research not prescriptive methods and there are a number of careful and common sense caveats to be considered. This is a powerful summary of the effective strategies that can be drawn upon to improve the writing of children between the ages of ten and eighteen.

The direct focus on educational attainment in writing continues in the article by Harris and Graham on *Self-regulated strategy development in writing*. This is an approach to writing instruction developed over many years and the chapter is full of detail on how this approach can be successfully implemented in the classroom. The authors note that their approach is centred on 'theoretical pragmatism' and that it is more important to ask the right questions rather then be driven by just one approach or one theory.

In order to identify and assist struggling writers in the classroom, we need accurate assessment tools. Focusing on transcription skills, Barnett and colleagues describe, in their article, the development of a test to measure handwriting speed (the DASH). The publication of standardized norms of handwriting speed allows researchers to move forward in their understanding of the complex interplay between handwriting fluency and success in writing more generally. It also enables practitioners to identify those with difficulties and plan appropriate support. Such support can take various forms including special tuition in handwriting, extra time in examinations and the teaching of keyboarding skill and use of other technology.

There has been a large investment in the use of information technology in the classroom over the last decade. However, a recent research review on technology for literacy in the UK (Torgerson & Zhu, 2003) made the startling conclusion that there was no evidence that information technology was making any difference to literacy attainment. The article by MacArthur reviews in detail current knowledge known about the impact of technology on children learning to write. The author demonstrates that there can be benefits of using information technology in the classroom particularly for struggling writers. MacArthur also makes a clear statement that children need to be carefully shown and instructed in how to get the best out of any new technological tool for writing. He suggests that many schools do not even allow children to get the best out of simple word processing tools through not providing enough practice or instruction in typing. New tools are of little use unless young writers know how to use them to best effect.

Taken together, these papers emphasize the complexity of the writing process and the various levels of analysis that can be used, ranging from the purely biological (brain activation) to overt behaviour. This corpus of work illustrates the breadth of current research, spanning different components of the writing process including the generation of ideas, linguistic planning, spelling, and handwriting. Such a combination of different approaches is needed to obtain a better understanding of the writing process, which we hope will in turn contribute to improved practice and performance in the classroom.

Acknowledgements

We express our sincere thanks to Professor Julie Dockrell and Professor Andrew Tolmie for their support of the conference and their valuable contribution to the review process.

References

COST Action IS0703: The European Research Network on Learning to Write Effectively (2007). Memorandum of Understanding (MoU) for the implementation of a European Concerted Research Action designated as COST Action IS0703: The European Research Network on Learning to Write Effectively (ERN-LWE). Retrieved 1 December 2008 from http://www.ph-heidelberg.de/org/writing/sig/html/Memorandum_COST.pdf

DCSF (2007). Press release from Department for Children, Schools and Families, 11 December 2007. Retrieved 1 December 2008 from http://www.dcsf.gov.uk/pns/html

Graham, S. (2008). Research on writing development, practice, instruction, and assessment. *Reading and Writing, 21*, 1-2.

Graham, S., & Perin, D. (2007). *Writing next: Effective strategies to improve writing of adolescent middle and high school.* Washington, DC: Alliance for Excellence in Education.

Hooper, S., Swartz, C., Wakely, W. B., de Kruif, R. E. L., & Montgomery, J. W. (2002). Executive functions in elementary school children with and without problems in written expression. *Journal of Learning Disabilities, 35*, 57-68.

Levy, C. M., & Marek, P. (1999). Testing components of Kelloggs multicomponent model of working memory in writing: The role of the phonological loop. In M. Torrance & G. C. Jeffery (Eds.), *The cognitive demands of writing: Processing capacity and working memory in text production* (pp. 25-41). Amsterdam, The Netherlands: Amsterdam University Press.

MacArthur, C. A., & Graham, S. (1987). Learning disabled students' composing under three methods of text production: Handwriting, word processing, and dictation. *The Journal of Special Education, 21*, 22-42.

McCutchen, D. (2000). Knowledge acquisition, processing efficiency, and working memory: Implications for a theory of writing. *Educational Psychologist, 35*, 13-23.

National Commission on Writing (2005, July). Writing: A powerful message from state government. Retrieved December 1st 2008 from http://www.writingcommission.org/report/html

Rijlaarsdam, G., Braaksma, M., Couzijn, M., Janssen, T., Kieft, M., Broekkamp, H., *et al.* (2005). Psychology and the teaching of writing in 8000 and some words. In pedagogy – learning for teaching. *British Journal of Educational Psychology Monograph series II*, (3), 127-153.

Shanahan, T. (2006). Relations among oral language, reading and writing development. In C. MacArthur, S. Graham, & J. Fitzgerald (Eds.), *Handbook of writing research* (pp. 171-185). New York: Guilford Press.

Swedlow, J. (1999). The power of writing. *National Geographic, 196*, 110-132.

Torgerson, C., & Zhu, D. (2003). *A systematic review and meta-analysis of the effectiveness of ICT on literacy learning in English, 5-16. Research evidence in education library.* London: EPPI-Centre, Social Science Research Unit, Institute of Education.

Torrance, M., & Galbraith, D. (2006). The processing demands of writing. In C. MacArthur, S. Graham, & J. Fitzgerald (Eds.), *Handbook of writing research* (pp. 67-80). New York: Guilford Publications.

Teaching and Learning Writing, 5–26
BJEP Monograph Series II, 6
© 2009 The British Psychological Society

Society

www.bpsjournals.co.uk

Writing as discovery

David Galbraith*

Staffordshire University, Staffordshire, UK

Background. Although writing is commonly characterized as a process of discovery, there are contrasting conceptions of what this implies about the writing process. Classical models of the cognitive processes in writing treat discovery as a side-effect of the processes required for effective communication, and associate it with the adaptation of thought to rhetorical goals.

Aims. In this paper, I argue that these models overemphasize the role of explicit thinking processes in writing at the expense of more implicit text production processes.

Arguments. Following a review of research investigating the conditions under which writers discover new ideas through writing, which I argue contradicts important features of the classical account of discovery, I outline an alternative dual-process model of writing which I claim provides a better account of the empirical data.

Conclusions. The model identifies two conflicting processes in writing: an explicit planning process, incorporating many of the features assumed by classical models of writing, and an implicit text production process, which operates according to connectionist processing principles. The basic features of these processes are described, and the complementary role they play in writing is discussed.

Writing is commonly described as a process of discovery, and there is general agreement within the field that writers develop a deeper understanding of what they are writing about in the course of writing. However, beneath this apparent consensus, there are long-standing differences in how the general assumption is interpreted, reflecting different theoretical assumptions about what discovery in writing is. Classical theories of rhetoric, for example, focus on identifying the most effective methods for persuasive communication, and treat the search for persuasive ideas (under the guise of the art of invention) as a means to this more general end. Discovery, in other words, is seen as a by-product of the strategies required for effective communication. At the other end of the continuum, romantic approaches to writing treat discovery as intrinsic to the process of writing, characterizing the process itself as a matter of finding out what to say in the course of writing, and emphasizing that in order for this to happen, writing should be a matter of spontaneous self-expression, free from external constraints.

*Correspondence should be addressed to David Galbraith, Centre for Educational Psychology Research, Faculty of Sciences, Staffordshire University, College Road, Stoke-on-Trent ST4 2DE, UK (e-mail: d.galbraith@staffs.ac.uk).

DOI:10.1348/978185409X421129

Current models of the cognitive processes involved in writing have tended to take the classical side of this debate. They share three interrelated features. They focus almost exclusively on the thinking behind the text, and treat language production as a matter of translating the products of thought into words. They assume that variations in the way content is generated during writing are a consequence of variations in the thinking behind the text, particularly in the extent to which it is directed towards external, communicative goals. And they assume that a fundamental conflict in writing arises when writers try to carry out the high level thinking required to satisfy these rhetorical goals at the same time as formulating their thought in full text.

In the most fully developed cognitive account of writing as a process of discovery, Bereiter and Scardamalia (1987) characterize the essential difference between novice and more expert writers as a contrast between a knowledge-telling model of writing and a knowledge-transforming model of writing. Following earlier research by Hayes and Flower and their colleagues comparing experts and novices thinking aloud while writing (see, for example, Flower & Hayes, 1980, 1984; Hayes & Flower, 1986; Hayes, Flower, Schriver, Stratman, & Carey, 1987), they characterize knowledge telling as essentially a 'think–say' or 'what next?' method of composition. It involves retrieving content in response to its organization in memory and in accordance with stored discourse schemas, and translating it directly into prose. The resulting text reflects the structure of knowledge in the writer's own mind, modified only as much as is required to conform to the conventions of the genre in which they are writing. Knowledge transforming, by contrast, involves developing an explicit representation of the rhetorical problem as a hierarchy of goals and subgoals, and requires the active transformation of content in order to satisfy these goals. Figure 1 shows how this was formalized as an explicit model of the cognitive processes involved.

The first feature to note about this model is that the knowledge-telling process is incorporated in the model as the process responsible for formulating thought in words. It is therefore assumed to play no role in itself in the knowledge-transforming process but is simply responsible for translating the output of higher level thinking into words. The crucial difference in the thinking involved in the knowledge-telling and knowledge-transforming models stems from differences in how novices and experts carry out the interaction between two problem spaces: a content problem space, in which the writer's content knowledge is represented, and which is operated on by general thinking processes, and a rhetorical problem space, which consists of a functional representation of the text in terms of the writer's rhetorical goals. According to Bereiter and Scardamalia, novices treat writing as a matter of translating from content space into rhetorical space. Thus, although such writers may represent the rhetorical situation to themselves, this is only used as a constraint to guide the way content is presented in text. Writing is driven by operations in the content problem space and these are the main guiding force governing the content and organization of the text. Experts, by contrast, treat writing as a two-way interaction between the content and rhetorical spaces. They develop a more elaborate representation of their rhetorical goals and use this to develop a fuller representation of the text in rhetorical problem space. The crucial feature being that this more elaborate representation of the underlying rhetorical functions of the text is used to set goals to be achieved in content space, and it is the modification of content in order to satisfy these goals which leads to the development of the writer's thought during writing. It is this which, to use Bereiter and Scardamalia's words (1987, p. 302) is responsible for 'the peculiar value that many have claimed for writing as a way of developing one's understanding'.

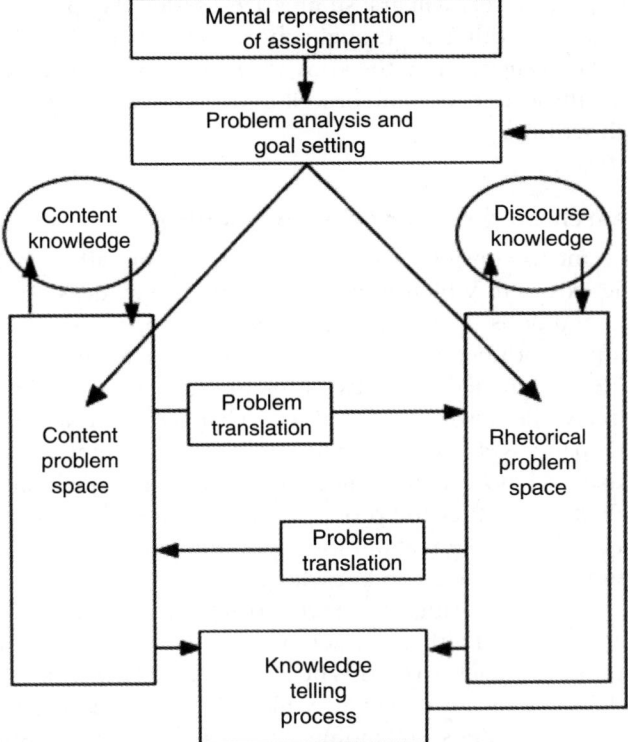

Figure 1. Bereiter and Scardamalia's (1987) knowledge-transforming model of writing.

The final ingredient of cognitive approaches to discovery is concerned with the most effective way of combining the higher level, thinking processes involved in planning and the lower level, linguistic processes involved in text production. Research on drafting strategies (e.g. Glynn, Britton, Muth, & Dogan, 1982; Kellogg, 1988, 1994) has typically assumed that their function is to reduce cognitive load, and has seen this as arising from the requirement to carry out high level thinking at the same time as producing full text. The generally agreed solution to this problem is to separate the demands of thinking from those of producing text. Thus Kellogg (1988, 1994) has consistently found that outlining ideas in note-form before writing leads to the production of better quality text, and that this is a consequence of focusing attention initially on the generation and organization of ideas before then shifting it to the problem of expressing ideas clearly in language.

Taking these strands of research together, the classical accounts of writing suggest that discovery depends on the extent to which the writer directs their writing towards rhetorical goals, rather than simply translating existing thought into text, and on the extent to which they are able to focus exclusively on strategic thinking, rather than trying to combine it with full text production. However, despite this clear prediction about the conditions under which writers should develop their understanding of a topic, there has been very little research that directly tests effects of writing on thought. This is in large part because the general assumption that knowledge transformation is a by-product of the processes required for effective communication has meant that most research has focused on identifying the processes involved and not on their effects on the writer's thought.

In what follows, therefore, I will first summarize a series of experiments which aimed to assess the effects of writing on thought more directly. I will then argue that the findings of this research suggest that the knowledge-transforming model provides only a partial account of these effects, and describe an alternative dual-process model of discovery through writing.

Empirical research on discovery through writing

The first study I want to consider was carried out by Galbraith (1992), and aimed to assess directly the extent to which writers developed new ideas about a topic under different writing conditions. In order to do this, participants were asked to list their ideas about the topic, both before and after writing. They were then asked to rate the similarity of the ideas contained in the two lists. In order to assess the extent to which the production of new ideas was associated with changes in the writer's understanding of the topic, participants were also asked to rate how much they felt they knew about the topic immediately before and immediately after writing about the topic. This enabled him to identify whether the processes carried out during writing had led to a change in what the writer thought about the topic, and whether any such changes were associated with subjective changes in knowledge.

Given this method of assessing the extent to which writing led to changes in the writer's understanding, Galbraith then set out to test the two main claims of the knowledge-transforming model. To do this he first selected two groups of writers whom he assumed would differ in the extent to which they directed their writing towards rhetorical goals, using Snyder's self-monitoring scale (Snyder, 1986). According to Snyder, high self-monitors are 'particularly sensitive to the expression and self-presentation of relevant others in social situations and use these cues as guidelines for monitoring (that is regulating and controlling) their own verbal and non-verbal self-presentation'. By contrast, low self-monitors' 'self-presentation and expressive behaviour . . . seems, in a functional sense, to be controlled from within by their affective states (they express it as they feel it) rather than moulded and tailored to fit the situation'. Galbraith selected these two types of writers because they seemed to embody the contrast between knowledge-telling and knowledge-transforming approaches to writing: low self-monitors would be expected to prioritize the direct expression of their beliefs about the topic, whereas high self-monitors would be expected to generate content to satisfy their rhetorical goals. A recent study by Klein, Snyder, and Livingston (2004), showing that high self-monitors vary the thoughts they list before a discussion with different audiences, whereas low self-monitors do not, supports this assumption.

In addition, in order to test whether writers' ability to transform their knowledge was affected by cognitive load, he asked these two groups of writers either to write notes in preparation for an essay (planning) or to write an essay without pre-planning (text production).

If discovery depends on the extent to which writers generate content in response to rhetorical goals, one would expect the high self-monitors to produce more new ideas after writing than the low self-monitors. If, furthermore, the process involves deliberate problem solving and this is impaired when working memory is overloaded, one would expect a greater number of new ideas to be produced after planning in note-form than when writers had to produce full text at the same time as planning.

As can be seen in Figure 2, this was, partly, what Galbraith found. The high self-monitors discovered more new ideas after writing notes than the low self-monitors did,

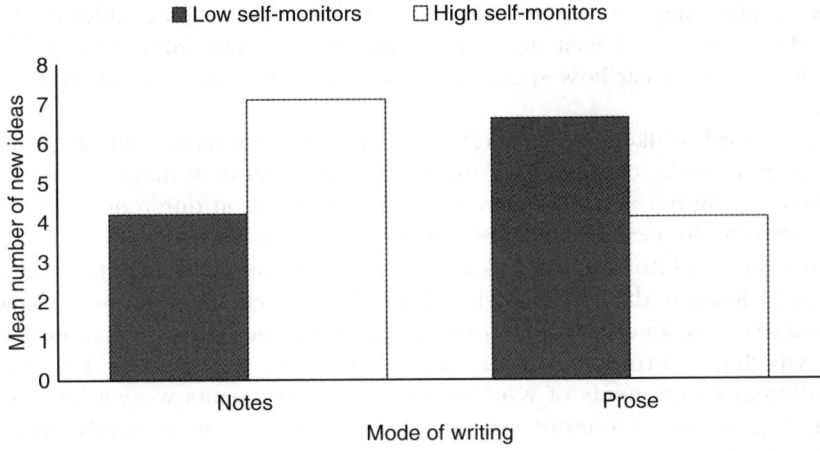

Figure 2. Mean number of new ideas produced after writing as a function of self-monitoring and mode of writing (Galbraith, 1992).

and this was reduced when the high self-monitors had to write full text. This suggests that the generation of new ideas depends on the extent to which content generation is directed towards the satisfaction of rhetorical goals and that it is reduced when the writer has to deal with the extra cognitive load of producing well-formed text. However, in direct contrast to what the knowledge-transforming model would predict, these new ideas were *not* associated with subjective increases in writers' knowledge. Furthermore, far from generating fewer new ideas when they wrote full text, as one would expect if they were simply knowledge telling, the low self-monitors generated a high number of new ideas after writing full text, just as many in fact as the high self-monitors did when they made notes. There was also a clear positive correlation between the number of new ideas the low self-monitors produced in this condition and increased knowledge of the topic. In other words, discovery appeared to occur when writing was assumed *not* to be directed towards rhetorical goals, and when cognitive load should be at its highest.

Overall, Galbraith (1992) concluded that, although there was evidence that adapting thought to rhetorical goals does affect the generation of content, this was not associated with the development of the writer's understanding. In addition, there was also evidence that dispositionally guided text production, far from being a matter of retrieving existing ideas from memory, involved actively creating novel content, and that this led to the development of the writer's understanding. Subsequent research explored the effects of these two different types of process in more detail.

Rhetorical planning

Kellogg's (1988, 1994) research on outlining has established that it does have a beneficial effect on text quality. However, it's not clear from this research whether the effectiveness of outlining depends further on *how* it is carried out; specifically, whether it also depends on the extent to which writers generate new ideas to satisfy rhetorical goals. Given Galbraith's (1992) results suggesting that writers vary in the extent to which they do this, and Bereiter and Scardamalia's (1987) general claim that the effectiveness of planning depends on the extent to which it involves knowledge transforming, one would certainly expect that it should. Furthermore, although

Kellogg's research suggests that outlining has this effect because it enables the writer to separate the demands of idea generation and organization from those of full text production, it is less clear how specifically these processes are carried out in working memory.

Galbraith, Ford, Walker, and Ford (2005) set out in to investigate these questions by asking writers to make outlines for a brief article for a student magazine while at the same time carrying out secondary tasks designed to load on different components of working memory. To measure the extent to which writers transformed their ideas they divided up outlining into two phases – an initial, generating phase in which participants were asked to generate their ideas freely, followed by an organizing phase, in which they were asked to create an organized outline of the text to be written – and measured the extent to which they introduced new ideas during the organizing phase. To examine the role of different components of working memory, participants were asked to do this while carrying out one of four different secondary tasks: (i) random number generation, designed to load on the central executive component of working memory, (ii) a spatial tracking task, designed to load on the spatial component of working memory, (iii) a visual task, designed to load on the visual component of working memory, and (iv) a foot-tapping task, designed to provide a control condition involving a general secondary task not loading on any specific component of working memory. After creating their outlines, all participants were asked to write their articles (without a secondary task). This experiment produced two important findings.

First, there was a highly significant multiple correlation between three features of the outlines and the quality of the final text – the amount of content in the plan, the number of new ideas introduced during outlining, and the extent to which the plan included explicit rhetorical groupings of content – with each feature contributing independently to the relationship. This pattern of results is compatible with the knowledge-transforming model's claim that the generation of novel ideas during planning in order to satisfy rhetorical goals is related to the quality of the final text. Furthermore, given that all the participants in the experiment made outlines, it suggests that *how* writers construct their outlines is important, rather than just whether or not writers make one at all.

Second, both random number generation and spatial tracking secondary tasks reduced the effectiveness of outlining compared to the control condition, whereas the visual secondary task had no effect. The effect of random number generation is not particularly surprising: it is a very demanding secondary task, and in effect prevented the participants from outlining at all before writing. The effect of the spatial tracking task is more interesting because it specifically reduced the extent to which writers introduced new ideas during the second organizing phase of outlining, but had no effect on the number of ideas they were able to list during the initial generation phase. Furthermore, the resulting articles were rated as significantly lower in quality than those produced by the control group. Galbraith *et al.* suggest that this is because writers need to represent different ideas simultaneously in working memory in order to evaluate the global structure of the text to be written and identify new content to satisfy rhetorical goals.

The results of this experiment, together with the results of Galbraith (1992), suggest that knowledge transforming (as a process rather than an effect on thought) does play an important role in enabling writers to improve the quality of their texts. As the classical models of writing assume, the effectiveness of planning does appear to depend on the extent to which it is directed towards rhetorical goals and on the extent to which it is carried out separately from the demands of full text production. In addition, they suggest that this involves constructing a spatial representation – or mental model – of the global structure of the text in working memory. However, Galbraith' (1992) finding that new ideas introduced during planning were not related to changes in writer's subjective ratings of knowledge calls into question Bereiter and Scardamalia's (1987, p. 302) claim that this kind of knowledge transforming process is responsible for 'the peculiar value that many have claimed for writing as a way of developing one's understanding'. It may play a valuable role in writing but it doesn't appear to lead to discovery.

Dispositionally guided text production

An important question about the effect of dispositional text production is how it relates to pre-planning. In the essay condition of Galbraith's (1992) study, participants had to write a well-formed version of their essays in a single draft and no attempt was made to control the extent to which they planned this ahead of time. Although relatively few participants actually wrote an outline before starting their texts, many of them still could have made a mental plan before starting to write, and the fact that they were required to produce a well-formed text meant that inevitably they had to take into account the rhetorical constraints for the essay. They were not simply writing down their thoughts as they came to mind.

Galbraith (1999) set out to explore this issue by explicitly manipulating the extent to which writers planned before writing. He asked two groups of undergraduate low and high self-monitors to write essays discussing the issue of whether terrorism was justifiable under three different planning conditions: (i) unplanned, in which writers were simply asked to write out their thoughts as they came to mind without worrying about how well organized the text was, (ii) synthetically planned, in which writers were given 5 min (after generating the initial list of ideas used as part of the measure of idea change, but before writing the text) in which to write down a single sentence summing up their response to the topic, (iii) outline-planned, in which writers were again given 5 min to plan before writing, but were asked to construct an outline of the text to be written. In addition, in both the planning conditions, writers were asked to try to produce a well-organized text but not to worry about well expressed the text was. The same measures were used as in the experiment by Galbraith (1992), except that as well as being asked to rate their understanding of the topic participants were also asked to rate how organized their thoughts about it were before and after writing.

The first important finding was that, as in the Galbraith (1992) study, the low self-monitors produced significantly more new ideas after writing than the high self-monitors. As can be seen in Figure 3, this difference was most pronounced in the synthetic planning condition. Furthermore, this was the only condition in which there was a positive relationship between the number of new ideas and subjective increases in understanding of the topic. In other words, although low self-monitors also produced a relatively high number of new ideas in the other planning conditions, it was only in the synthetic planning condition that these were associated with developments of the writer's understanding. Galbraith concluded that it was only in the synthetic planning condition that dispositional text production took place uncontaminated by other processes. In all other conditions, he claimed that text production was directed by either rhetorical goals (high self-monitors) or by an explicit plan for the text (unorganized in the unplanned condition, or organized in the planned condition). This implies that a key characteristic of synthetic planning compared to the

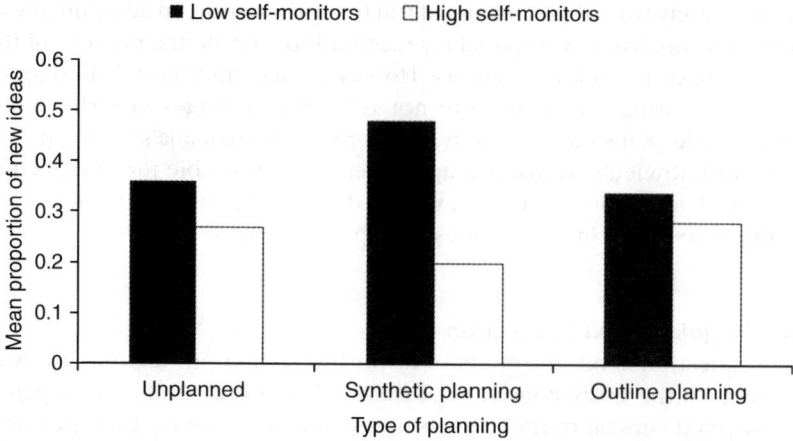

Figure 3. Mean number of new ideas produced after writing (measured as a proportion of ideas produced before writing) as a function of self-monitoring and type of planning (Galbraith, 1999).

other conditions is that writing is directed by a single overall goal, rather than by a linear set of stored ideas.

Evidence to support this interpretation came from two other features of the data. First, the majority of high self-monitors in all conditions (91%) reported increases in the organization of their thought after writing, and this was significantly higher than for the low self-monitors (71%). This supports the assumption that, although writing directed towards rhetorical goals may not lead to development of understanding, it may increase the organization of thought. Second, although it was not possible to assess the relationships between new ideas and changes in organization for the high self-monitors because of the restricted range of the data, it was possible to do this for the low self-monitors. This showed a significant positive correlation between the number of new ideas produced after writing and increases in subjective organization of thought within the low self-monitors' outline-planned condition, but not in either the synthetically planned or unplanned conditions. In other words, there was clear evidence for the presence of an explicit organizing process in conditions other than the low self-monitors' synthetically planned condition, and that, although this was associated with the generation of new ideas, these were not associated with developments of the writer's understanding.

Taken together, these findings support the assumption that new ideas can be produced by a range of different processes and that these vary depending on the form of planning carried out and the goals towards which writing is directed. In particular, they suggest that new ideas can be produced by: (i) dispositional text production, which is reduced when writing is planned or directed towards rhetorical goals, and which is associated with developments in the writer's understanding of the topic and (ii) explicit planning directed towards rhetorical goals, which does not lead to developments in the writer's understanding, but does lead to increases in the organization of thought.

This conclusion also implies that, by itself, the measure of the number of new ideas produced after writing is not capable of distinguishing between the different processes responsible for producing them, and that a direct measure of the degree of organization of ideas is required. In a recent study, Galbraith, Torrance, and Hallam (2006) attempted to do this. Using the same general procedure as in earlier experiments, they asked writers to produce lists of ideas before and after writing. But, in addition, after the list had been produced they presented the participants with all possible pairs of the ideas in the list in a random order and asked them to rate the extent to which each pair was mutually supportive or contradictory. They then used these ratings to calculate a measure of the 'harmony' of the ideas before and after writing. This assesses the mutual coherence of a set of ratings, and essentially indicates the extent to which a set of ideas are united by a common theme (see Galbraith *et al.*, 2006, for further details). As with the previous experiment, high and low self-monitors were asked to write either synthetically planned or outline-planned essays. In addition, a control condition, in which participants listed and rated ideas about the same topic before and after writing, but wrote about a different topic in between, was also included in order to assess for general non-content effects of writing.

As can be seen in Figure 4, this study found essentially the same effects on the number of new ideas produced after writing as earlier studies. The low self-monitors produced significantly more new ideas than the high self-monitors in the synthetically planned condition, and this was also greater than the number of new ideas produced in the control condition, where participants wrote about a different topic. They also produced a relatively high number of new ideas in the outline-planned condition, which is slightly surprising, but is compatible with the range of variation found in previous studies. As in previous studies, the high self-monitors produced a higher number of new ideas in the outline-planned condition than in the synthetically planned condition, as would be expected if they engage in more explicit planning when required to make an outline before writing. (It is worth noting, though, that this was not significantly greater than the number of new ideas produced in the control group, which suggests that the effect may be in part due to direct processing of the lists produced before and after writing rather than changes due to writing about content in between the production of the lists.)

This experiment appears, then, to have successfully replicated the previous studies in finding evidence for the generation of novel ideas through two different processes: dispositionally guided text production in the case of low self-monitors' synthetically

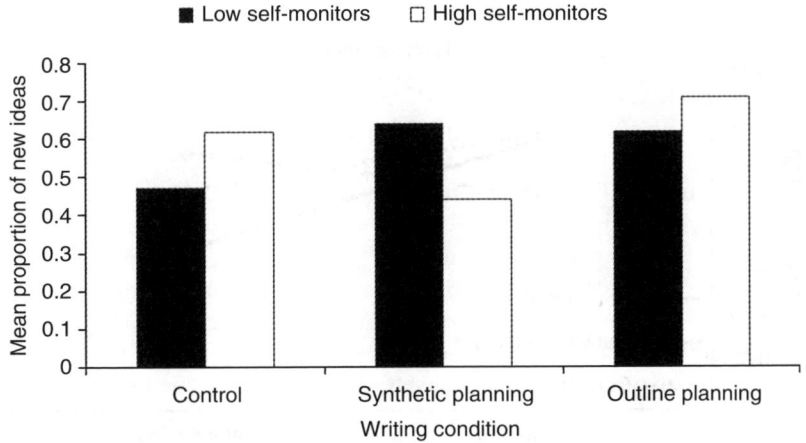

Figure 4. Mean number of new ideas produced after writing (measured as a proportion of number of ideas produced before writing) as a function of self-monitoring and writing condition (Galbraith *et al.*, 2006).

planned essays, and explicit planning combined with text production in the case of the low and high self-monitors outline-planned essays. Given that similar numbers of new ideas are produced in these three conditions, the key question is whether the presumed difference in processes will be reflected in differences in the effects on the organization of ideas. Figure 5 shows the mean harmony before and after writing in the different conditions, plotted separately for low and high self-monitors (logs were taken to normalize the distributions of the scores).

As can be seen in Figure 5, there was one highly significant difference in this data between the high and low self-monitors (none of the other differences in organization before and after writing were statistically significant). In the outline planning condition (the solid line in the figure), where the two groups of writers produced similar numbers of new ideas, the ideas produced by the low self-monitors after writing were just as coherently related to one another as they were before writing. In other words, the new ideas produced by the low self-monitors appeared to have been successfully integrated with their existing ideas. By contrast, for the high self-monitors there was a marked reduction in the coherence of their ideas after writing outline-planned essays.

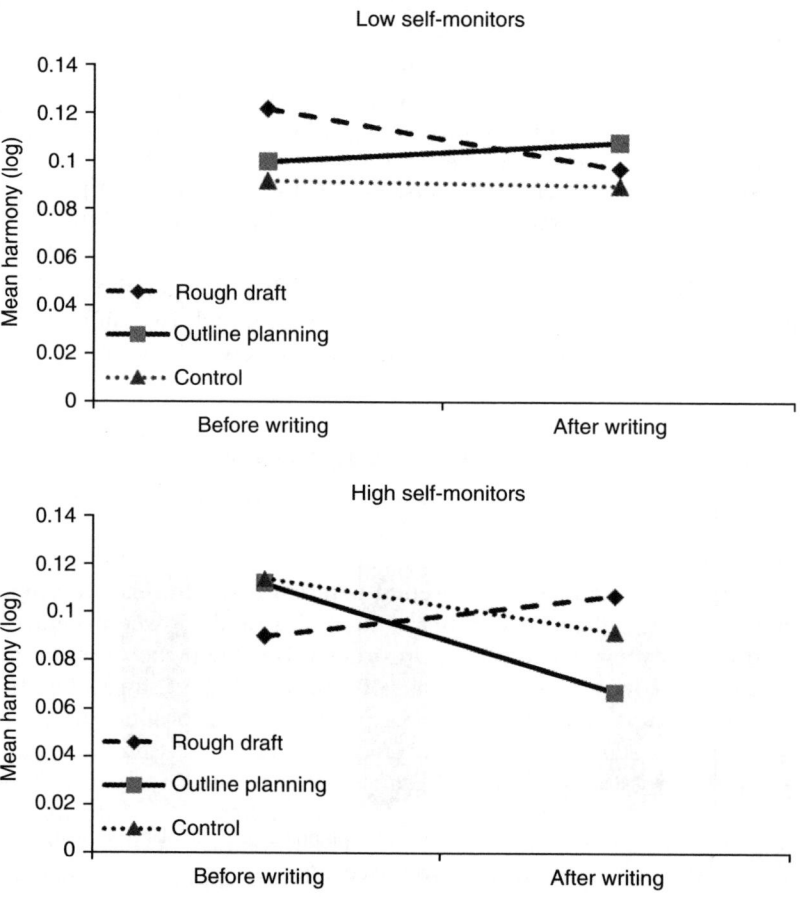

Figure 5. Mean harmony (log) before and after writing as a function of self-monitoring and writing condition (Galbraith *et al.*, 2006).

This implies that, although the two groups produced similar numbers of new ideas in this condition, the processes responsible were very different. Galbraith *et al.* suggest that the difference is between a top-down and a bottom-up planning process. According to this interpretation, high self-monitors modify the content of their plans directly, introducing new ideas in order to make their plans better able satisfy rhetorical goals, and then try to produce text which satisfies their higher level plan, producing further new ideas in order to so. The result is that, although their ideas satisfy their extrinsic rhetorical goals, they are not coherently interrelated in terms of their personal understanding. By contrast, the low self-monitors modify their plans less before writing and generate text dispositionally, only modifying their plans in order to accommodate novel content produced in the course of text production. The result is that their ideas are coherently interrelated in terms of their personal understanding.

There are two puzzling features of this data. The first is the disparity between the findings of this study, where harmony was used as a measure of organization of ideas, and the Galbraith (1999) study, where a subjective rating of organization was used. In the Galbraith (1999) study, virtually all the high self-monitors (91%), including those in the outline planning condition, reported subjective increases in the organization of their thought after writing, yet in this study the data suggest a marked decrease in the organization of their thought. The solution to this apparent paradox lies, I think, in the different nature of the two measures. The harmony measure is an implicit measure: it is calculated on the basis of the consistency of the participants' pair-by-pair judgements, rather than on a direct assessment of the global structure of their thought. By contrast, the subjective measure is presumably based on the writer's subjective appraisal of their mental model of the global structure of their text. If this is correct, then it provides a natural interpretation of the findings, which is compatible with the top-down planning explanation of the high-self-monitors' data. High self-monitors introduce new ideas in order to make their explicit plan for the text more coherent, hence they experience a subjective increase in the organization of their thought. However, because these ideas are not generated dispositionally, in terms of their personal understanding, their pair-by-pair ratings of the relationships between ideas are not consistent overall. When interpreted in this way, these data would actually be very consistent with earlier findings. The implicit measure of harmony would be a measure of the writer's personal understanding of the topic, and the decrease in this experiment would correspond to the consistent failure to find effects of rhetorical planning on the writer's subjective ratings of personal understanding of the topic in previous experiments.

The second puzzling feature is the lack of difference between the effects of low self-monitors' synthetically planned and outlined planned texts. In this experiment, these two conditions produced similar number of new ideas and showed a similar ability to integrate these with their existing ideas in order to maintain the overall organization their thoughts. This contradicts the findings of Galbraith (1999) suggesting that outline planning reduces the extent to which dispositonal text production leads to the development of understanding and instead leads to developments in the organization of existing ideas. It is possible that this is because there are subtle tradeoffs between the production of new ideas and the development of understanding and organization which the present measures are not able to capture. The resolution of this puzzle, and a full explanation of the disparity between high self-monitors' explicit judgements and their implicit ratings, must await further research looking directly at the processes involved when writers write under these different conditions.

Summary of conclusions

These studies call into question whether the knowledge-transforming model provides a full account of discovery through writing. They raise two main problems. The first is that, although there is evidence that planning directed towards rhetorical goals does lead to the modification of thought, and that this is related to the quality of the final text, it is not clear that this is also associated with developments of the writer's understanding. The second problem is that there is also clear evidence that dispositionally-guided text production, far from being a simple matter of translating predetermined content into words, is an active knowledge-constituting process in its own right.

Synthesizing ideas

In this section, I will first consider some conceptual problems with existing models of writing that make it hard for them to account for knowledge-constituting during dispositional text production, and then sketch out an alternative account based on connectionist processing principles that I think can account for this feature of text production.

Conceptual problems with existing models

Both Hayes and Flower's (1980) original model and Bereiter and Scardamalia's (1987) model have two problems when it comes to accounting for the generation of novel ideas during writing. They characterize idea generation as a retrieval process and treat it as separate from translation, which is seen as a matter of translating the output of planning into words. In Hayes and Flower's model of the idea generation subcomponent of planning (see Figure 6), for example, content in memory is retrieved in response to probes developed from the writer's goals and the writing assignment. Similarly, in Bereiter and Scardamalia's knowledge-telling model, content generation is described in terms of two operations: 'Construct memory probes' followed by 'Retrieve content using memory probes'.

It is difficult to see how content which is simply retrieved from a memory store can be 'new'. At best, it might vary depending on the memory probes used to retrieve it, with the result that writers might retrieve different content depending on whether they were simply generating ideas in response to probes associated with the topic (e.g. knowledge telling) or in response to probes associated with a more developed representation of the rhetorical situation (e.g. knowledge transforming). Bereiter and Scardamalia (1987, pp. 349–351) acknowledge this problem when they discuss memory search procedures, pointing out that, 'One of the most formidable challenges to theories of language use is to explain how it is that skilful speakers and writers are able so quickly to think of material fitting multiple constraints'. They consider the possibility that this could be a consequence of spreading activation within a network of fixed semantic units but conclude that it would be impossible for such a network to store explicitly all the different possibilities that might be required by different rhetorical contexts. Instead, they suggest a process of heuristic search, in which the rhetorical problem is progressively redefined until it 'provides cues that activate appropriate nodes in memory'. But it's not clear how, given their assumption that memory nodes consist of fixed units, this resolves the issue. Surely, all that heuristic search – or more refined rhetorical planning – achieves in this context is retrieval of more specific content.

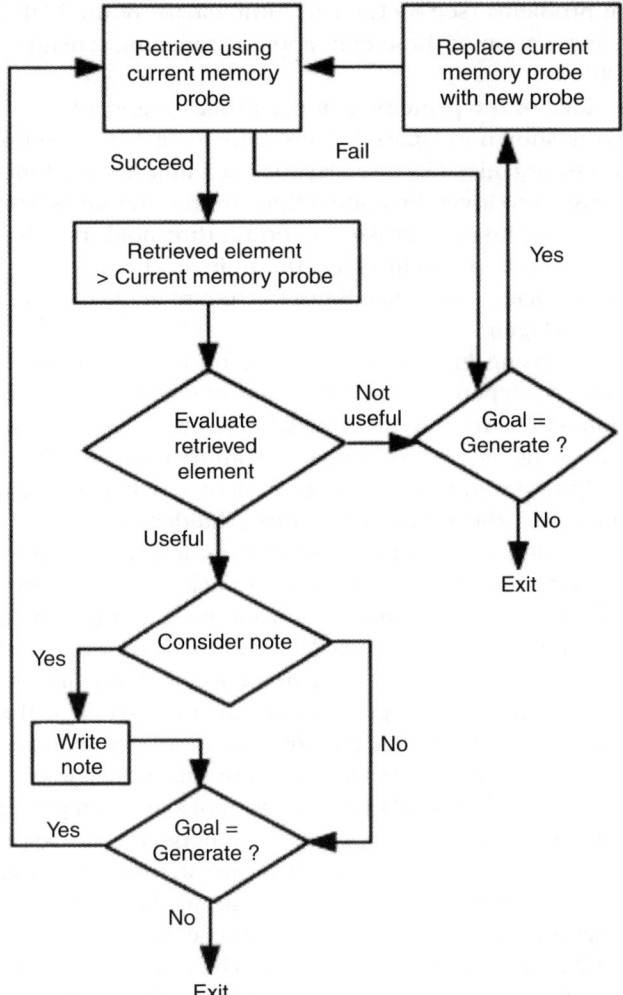

Figure 6. The generating component of the writing process as conceived in Hayes and Flower's model (1980, p. 13).

In other words, although they recognize the problem, it's not clear that heuristic search provides a solution to it.

Synthesizing implicit knowledge

Classical models of writing assume that knowledge is explicitly represented as fixed units in memory. This makes it hard to see, as the quote from Bereiter and Scardamalia above acknowledges, how the writer could produce novel content satisfying multiple constraints. It also makes it hard, in principle, to capture the sense of discovery as genuinely creating something new rather than simply being a matter of re-organizing existing content so that it is appropriate for a novel context. Since these models were developed, however, alternative models of knowledge representation based on theories of parallel distributed processing have emerged, which provide elegant solutions to these problems (see McClelland, Rumelhart, & the PDP Research Group, 1986; and, for an application of these concepts to modelling semantic memory, Rogers & McClelland, 2006).

To give you an idea of the principles of the processing involved, consider the very simple, 'toy' network shown in Figure 5. This consists of a set of simple units, roughly analogous to neurons, organized in three layers. Each unit has the function of summing up the activation passed to it via the connections from other units (shown as arrows in the diagram), and when this sum crosses a certain threshold, passing on activation to other units in the network. By themselves, the units in the network do not represent anything at all, they are simply little machines for summing up and passing on activation through the network (Figure 7).

The work of processing information is done by the connections between units, which vary in strength depending on the network's learning history. Thus, when a pattern of activation is presented at the input layer (consisting of say a pattern of light on the retina or, more abstractly, a set of semantic features) some of the units in the input layer will be strongly activated whereas others will be much less so. Each unit will then pass its activation on to the units in the next, hidden, layer, with the amount of activation it passes on depending on the strength of the connection it has with each of the units it is connected to. In this example, which is fully connected, and where activation is only fed forward through the network, each unit passes varying degrees of activation on to all the units in the next layer. Thus, if the unit on the far left-hand side of the input layer has a strong positive connection with the unit on the far left-hand side of the hidden layer it will strongly activate this unit, while at the same time, if it has a strong negative connection with the unit on the far right-hand side of the hidden layer, it will act to strongly reduce the activation of this unit. The overall effect on the units in the hidden layer will depend on the pattern of activation presented at the input layer and the varying strengths of the connections between this layer and the units in the hidden layer. The hidden layer will in turn pass activation forward to the output layer, which will then produce a response to the input the network has received.

For present purposes such networks have two crucial features. The first is that content is not stored in the hidden layer, waited to be retrieved by a set of cues. Instead it is synthesized, by the network as a whole, as a response to the input. To the extent that

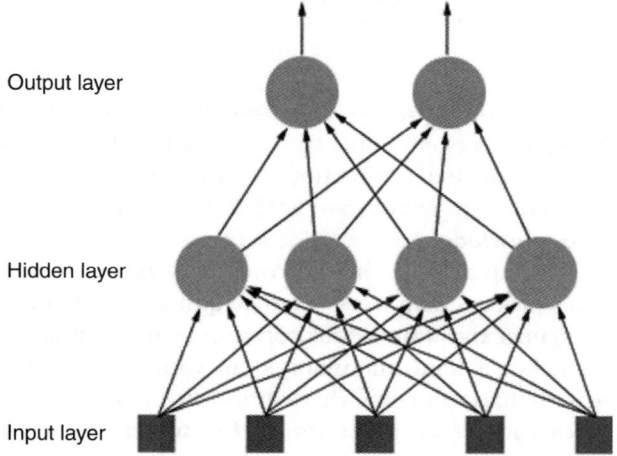

Output layer

Hidden layer

Input layer

Figure 7. A simple feedforward network.

anything is represented at all in such networks, it will consist only of a transient pattern of activation across the units in the hidden layer at the time that it responds to the input. Furthermore, none of the units themselves will necessarily correspond to interpretable features of the world: it is the pattern as a whole which forms the transient representation of content. And, because of the graded way in which each unit respond to activation it receives, each instance of a particular piece of content will be represented by a subtly different pattern of activation, varying as a function of the context in which the input is presented. In such networks, then, content is synthesized, as and when it is needed, in a contextually appropriate form, rather than being retrieved in a fixed form from memory. Furthermore, because information is processed in parallel, such networks provide a simple solution to the problem raised by Bereiter and Scardamalia of producing a rapid, and contextually flexible, response to multiple constraints.

The second crucial property of such networks is that knowledge is stored implicitly in the strength of the connections between units. It is these connections that are modified during learning. There is a range of ways in which such learning can take place but they all involve modifying the strength of the connections between units. The key feature is that the same set of units and connections is used to produce responses to all its different inputs. So training such a network consists of presenting a set of input and output pairs one after another and the network is required to find a single set of connections capable of simultaneously producing the full range of responses to the different inputs. Once the network has learned a set of input–output relationships, then, it will have a fixed set of connections between its units which enable it to reliably produce the full range of responses to its different inputs. It is this fixed set of connections which constitute the network's knowledge. But this knowledge cannot be inspected directly: instead it guides the way in which responses are produced and so only emerges as explicit knowledge once a response has been produced in context. Note also that, because the connections between units have to be capable of representing the full range of input–output pairs in a domain, they all have an influence on the strength these connections have. Any individual response is therefore influenced by all the other responses that the network can make; each individual response that the network makes is a reflection of the totality of its knowledge.

Writing as a knowledge-constituting process

Galbraith (1999) used these two basic principles of connectionist processing – the synthesis rather than retrieval of content and the implicit rather than explicit organization of knowledge – to provide an account of how dispositionally guided text production could lead to developments of a writer's understanding. In its most general form, this claims, first, that text production is a process of discovery because it is a synthetic process, in which, to paraphrase E. M. Forster, the writer only finds out what they think when they see what they say. The writer synthesizes a response to a set of constraints, rather than searching for stored content corresponding to a set of memory probes. Second, this process is guided by the implicit organization of the writer's knowledge – the writer's disposition towards the topic (as represented in the fixed set of connections within a connectionist network) – rather than by external rhetorical goals.

The particular way that he claims these principles are applied in the context of writing is represented by the sketch in Figure 8. The writer's disposition is represented by the network of interconnected units at the centre of the diagram. This represents a particular form of connectionist network – a parallel constraint satisfaction network – in

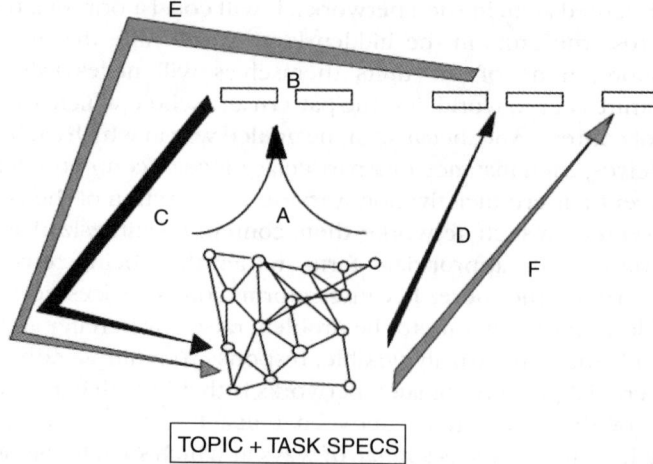

Figure 8. Writing as a knowledge constituting process (Galbraith, 1999).

which, all the units are connected with one another by positive or negative connections. These fixed connections represent the implicit organization of the writer's disposition and are responsible for guiding the way activation is passed round the network in response to external constraints.

These external constraints (or input to the network) consist of the topic and task specification and are shown at the bottom of the diagram. When these are specified, they activate each unit within the network. Activation is then passed round the network according to the strength of the connections between units, with negatively connected units trying to turn one another off and positively connected units trying to turn one another on. Eventually the network settles into a stable state, with some of its units highly activated and others deactivated: this pattern of activation represents the writer's response to the external constraints and corresponds to the message they want to convey. This message is then formulated in language (represented by the arrow labelled A) and written down as an utterance (labelled B in the diagram).

This central part of the diagram, then, represents the way that an individual utterance is synthesized by the writer's disposition in response to a set of external constraints. It is meant to emphasize the synthetic nature of the process and the fact that this is organized by the fixed set of connections constituting the writer's implicit knowledge of the topic. It provides a formal specification for the writer's disposition and shows how this could in principle guide the formulation of an idea or utterance.

A crucial feature to note is that this is only a partial, 'best fit' to the initial set of constraints embodied in the topic and task specifications. When the network is first activated by these constraints all the units will be activated to a greater or lesser extent – this initial pattern of activation reflects *all* the possible content that could be expressed in response to the topic and task specifications. Once the network starts to pass activation between the units themselves, however, this initial pattern of activation will change as the positive and negative links representing the writer's disposition pass activation back and forth until it reaches a stable state compatible with the internal relationships between units. In effect, the disposition selects a pattern of activation across its units that is compatible with its own internal constraints.

The second key component of the model concerns what happens after an utterance is output. One possibility is that the writer interprets what they have written and evaluates it in terms of their plans and goals. They might then formulate a new set of specifications corresponding to the next step in their plan, or designed to better satisfy their goals, and this would form the input to a new synthesis. This would involve least modification to classical models of writing because it would restrict the influence of the writer's disposition to the unpredictable formulation of individual utterances. The writer's disposition would be important insofar as it would be required to guide the formulation of individual utterances, but not so far as the generation of a succession of utterances was concerned, which would be controlled by the standard rhetorical planning processes specified in classical models of writing.

However, Galbraith (1999) makes a stronger claim than this. He suggests that, after the initial utterance has been output, a set of feedback connections (labelled C in the diagram) from the output, as it is represented in working memory, pass inhibitory activation back to the writer's disposition. This has the effect of reducing the activation of units corresponding to the writer's initial message, and means that when the same set of initial constraints from the topic and task specifications are input into the network again, a different pattern of activation will result following constraint satisfaction. This will roughly correspond to the disposition's selection according to its internal constraints from the 'remainder' of the content activated by the initial set of external constraints. The resulting utterance is labelled D in the diagram. Further passages of inhibitory feedback (labelled E) and utterance production (labelled F in the diagram) represent further cycles of text production.

Overall, then, this claims that dispositional text production is not just a matter of synthesizing individual utterances under the guidance of the writer's disposition, but that it also involves an interaction between the writer's disposition and the emerging text. Because any individual utterance is only a partial representation of the network's response to the topic and task specifications, in order for the writer's disposition to be fully captured in the text, it has to be allowed to guide processing over successive sentences, free from external planning.

A dual-process model of writing

Now that we have specified the processes involved in dispositional text production, I want to explain how this contributes to a dual-process model of writing and what changes this involves to existing models of writing.

The first important feature of the dual-process model is that it incorporates the main features of the planning components of Hayes and Flower, and Bereiter and Scardamalia's models. These are seen, however, as providing a partial account of one of the components of writing rather than a general account of the process as a whole. The main characteristics of the model and the contrasting nature of the two processes involved are summarized in Table 1.

The model assumes that one of the systems involved in writing – the *knowledge-retrieval* system – does, as the classical models of writing claim, draw on an explicit store of knowledge, and that this does involve the retrieval of knowledge from long-term memory, and that this may or may not be evaluated and manipulated in working memory in order to satisfy rhetorical goals. However, because this system operates on existing stored knowledge it cannot by itself lead to the discovery of new ideas. At most, it may lead to the reorganization of existing knowledge. This is, nevertheless, a vital part of the writing process. It enables the writer to take a set of miscellaneous ideas and put them together into a coherent knowledge object, which can be retrieved on later occasions as

Table 1. Contrasting characteristics of the two systems involved in the dual-process model.

Features of system	Knowledge-retrieval system	Knowledge-constituting system
Form of representation	Explicit representation of knowledge in separate fixed units	Implicit representation of knowledge in connections between units
Generation of content	Retrieval from memory	Synthesis
Organization of content	Associative spread of activation within long-term memory or goal-directed manipulation of content in working memory	Feedback from content in working memory to writer's disposition

a coherent package. Furthermore, it plays a crucial role in writing because it enables the writer to organize and present their ideas in text so that they satisfy their rhetorical goals.

This system operates best under the conditions assumed by classical models of writing. It requires ideas to be represented in a fixed and abbreviated form (as notes 'labelling' ideas for example) so that the limited capacity working memory system can focus its resources on evaluating the extent to which they satisfy their rhetorical goals and their potential contribution to the overall structure of the text. The results of Galbraith *et al.*'s (2005) experiment on the contribution of different components of working memory to planning suggest, in addition, that the spatial component of working memory plays a particularly important role in enabling the writer to construct a coherent mental model of their text as a whole.

The model also accepts the distinction between knowledge-telling and knowledge-transforming approaches to writing. Knowledge telling occurs when the writer simply retrieves content from memory without considering how to adapt it to rhetorical constraints; whereas knowledge transforming involves a more strategic search and evaluation of stored content in order to satisfy rhetorical goals. The dual-process model highlights, however, that both these processes are essentially memorial processes, involving the retrieval and manipulation of existing content. In particular, it highlights the fact that knowledge telling is not just 'writer-based' but is also a matter of assuming that writing involves the recalling rather than the synthesis of content. This is why, as Bereiter and Scardamalia (1987) point out, it is particularly prevalent in educational contexts where writing is used as a means of testing whether students have acquired relevant knowledge from their lessons.

The second component of the model – the *knowledge-constituting* system – is assumed to operate by using an implicit representation of knowledge, and to involve the synthesis rather than the retrieval of content. Furthermore, it is assumed to be capable, not just of synthesizing individual utterances but also, through inhibitory feedback from working memory to the writer's disposition, of producing a sequence of content without requiring external goals to drive the process. This process, in other words, is intrinsically a process of discovery: the knowledge implicit in the connections between units is only realized as explicit content once it has been formulated as potential text. The extent to which this leads to a change in the writer's understanding depends on the extent to which the content produced by the synthetic process corresponds to pre-existing content in the explicit memory system. When it does, although the process may be synthetic, the fact that the content produced corresponds to existing content will mean that the writer will not experience a development of their understanding. When, however, the synthesized content does not correspond to pre-existing content, the writer will experience a development in their understanding.

The knowledge-constituting process is assumed to operate best when writers formulate their thought in explicit, connected sentences and when these are dispositionally synthesized, rather than consciously designed to satisfy external goals. Indeed, it is assumed that it is precisely because of the need to formulate a statement based on one's knowledge or past experience that the content generating component of the language production system is organized in this way. The holistic way in which the strength of the connections between units are developed means that multiple past experiences – in principle the totality of the writer's past experiences – determine the content of any given utterance. Rather than depending on the writer surveying a range of content in memory and trying consciously to determine how to formulate a sentence compatible with them all, the accumulation of past experiences in a set of fixed connections enables the writer to bring their past experience to bear rapidly and implicitly without the need for a conscious survey of memory. Furthermore, this process operates best when successive sentences are produced synthetically in the context of the preceding text, rather than in response to content which is explicitly recalled from memory.

It is worth noting here, that, although the details of what is involved are very different, the broad outlines of this dual-process account are similar to current approaches to other psychological phenomena. In particular, dual-process accounts of reasoning (see Evans, 2008, for review) distinguish between an implicit processing system, which involves rapid and parallel processing of information, and an explicit system, which operates slowly and sequentially and involves the manipulation of mental models in a limited capacity working memory system. There is also evidence from neuropsychological research for two different, but interconnected, memory systems: an explicit memory system located in the hippocampus, and an implicit memory system located in the neo-cortex (see McClelland, McNaughton, & O'Reilly, 1995, for a discussion of how these two systems relate to connectionist models).

Relationship between the two systems

The two processes are both necessary for effective writing. The knowledge-retrieval system and the associated manipulation of mental models in working memory are required in order to explicitly organize the text and ensure that it satisfies rhetorical goals. They also play a crucial role in identifying gaps in the global structure of the text and in guiding the search for relevant potential content, as well as identifying potential aspects of the topic that need to be included in the text. The knowledge-constituting process synthesizes content activated by the knowledge-retrieval process into explicit, connected sentences, and in the course of this may produce novel content that clarifies the writer's understanding. In this respect, it provides a mechanism whereby problems identified in rhetorical space can be realized in text. Rather than the heuristic search specified by Bereiter and Scardamalia, in which appropriate existing content is identified by the progressive refinement of memory probes, this involves synthesizing implicit content activated by the rhetorical goals, and discovering what the relevant content is in the course of text production. However, since this is essentially a linear process in which attention is focused on each individual utterance as it is produced, the writer has to deliberately identify the distinct ideas in this text after they have been produced and then consider reflectively how it can be integrated into the global structure of the text. The joint result of these two processes is the creation of a coherent knowledge object, which satisfies rhetorical goals, and hence which is capable of existing independently of the writer, but which at the same time fully captures the writer's implicit understanding of the topic.

The model implies a fundamental conflict between two sources of content organization in writing. The knowledge-retrieval process organizes content in terms of the relationships between pre-existing ideas in explicit memory and the writer's rhetorical goals, whereas the knowledge-constituting process is guided by the implicit organization of the writer's disposition. The result is that when the writer turns from planning to producing text, they find that that the sequence of utterances that emerges does not conform to the sequence required by their plan. Equally, while the writer is constituting their thought, the emerging sequence is disrupted when it is interrupted by planning. The conflict is not so much because of the conflicting demands of two different processes – planning and text production – on a limited set of cognitive resources but rather between two conflicting impulses: the impulse to maintain a pre-determined plan, and impulse to follow an unfolding train of thought. The writer is being pulled in two different directions at once.

Furthermore, this is not simply a cognitive conflict. It is deeply related to the writer's conception of self. The writer's explicit representation of what they have to say includes a sense of how this will be received by the reader. Having a clear and coherent model of what it is they want to say enables the writer to anticipate and control the impression that they make. In addition, an important goal in constructing and manipulating this representation is that it should correspond to the writer's self-image. These factors are likely to generate a desire to (a) construct a clear mental model of the text before writing and (b) to try to maintain this model during text production. To the extent that text production is unpredictable it will threaten this goal. At the same time, insofar as text production enables the writer to realize their implicit knowledge in the text, it becomes an important means of self-actualization. The two different processes, therefore, embody a tension between the writer's need to maintain a current self-image and the desire to actualize the potential self latent in their implicit disposition towards the world. One of the potential virtues of the dual-process model is that, to the extent that it prompts us to identify the presence of these different processes during writing, it should also allow us to explore the effects of the writer's self-concept on their writing and thought.

Given these considerations, it is perhaps no surprise that the individual difference variable of self-monitoring should have shown such consistent differences in the effects of writing on thought. High self-monitors are, by definition, concerned with managing and controlling the presentation of the self. In terms of the dual-process model, one would therefore expect them to prioritize the knowledge-transforming component of writing, and to use the resulting mental model to guide and control text production. By contrast, low self-monitor's prime concern is assumed to be to allow their implicit disposition towards the topic to be realized in what they say. Accordingly, one would expect them to prioritize the synthetic, knowledge-constituting component of writing over the memorial knowledge-transforming component.

Conclusion

The classical models of writing proposed by Hayes and Flower, and Bereiter and Scardamalia overemphasize the importance of explicit thinking processes in writing and hence treat text production processes as a relatively passive component of the writing process. In consequence they treat 'discovery' as a side-effect of the explicit, goal directed thinking processes they regard as required to produce effective, reader-based prose, and characterize the central conflict in writing as an essentially cognitive conflict between thinking and text production processes. An important consequence of this emphasis has been that effects of writing on thought have typically been inferred from general properties of the processes assumed by the models, rather than being directly tested.

In this paper, I have made two broad claims about these models. First, I have claimed that they are unable to account for the findings of empirical research that has directly examined the effects of writing on thought. In particular, this research questions the extent to which explicit thinking processes directed towards rhetorical goals do lead to a development of writer's understanding, and suggests that dispositionally guided text production is not a passive output process but is an active knowledge-constituting process in its own right. Second, I have outlined an alternative conception of the basic processes involved in writing, based on connectionist principles of processing, which casts the basic components of the writing process in a different light. It sees the two fundamental components of the production process not as thinking and language production, but instead as knowledge-retrieval and knowledge-constituting processes. Knowledge-retrieval processes involve the retrieval of existing knowledge from long-term memory and are essentially memorial processes. By contrast, the knowledge constituting process is a synthetic process, which underlies productive thought and language production. Content produced by these two processes is organized in a fundamentally different way. Content produced by the knowledge-retrieval process is organized by the explicit manipulation of ideas in working memory in order to satisfy extrinsic goals. Content produced by the knowledge-constituting process is organized implicitly by the fixed connections within a parallel constraint satisfaction network corresponding to the writer's disposition towards the topic.

This model treats discovery as an intrinsic part of the writing process. In consequence it claims that the fundamental conflict in writing is between two different forms of organization – explicit organizing processes carried out in working memory and the implicit organization which guides the knowledge-constituting process – rather than between thinking and text production processes. Furthermore, this is not simply a cognitive conflict. The writer's disposition is equivalent to their implicit self, and hence the conflict between the two forms of organization is also a conflict between explicit and implicit self-knowledge.

In this respect, the model can be seen as an attempt to reconcile romantic and classical conceptions of writing. Romantic conceptions of writing, which emphasize self-expression free from external constraints, focus on the synthetic, knowledge-constituting component of writing. Classical conceptions of writing, which emphasize strategies for effective communication, focus on the knowledge-retrieval component of writing. In stressing that effective writing is the joint product of knowledge-retrieval and knowledge-constituting processes, the dual-process model claims that these two conceptions of writing should be treated as complementary rather than conflicting, and provides a framework within which this can be achieved.

References

Bereiter, C., & Scardamalia, M. (1987). *The psychology of written composition*. Hillsdale, NJ: Erlbaum.

Evans, J. (2008). Dual-processing accounts of reasoning, judgement and social cognition. *Annual Review of Psychology, 59*, 255–278.

Flower, L. S., & Hayes, J. R. (1980). The cognition of discovery: Defining a rhetorical problem. *College Composition and Communication, 31*, 21–32.

Flower, L. S., & Hayes, J. R. (1984). Images, plans and prose. The representation of meaning in writing. *Written Communication, 1*(1), 102–160.

Galbraith, D. (1992). Conditions for discovery through writing. *Instructional Science, 21*, 45–72.

Galbraith, D. (1999). Writing as a knowledge-constituting process. In M. Torrance & D. Galbraith (Eds.), *Knowing what to write: Conceptual processes in text production* (pp. 139–160). Amsterdam: Amsterdam University Press.

Galbraith, D., Ford, S., Walker, G., & Ford, J. (2005). The contribution of different components of working memory to planning in writing. *L1 – Educational Studies in Language and Literature, 15*, 113–145.

Galbraith, D., Torrance, M., & Hallam, J. (2006). Effects of writing on conceptual coherence. *Proceedings of the 28th Annual Conference of the Cognitive Science Society*, 1340–1345.

Glynn, S. M., Britton, B., Muth, D., & Dogan, N. (1982). Writing and revising persuasive documents: Cognitive demands. *Journal of Educational Psychology, 74*, 557–567.

Hayes, J. R., & Flower, L. S. (1980). Identifying the organization of writing processes. In L. W. Gregg & E. R. Steinberg (Eds.), *Cognitive processes in writing* (pp. 3–30). Hillsdale, NJ: Erlbaum.

Hayes, J. R., & Flower, L. S. (1986). Writing research and the writer. *American Psychologist, 41*(10), 1106–1113.

Hayes, J. R., Flower, L. S., Schriver, K. A., Stratman, J. F., & Carey, L. (1987). Cognitive processes in revision. In S. Rosenberg (Ed.), *Reading, writing and language learning* (Vol. 2, pp. 176–240). Cambridge: Cambridge University Press.

Kellogg, R. T. (1988). Attentional overload and writing performance: Effects of rough draft and outline strategies. *Journal of Experimental Psychology: Learning, Memory and Cognition, 14*, 355–365.

Kellogg, R. T. (1994). *The psychology of writing*. New York: Oxford University Press.

Klein, O., Snyder, M., & Livingston, R. W. (2004). Prejudice on the stage: Self-monitoring and the expression of group attitudes. *British Journal of Social Psychology, 43*, 299–314.

McClelland, J. L., McNaughton, B. L., & O'Reilly, R. C. (1995). Why there are complementary learning systems in the hippocampus and neocortex: Insights from the successes and failures of connectionist models of learning and memory. *Psychological Review, 102*, 419–457.

McClelland, J. L., Rumelhart, D. E., & the PDP research group (1986). *Parallel distributed processing: Vols. 1 and 2*. Cambridge, MA: MIT Press.

Rogers, T., & McClelland, J. (2004). *Semantic cognition*. Cambridge, MA: MIT Press.

Snyder, M. (1986). *Public appearances, private realities: The psychology of self-monitoring*. New York: W.H. Freeman and Company.

Teaching and Learning Writing, 27–44
BJEP Monograph Series II, 6
© 2009 The British Psychological Society

The
British
Psychological
Society

www.bpsjournals.co.uk

From talking to writing: Linguistic development in writing

Debra Myhill*
University of Exeter, Exeter, Devon, UK

Background. Previous research in linguistic development in writing has primarily addressed the acquisition of writing, early linguistic development of writing, and spoken–written interactions in the primary phase. This study explored linguistic development in older writers in the secondary phase.

Aims. The aims of this 2-year study were to investigate both the linguistic constructions in secondary-aged students' writing, and to explore their understanding of their own writing processes.

Sample. The data reported here draws on the first year data collection: a sample comprising two pieces of writing, narrative, and argument, drawn from pupils in year 8 (aged 12–13) and year 10 (aged 14–15). The writing sample was stratified by age, gender, and writing quality.

Methods. The writing was subject to linguistic analysis at both sentence and text level, using purpose-built coding frames and a qualitative analysis sheet.

Results. The linguistic analysis indicates that the patterns of linguistic development show that the influences of oral speech characteristics are strongest in weaker writing than good writing.

Conclusions. Cognitive research into the translation from thought to text needs to address more explicitly the fact that good writing requires not only production of text, but also shaping of text. Although, it is well-understood that learning to be a writer draws on 'talk knowledge', this study makes it clear that one key element in learning to write with accomplishment is, in part at least, learning how not to write the way you talk, or rather acquiring adeptness in transforming oral structures into written structures.

The history of research in the learning and teaching of writing is not characterized by a unified and incremental body of empirical, theoretical, and professional knowledge. Rather, it is a multi-layered, disparate and, at times, fragmented set of understandings concerning writing instruction. This is largely due to the very different methodological paradigms which are employed in research into writing. This is exemplified beautifully

*Correspondence should be addressed to Debra Myhill, School of Education and Lifelong Learning, St Luke's Campus, Heavitree Road, Exeter Devon EX1 2LU, UK (e-mail: D.A.Myhill@exeter.ac.uk).

DOI:10.1348/978185409X421895

in the recent *Handbook of writing research* (Macarthur, Graham, & Fitzgerald, 2006), where the first five chapters, outlining theories and models of writing, shift from socio-cultural perspectives to cognitive psychological perspectives with relatively little in common. The affiliations of the list of contributors point to the multi-disciplinary nature of education as a field of enquiry: the contributors variously come from Faculties of Psychology, Education, English, the Arts, and Linguistics. In a book such as the present one, which is directed towards a discourse community familiar with the cognitive tradition, it is worth noting that cognitive perspectives are often positioned as of little value in educational settings which are, by their very nature, social settings. Indeed, Prior (2006, p. 54) states that socio-cultural theory is 'the dominant paradigm for writing research today' and Nystrand (2006) critiques cognitive research in writing for depicting 'writers as solitary individuals struggling mainly with their thoughts' (p. 20). However, a comprehensive educationally valid pedagogy for writing needs to adopt a pluralist stance and draw with insight on theoretical and empirical understandings from socio-cultural, psychological, and linguistic domains. Our own research, in an attempt to develop this multi-disciplinary integration, has been framed by what we have called a tripartite model of enquiry, which looks at writing from writer-, reader-, and text-oriented viewpoints. Superficially, each of these may seem to be located principally within one paradigm (writer = cognitive; reader = socio–cultural; text = linguistic) but in practice, each orientation draws, albeit with different weight, on all three perspectives. In exploring the nature of linguistic development in writing, this chapter adopts a text-oriented stance: reader- and writer-oriented perspectives have been reported elsewhere (Myhill & Jones, 2007; Myhill, 2009).

Linguistic development

The potential of linguistic analysis for providing appropriate descriptions of development in writing has not yet been fully realized. Over 20 years ago, Collins and Gentner (1980) argued for 'a new kind of linguistic analysis' which would offer 'a linguistic theory of good structures for sentences, paragraphs, and texts' (p. 53) and which would have corresponding implications for the teaching of writing. In a similar vein, Kress (1994) critiqued linguistics for failing to provide 'the theoretical and methodological tools either for the analysis of writing . . . or for the analysis and understanding of the developmental processes and stages in the learning of writing' (p. 3). And yet, there remains a fairly limited body of research in this area, and what there is has rarely been translated into classroom practice. In particular, there is relatively little extant enquiry into writing development in the secondary age range, mirroring the general tendency for language acquisition and language development studies to focus on the pre-school and primary phases. As Perera (1987) notes, 'knowledge about the later stages of acquisition is slight in comparison with the considerable amount of information that has been accumulated about the first three years' (p. 12).

Perera's (1987) study of linguistic development in children's writing aged 8–12 remains the most comprehensive study available. She took as her starting-point a recognition that there was no clearly defined psycholinguistic theory of grammatical complexity, and investigated grammatical complexity by considering the sequence in which children acquire constructions, taking adult constructions as a sign of greater linguistic maturity. Her detailed analyses highlighted that the use of such things as the passive voice, subordination, and greater lexical density increase as writers get older.

This corresponds with both Crowhurst and Piche (1979) and Verhoeven *et al*.'s (2002) findings that syntactic complexity developed with the age of the writer, and Allison, Beard, and Willcocks (2002) findings regarding increased subordination use. The length of syntactical units also appears to increase with age: for example, the length of noun phrases (Perera, 1987), and the length of clauses (Harpin, 1986). These studies all appear to indicate that linguistic development is marked by an increased frequency of usage of a range of linguistic constructions.

One of the very few studies to look across the age range from primary to secondary (Hunt, 1965) provides somewhat contradictory evidence. This study looked at writing from writer in the 4th, 8th, and 12th grades in the US schools in an attempt to determine whether there were developmental trends in the frequency of various grammatical structures. His data suggested that the structures he studied 'are virtually all used by fourth graders and are used often enough and successfully enough to indicate that fourth graders command them. The study provides no justification for teaching some structures early and others late' (Hunt, 1965, p. 155). Two more recent studies also consider writers beyond the primary phase. Haswell (2000) used factor analysis to investigate linguistic development in college writers and, just as with younger writers, found that development was marked by an increase in both syntactical complexity and elaboration within the sentence. Massey, Elliott, and Johnson (2005) adopt a rather different methodology and rather than considering development as a chronological factor look at indices of development across ability groupings, using General Certificate of Secondary Education (GCSE) grades. They found that there was more co-ordination present in the lower grades with a more limited use of subordination and that word length increased with increasing grades.

However, a simplistic identification that syntactic maturity increases with age, and ability, though useful, is a rather narrow conceptualisation of linguistic development. Harpin (1986) argues that 'a simple linear model of growth towards linguistic, and particularly, syntactic maturity is clearly inadequate' (p. 169). In particular, it adopts a uni-dimensional view of language, and of text and is less concerned with meaning making and with reader-writer relationships. Allison *et al.* (2002) warn against formulaic approaches to teaching or assessment which veer towards merely identifying the presence or absence of syntactic features: instead they caution that the presence of linguistic constructions 'has to be set against the sense of authenticity in a piece of writing, as a child weaves the tapestry of vocabulary and grammar in ways which seem best to meet a particular communicative need at a particular time' (p. 109). Likewise, in the context of college writing where he had found that sentence length increased with maturity, Haswell (2000) reminds us that it is not sentence length *per se* which is significant, but what a particular sentence achieves in terms of 'serving specific rhetorical motives, opting for syntactic, and tonal choices that heighten register, generate rhetorical emphasis, and increase readability of thought units of a certain logical complexity' (p. 338).

Lack of psychological research on language production

If linguistic development is concerned with increasing maturity and sophistication in management of production of words, sentences, and texts, then it is important to understand the process of moving from an idea in the head to the words on the page. Most models of language production investigate speech production, rather than written production, and consider the process by which a speaker converts thought into spoken utterance (Badecker & Kuminiack, 2007; Bock & Levelt, 1994) and Bock and Levelt's (1994) model of speech production has been applied to writing (Alarmargot & Chanquoy, 2001, p. 13) as a mechanism for explaining language production in text. Hartsuiker and Westenberg (2000) and Cleland and Pickering (2006) have argued, through syntactic priming analyses, for 'a model of language production where syntactic information is shared between written and spoken' (p. 194). In general, models of language production argue for either a three-stage process comprised of conception, formulation, and articulation (Stallings, MacDonald, & O'Seaghda, 1998, p. 394), or a two-stage model comprising conceptualization and formulation (Cleland & Pickering, 2006, p. 186). The formulation stage, when the idea is shaped into words and sentences, has been further sub-divided into the functional processing stage, when the principal lexical items are retrieved from memory, and the positional processing stage, when the syntactical structures are shaped.

Within cognitive models of the writing process, this is the translating stage (Alarmargot & Chanquoy, 2001; Hayes & Flower, 1980). Translation is broadly conceived of as a process which bridges the gap between the initial conception of a thought or message and its eventual production as syntactically organised text. It involves both the selection of appropriate vocabulary and the structuring of words into sentences, and the organization of sentences into paragraphs, and texts. Collins and Gentner (1980) see this as the imposition of linguistic order upon ideas, a top-down process in which 'the idea must be expanded downward into paragraphs, sentences, words, and letters' (p. 67) and in similar vein, Negro and Chanquoy (2005) maintain that during translation 'the ideas collected during planning have to be formulated into words, and these words need to be ordered into grammatically and syntactically correct sentences to form a cohesive text' (p. 106). However, there is limited empirical enquiry into what occurs during the translation stage – the Hayes and Flower (1980) model has a box labelled 'translation' but there are no sub-processes identified. Two recent accounts of the translating process provide more detailed explanations of the sub-processes, and these have been represented in Table 1.

Table 1. Theoretical overviews of the translating process

Four stages to the translating process	Three operations ensure proper translating
• Elaboration (retrieving the idea from the plan)	(a) The selection in the mental lexicon of appropriate words to formulate ideas
• Linearization (first transformation of the idea into a syntactico-semantic structure, a pre-verbal message)	(b) The generation of sentences
• Formulation (shaping the pre-verbal message into words)	(c) The elaboration of the textual coherence and cohesion using appropriate linguistic devices
• Execution (planning and graphic execution of the linguistic product)	
Alamargot and Chanquoy (2001, p. 65)	Negro and Chanquoy (2005, p. 106)

But 'the study of how speakers turn messages into utterances' (Bock, 1995, p. 181) is not a wholly satisfactory parallel for how writers turn messages into written texts: the demand on cognitive resources for writing is higher than for speech. Immature writers have to cope with the demands of transcription and even when these processes have become automatized, writing requires a more sophisticated shaping of language to meet the needs of an absent reader in contrast to the instant feedback provided by a conversation partner. Nor is it evident that 'the same set of sentences seem to be acceptable in written or spoken language', as Cleland and Pickering (2006, p. 185) claim, particularly given what we know from linguistics research about the significant linguistic differences between speech, and writing, including syntactical differences. Alamargot and Chanquoy (2001, p. 76) acknowledge that 'writing models remain unclear concerning the formulation of sentences from a preverbal message' and Cleland and Pickering (2006, p. 186) note that the limited research on sentence production focuses mostly on 'composition, planning, and revising', or the role of working memory. This inattention to written sentence production may be because it is not perceived to be cognitively complex: Negro and Chanquoy (2005, p. 106) postulate that the formulation stage of writing is easier to automate because it involves 'mainly the application of fixed rules'.

These understandings of sentence production over-simplify the process of writing to one which is merely a reproductive process of linguistic conversion of pre-verbal thought to syntactically correct writing; the very word 'translating' implies a linear trajectory from one mode to another, which once accomplished is complete. If syntactically correct sentences were the end point of this process, then this way of thinking might be sufficient, but successful writing is a transformative act, governed not simply by the content of the communicative message but governed also by the nature of the relationship with the intended reader and the challenge of creating text which is not simply speech written down. It is important to acknowledge that writing is 'material social practice in which meaning is actively made, rather than passively relayed or effortlessly produced' (Micciche, 2004, p. 719).

Role of speech into writing

Whilst research into linguistic development may be limited and whilst cognitive psychology may be less secure in its accounts of linguistic production in writing, an understanding of the important relationships between speech and writing has been much more comprehensively investigated. Although speech and writing are in reality on a continuum, with some spoken genres, such as a formal speech, being very like writing, and some written genres, such as texting, or email messaging being very close to speech, the linguistic distinctions between informal speech and formal writing (at either end of the speech–writing continuum) are well understood. Writing is more lexically dense and integrated than speech (Czerniewska, 1992; Perera, 1987), and this is typically achieved through the use of constructions such as non-finite subordinate clauses, verbless subordinate clauses, ellipsis, nominalization, participial subordination, and attributive adjectives. Moreover, the constructions used are frequently longer, and more complex (Chafe, 1982; Drieman, 1962) and make greater use of passives (O'Donnell, 1974; Perera, 1984). Co-ordination, on the other hand, is a pattern of speech (Czerniewska, 1992; Kress, 1994), reflecting the greater use of repetition and chaining in speech in contrast to the joining of clauses in writing 'by the hierarchical processes of subordination, which gives a more tightly integrated texture to the language' (Perera, 1987, p. 183).

For the developing writer, learning to write is, in part, about learning that writing is not speech written down: it is shaped and constructed differently and is governed by different grammatical and social conventions. A written sentence is not the same as a spoken utterance: the two texts below (English and Media Centre, 1984, p. 34) illustrate, clearly the way a confident writer reshapes her oral telling of a story for the written medium (Table 2).

Table 2. Contrasting spoken and written versions of a narrative event

Spoken version	Written version
Um. . .well this happened when I was little – well. . .er quite young. . .eight or nine, I think. . . and I had just got this new bike. All of us, I mean all the kids at school. . .had bikes cos, um it was quiet where we lived – it was a small town. . .not much cars, er. . .traffic. Lots of kids rode bikes to school. Anyway this day I was just leaving school – I was a bit late cos I had to see this teacher – she was always keeping me in – and the playground was just about empty only these boys were near the bike shed	At last my new bike had arrived, and I was riding to school like all my friends. All day in lessons I'd thought about the bike and imagined myself riding out of the school gates with them, waving to those poor unfortunates who had to walk home. The day seemed endless, and then just as the last bell went Mrs Fitzgerald said, 'Rosa, I'd like to see you before you go.' I was furious but there was nothing I could do: I had to wait behind

These linguistic differences between spoken and written discourses represent more than an understanding that sentences are shaped differently from utterances: they are central to beginning to understand the demands of both text conventions and the needs of an absent reader. Crystal (1995, p. 291) usefully draws attention to some of these important contrasts. Speech is time-bound and dynamic and once uttered cannot be 're-heard' or corrected, whereas writing is space-bound and static, and can be re-read and revised. Because of this, complex advance planning is less usual in speech than writing, and informal speech, in particular, is often spontaneous and unplanned. Most spoken dialogue is conducted face-to-face and so both speaker and listener can use facial expressions, modulation, and gesture to support meaning, whereas writing distances the reader, and removes the possibility of immediate feedback. Writing cannot rely on the context for the creation or clarification of meaning and so the writer has to anticipate the reader's response. Wells and Chang (1986, p. 123) note that young writers sometimes face difficulties in making this transfer from speech to writing: the lack of feedback from a conversational partner puts 'the major responsibility for sustaining the flow and connectedness of the text' firmly on the writer.

Young writers, therefore, need to master both the grammatical construction of written sentences and an ability to imagine how a reader might read their text. Achieving mastery of the sentence as a written 'unit of discourse' appears to happen earlier than the development of reader awareness. Loban (1976) found written and oral language seemed to develop in parallel, but he did find a pattern whereby linguistic constructions identified in speech were not observed in writing until approximately a year later. Perera's (1986) study of speech and writing development that as children grew older their speech and writing became more clearly differentiated: 'on the one hand, as they get older they use in their writing grammatical constructions that are more advanced than those they use in speech; on the other hand, they use in their speech an increasing proportion of specifically oral constructions' (p. 91). There were very few oral constructions in the writing of 8-year-olds and Perera (1986) argues that this indicates that 'children are differentiating the written from the spoken language and are not simply writing down what they would say' (p. 96). This absence of transfer of speech forms into written forms is not universally recognized, however. Pea and Kurland (1987, p. 293) maintain that young writers adopt a linear process of writing, what they call a 'memory dump', which represents 'a literal translation of oral speech conventions into written language' and Massey *et al.*'s (2005, p. 64) study of writing in examinations found an increase of both non-standard forms and colloquial, informal language. They observe that 'Increasingly writing seems to follow forms which would have been confined to speech in 1980. Sometimes this seems appropriate, but often it looks more like poor judgement, or simply failure to appreciate the distinction'.

Making linguistic choices and shaping sentences and texts to satisfy the needs of an implied reader is more challenging. Flower (1979) argued that novices write 'writer-based prose' and experts write reader-based prose, mirroring Perera's description of writing development as being from writing for self to writing for another. Kroll (1978) calls this *'cognitive egocentrism'*, because at this stage writers have an undeveloped sense of 'other reader'. The distinction made by Bereiter and Scardamalia (1987) between the knowledge-telling and the knowledge-transforming phases will be familiar to most readers, but this also corresponds to developing from writing down what is in your head, more or less as it occurs, to thinking about how what you write might sound to another reader. The link between speech and writing is reiterated further in their contention that children, in general, are more confident with written narrative as it is relatively closed in oral discourse; but the reverse holds for opinion essays (Bereiter & Scardamalia, 1982, p. 10) which are a more 'writerly' form.

Methodology

The data reported in this chapter is drawn from a 2-year study, conducted in England and funded by the Economic and Social Research Council, investigating both the linguistic constructions in young people's writing, and their understanding of their own writing processes. In the first year, a sample of writing was collected comprising two pieces of writing, narrative, and argument, drawn from pupils in year 8 (aged 12–13), and year 10 (aged 14–15). The writing was completed in a naturalistic classroom setting, led by the usual class teacher in a lesson where the writing was a focus of the teaching, rather than an outcome from a different focus. The narrative was a personal piece, written from experience, whereas the argument sample was writing which expressed a clear viewpoint. The argument sample was more diverse in style than the narratives, including letters of complaint, formal argument essays, and leaflets presenting an argument. These different types of argument do have different genre features and future research in this area might well investigate more closely how children's writing varies between genres. The sample was also stratified by writing quality, using nationally understood assessment systems: National Curriculum levels in year 8 (age 12–13) and GCSE grades in year 10 (age 14–15). These grades were given by the class teacher and each grade was checked and verified by the Project Director. Overall, the sample comprised 718 full pieces of writing, stratified by age, gender, and writing quality (Table 3).

The writing was analysed at both sentence and text level, using purpose-built coding frames and a qualitative analysis sheet. The latter permitted exemplification of the quantitative patterns identified through the statistical analysis. Full details of the methodology and coding frames can be found on the project website (www.people.ex. ac.uk/damyhill/patterns_and_processes.htm) and in Myhill (2008) and Jones and Myhill (2007).

Findings

This chapter will draw on the statistical and qualitative data to explore the speech to writing interface, and to illustrate how one key aspect in linguistic development is

Table 3. Overview of the project sample

	Good		Average		Weak		Total year 8	Total year 10	Total
	Year 8	Year 10	Year 8	Year 10	Year 8	Year 10			
Narrative									
Boys	30	30	30	30	30	30	90	90	180
Girls	30	30	30	30	30	30	90	90	180
Total narrative	120		120		120		180	180	360
Argument									
Boys	30	30	30	30	28	30	88	90	178
Girls	30	30	30	30	30	30	90	90	180
Total argument	120		120		118		178	180	358
Total boys	120		120		118		180	180	358
Total girls	120		120		120		180	180	360
Total	240		240		238		358	360	718

learning how to shape sentences and make linguistic choices which do not draw directly on oral patterns or influences. Instead, the linguistic constructions of more assured writers demonstrate greater understanding of the needs of the reader and the conventions of the text genre, and greater confidence manipulating text to create a 'writerly' style, rather than an oral style.

Lexical choices

At the most elementary level of text, the word, the vocabulary choices that writers make reveal differing stages of development. The statistical analysis of word length, taken as a proxy for sophistication in lexical choice, indicated that word length increased with writing quality, as Table 4 illustrates.

Table 4. Differences in word length by writing quality

Number of characters per word	Mean	Statistical significance
Good	4.3	.00*
Average	4.1	
Weak	4.0	

The qualitative data illustrates much more clearly, however, how word length relates to text quality. In general, it reflects vocabulary choices which are drawn from a broader repertoire, showing writers using synonyms of vocabulary much more commonly used in speech. The table below illustrates that the words taken from the lower quality writing are more typical of spoken vocabulary, whilst the parallel synonyms found in higher quality writing reflect a more literary lexical capacity (Table 5).

The choice of verbs also demonstrated greater lexical sophistication in higher quality writing. In the argument writing samples, the weaker writing made greater use of 'I think' to express a personal opinion, whereas the more assured writing offered a range of verbs to fulfil the same function: for example, *I understand, I believe, I would suggest.* Sometimes, this involved not just substitution of a different verb, but a reconstruction of a sentence for rhetorical effect, as in the piece where the writer

Table 5. Contrasts in vocabulary choice by writing quality

Weak	Good
Lots/a lot	Majority
Stuff	Substances
Place	Environment
Give up	Sacrifice
Stories	Narratives
Against it	Opposed
Saying	Proposing
Nose	Nostrils
Made-up	Imaginary
Bad	Negative

asserts his viewpoint by informing his reader that 'I tell you now that it would'. Another pattern of usage was the greater prevalence of phrasal verbs in weaker writing, again a reflection of typical oral usages. Examples of these included: *stitch them up*; *nodding off*; *give up*; and *hang around*.

Sentence expansion

The theoretical accounts of differences between speech and writing, discussed earlier, note the greater lexical density of writing, established through presence of more participial non-finite clauses, more expansion through constructions such as noun phrases adverbials, and more attributive adjectives. Our study suggests that this is a difference which needs to be acquired and which is one of the markers of linguistic development. The frequency of finite verb use declined with writing quality: in other words, the most accomplished writing expanded and elaborated within the sentence, through constructions other than the finite verb. One element of this expansion is the use of the non-finite present participle clause, which increased with writing accomplishment. Indeed, 42% of all writing judged to be weak writing made no use at all of present participle clauses. These data are illustrated in Table 6.

Table 6. Differences in finite verb frequency by writing quality

Per 100 words	Mean	Statistical significance
Number of finite verbs		
Good	12.15	.000*
Average	12.90	
Weak	14.18	
Number of non-finite present participle clauses		
Good	1.7	.001*
Average	1.4	
Weak	1.1	

These different patterns are exemplified clearly in the extracts below. The first extract, with the finite verbs underlined, expands noun phrases to provide explanatory detail for the reader. In part, this is achieved through the use of adjectives (a 'strained expression'; 'children, pale faced, and yawning') but also through a prepositional phrase to expand the head noun ('a man *in a brown suede coat*'). The writer also uses adverbs to provide additional detail ('watching a sweet machine nearby, longingly, and expectantly'). This is essentially a descriptive section in a narrative whereas the second piece is concerned with narrative action. Here, the use of present participle clauses (emboldened), intensifies the action, creating a sense not only of what is happening but also of how it feels: the narrative participants are presented as victims of the weather, needing to find shelter and avoid being pummelled by the rain. In both pieces, the lexical density is increased through these constructions, and the reader is offered a more detailed and nuanced narration of events.

> A child *shouted* for food. His mother's strained expression *was* similar to that of a waitress, who *was* serving a man in a brown suede coat. His face *was* hidden. Two children, pale-faced and yawning, *were* watching a sweet machine nearby, longingly, expectantly.

> My mum *ran* to open the car and *climbed* in, all the time **sheltering** herself with her arm from the rain that *was* lashing down upon her. I *closed* the front door to our house and *put* my hood up. I too *ran* to the car, **attempting** to keep my hood from **blowing** down and **subjecting** me to the rain **pummelling** down from the sky.

In contrast, the third extract below is less assured in its narration. There are nine finite verbs in this extract, signalling how little detail or expansion is provided in the rest of the sentence. There are no present participle clauses, only one adjective (*end-of-play*) and one adverb (*then*); but there are a high number of non-lexical words (*and, when, the, a, to, of* etc). Furthermore, the construction 'It's when . . .' is more typical of speech than writing.

> It's when one person *catches* people and *asks* the person who *has* been caught weather they *want* a kiss, cuddle or a torcher. The end-of-play whistle *was* then blown and Hannah and her friends *had* to go to their classes; this *was* the part of school, which *she* didn't like.

The study also investigated the usage of past participle non-finite clauses and infinitive clauses, but found no statistically significant differences within the sample. Further research might usefully explore this in more detail to establish whether older or adult writers use more of these constructions, or indeed whether the predominant difference between speech and writing is, in fact, the present participle clause.

Co-ordination
A further distinction between speech and writing noted in the theoretical accounts, described earlier, was the greater use of co-ordination in speech. Again, our study indicates that the trajectory of linguistic development mirrors this speech–writing distinction – the better the writing, the less reliant it was on co-ordination, as the table below shows (Table 7).

The extract below illustrates this tendency: the narrative action is chained through a series of clauses joined by 'and' or 'so', which echoes the prosodic features of an oral recount, dominated by the chronology of the event, and the succession of events.

> We were playing tracker *and* we decided to go on the field next to the woods *so* we ducked under the sharp barbed wire fence *and* went to the field. There was a herd of cows *so* we chased them off the field by poking their buttocks with sticks. They ran away past a house on the field. Moments later a farmer came out of the little house *and* chased after us *so* we leged it into the woods *and* hid for a few minutes *and* then went back on the field *and* layed there for 5 mins.

Table 7. Differences in co-ordinated clause frequency by writing quality

Per 100 words	Mean	Statistical significance
Number of co-ordinated clauses		
Good	2.25	.000*
Average	2.71	
Weak	3.18	

It is worth noting that although, this piece of writing is so heavily co-ordinated, there are other signs of developing maturity – there is a present participle clause (*poking their buttocks with sticks*) which successfully elaborates on the act of chasing away the cows, and the use of 'Moments later' to start a sentence is a 'writerly' choice, in place of the more oral 'Then'.

Subordination and embeddedness

If co-ordination is a typical characteristic of speech, then subordination, and embedded clauses are typical of writing. An increase in the use of subordination was identified as a feature of linguistic development in primary aged writers by Perera (1984), Harpin (1986), and Allison *et al.* (2002). One might reasonably expect, therefore, that in older writers in the secondary phase, this pattern would be replicated. However, our study shows clearly that this is not the case – in fact, subordination is used with higher frequency in less-accomplished writing (see Table 8 below).

Table 8. Differences in frequency of finite subordination by writing quality

Per 100 words	Mean	Statistical significance
Number of finite subordinate clauses		
Good	3.99	.022*
Average	4.25	
Weak	4.53	

The reason for this, however, does relate strongly to linguistic development and to the relationship between speech and writing. The higher proportion of subordination in weaker writing can be accounted for in two ways. Firstly, weaker writing presented many examples of long sentences which, although they contained subordination, were poorly managed. Secondly, higher quality writing made greater use of the simple sentence, with no subordination or co-ordination. One element of the use of the simple sentence is to alter the rhythm of a text and to create emphasis. These patterns are exemplified in the three extracts below. In the first, from an able writer, a long sentence with subordination is followed by three simple sentences which offer further elaboration on the scene and a final emphatic statement of the narrator's perspective. The second extract, also from an able writer, illustrates how subordination is effectively managed in a long sentence, including the use of an embedded clause. The final extract, however, from a weaker writer has four sentences of similar length, no simple sentences and both co-ordinated and subordinated clauses, and other than simple communication of narrative events, it does not linguistically shape the sentences for any effect of meaning or emphasis.

> I threaded my way through milling tourists quietly absorbing their surroundings of sculpted marble columns and paintings of cherubs, nativity scenes and brilliant patterns that covered the ceiling. The only noise was the buzz of quiet talk and the shuffle of feet. Coloured light shone from the stained glass windows. I was bored.

> We feel, as I am sure many other students across the country will agree, that we are much more refreshed and ready to work on a Monday morning, than we are at the end of the week, when we are restless and have no energy left.

> Later i had an appointment at the hospital and had the stiches taken out. I was unlucky enough to have another accident where I also hit my head. This happened at school when playing around with some of my mates in the Sand pit. I had made up a game where we had to jump on to a bench and then into the Sandpit.

The connection between linguistic development and an increasing ability to discriminate between spoken and written forms may also be evident in the usage pattern of subordinators. There was a consistent trend in both age groups studied for some subordinators to be more prevalent in weaker writing than in higher quality writing: *where, when, because,* and *if* were more frequent in the least able writing, whereas *whilst, whether,* and *once* were more likely to occur in accomplished writing. Arguably, this reflects speech–writing differences, with weaker writers making greater use of the subordinators most common in speech. This hypothesis is strengthened by the pattern of usage of 'like' as a subordinator, which was not evident at all in good writing, but a distinct pattern in weaker writing. Most linguists would regard this as a non-standard usage, substituting for the standard for 'as though' or 'just as' and it is a reflection of the oral use of 'like' in informal speech. Typical examples of this usage of 'like' included:

- I could smell the sweet smell of lavender, like I was standing in a herb garden.
- I opened it with a defening creek, closing it behind me with a ear splitting shatter which echoed through the church like someone was screaming.
- It was and felt as smooth as a slypery snake which is what I liked the most about it, so like any other person would do I figured that I should go and ride it.
- It seemed like he had stopped trying to get him and gone away.
- It seemed like we were travelling forever.

Thematic variation

One aspect of developing what Flower (1979) called reader-based prose is being able to alter the emphasis in sentences to guide the reader's interpretation of them. In spoken dialogue, the speaker influences the listener's reception through features such as intonation, rhythm, pitch, and stress and through non-verbal communicative accompaniments, but in writing these influences have to be achieved in different ways. Similarly, the meaning-making colour provided in speech by paralinguistic features means that 'lack of variety in sentence patterns is not necessarily evident in oral language' (Perera, 1984, p. 187). By contrast, lack of variety of sentence structure in writing can lead to a monotonous flat rhythm and limited positioning of the reader to pick up meaning-making cues. Therefore, thematic variation, altering what comes at the start of a sentence, is particularly significant in marking linguistic development from speech to written forms: 'what the writer puts first will influence the interpretation of everything else that follows' (Brown & Yule, 1983, p. 133). In English, the subject is dominant in first position in spoken utterances, principally because the listener needs to hear early on what the topic of a sentence is; in writing, reversals, or disruptions of this pattern are less problematic because readers tend to read small blocks of text rather than single words and because sentences can be re-read. Linguistic possibilities for creating thematic variation include the use of adverbs or adverbials, non-finite clauses, subject–verb inversions, and fronting.

The data indicate clearly that weaker writing is more dependent on the oral pattern of subject dominance in the thematic position (Table 9).

Table 9. Differences in subject openings by writing quality

Per 100 words	Mean	Statistical significance
Number of sentences opening with subject		
Good	4.17	.010*
Average	4.36	
Weak	4.74	

However, the data also reveals that at this stage of writing development, it appears to be using adverbials to alter subject dominance which is learned or acquired first. The table (Table 10) below shows that the best writing in 8 year exhibited greater use of adverbials than other writing, but in year 10 this pattern has altered to average writing. In year 10, good writing also uses non-finite clauses ($p = .040^*$), and subject–verb inversions ($p = .021^*$) to achieve thematic variation, and the very few examples of fronting in the sample were more likely to be in good writing. Thus, higher quality writing in our study demonstrated not only greater thematic variation, but also greater variety in the linguistic constructions used to create variation.

Table 10. Differences in adverbial openings by year group and writing quality

Per 100 words	Mean	Statistical significance
Adverbial sentence opening: year 8		
Good	1.25	.022*
Average	1.05	
Weak	0.86	
Adverbial sentence opening: year 10		
Good	0.95	.434
Average	1.22	
Weak	0.97	
Adverbial sentence opening: whole sample		
Good	1.12	.085
Average	1.17	
Weak	0.92	

The examples below illustrate, the different types of thematic variation and represent writers who are developing assurance in managing the reader–writer relationship and understand the needs of the reader in contrast to the needs of a listener. Reading them aloud, it is very easy to hear how unlike natural speech they are, and how they have been transformed into written sentences with lexical and linguistic characteristics of 'writerly' prose.

Adverbials

After a tiring walk, we reached our destination: street lamps flickered cautiously then lit up, glaring hostilely in our faces.

In Third World countries that have not developed economically, millions of people are experiencing the hardship of the lack of food, clean water, and medication that we, in the Western World, expect, and take for granted.

Confidently crossing the playground in the morning, with my Dad nobly carrying my suitcase, I felt highly important to be embarking on such an adventure.

Non-finite clauses

Unhurt by the rubber I turned straight back, found the nearest thing which happened to be a book and tossed it back.

Draped in my England flag, wearing the colours of St George, I was so nervous.

Fronting

However, the parents often feel that their children are not yet ready for this extra burden. *For all*, finding this balance is essential. *For most*, finding this balance is tricky. *But, for some*, finding this balance is nearly impossible.

To Natalie, life meant working in a hairdressers and staying asleep to noon. The Navy just wasn't her style.

Subject–verb inversions

There, five feet above me was *my bed*.

Ahead were *the dim lights of the manor flickering in the wind*.

Theoretical implications

Our study has, we believe, demonstrated that linguistic perspectives provide a valuable complement to more common cognitive and socio-cultural investigations of writing development and can illustrate in very explicit ways differing trajectories of development. It is important, however, to see these as patterns or tendencies rather than as absolute staging posts in development and to align knowledge of linguistic development with cognitive and socio-cultural insights into writing processes. For example, the ability to advance-plan a sentence and manipulate linguistic possibilities within the constaints of the overall textual goal requires a high level of executive control. Both Kuhn (2006) and McCutcheon (1996) have argued that growth in executive control is a feature of adolescence. Likewise, the linguistic choices made need to function within a secure understanding of both readers and texts as culturally situated. Research in writing, therefore, needs to be more cognizant of these multiple perspectives: shaping and creating text to meet a reader's needs demands high-level cognitive resources, operating within socio-cultural expectations, and drawing on appropriately-developed linguistic repertoires.

It is also clear that linguistic theory has addressed early writing development more satisfactorily than later writing development and our own research has only begun to mine this rich seam. From a text-oriented perspective, further research might look more specifically at later development of the noun phrase, and investigate in more detail the different types of subordination used, and the range of adverbials used, for example. From a writer-oriented perspective, this study naturally raises questions about metalinguistic understanding and the extent to which writers' choices are made explicitly or tacitly. It is also evident that cognitive research into the translation from thought to text needs to address more explicitly the fact that good writing requires not only production of text, but also shaping of text.

Pedagogical implications

Although, it is well understood that learning to be a writer draws on 'talk knowledge', this study makes it clear that one key element in learning to write with accomplishment is, in part at least, learning how *not* to write the way you talk, or rather acquiring adeptness in transforming oral structures into written structures. This demands a degree of deliberateness in the process of writing which is more cognitively costly than simply writing down the words that come into your head, a process which merely 'preserves the straight-ahead form of oral language production' (Bereiter & Scardamalia, 1987, p. 9). It also requires the acquisition of a linguistic repertoire which is specific to writing and may have no parallels in talk. This implies that pedagogical attention to grammar needs re-orientation from assumptions about error and accuracy in writing to a stronger focus on rhetorical choices and rhetorical effects and means making more connections for developing writers between linguistic choices and meaning-making effects. In England, as a consequence of a renewed emphasis on grammar teaching, underpinned by policy frameworks, there has been a tendency to teach 'sentence variety' without any assured consideration of the effects of sentence variety or how that variety might be achieved. It appears that this is not an issue restricted to England: Paraskevas (2006) reports American students bemoaning teachers who encourage them to 'vary the way the begin their sentences without guidelines as to how this can be done' (p. 68). Instead, Paraskevas (2006) advocates developing understanding about sentences which will give writers 'the power to choose how they want to convey their meaning, how best to say what they want to say' (p. 68). Our study would suggest that one aspect of understanding which should be at the forefront of instructional attention is the difference between spoken utterances and written sentences and the particular linguistic constructions which tend to characterize this distinction.

The use of talk as an instructional support alongside writing also needs to be more carefully addressed. What is the talk for? Talk is a valuable tool in the writing classroom for generating and evolving ideas for writing and for reflecting on and sharing responses to writing through paired work or peer assessment. Our observations of the teaching of writing in our study suggest that these are the most prevalent instructional strategies for talk in the context of writing. Some teachers do, however, use talk for 'oral rehearsal', a term which has gained currency in literacy classrooms in England due to its place in policy documents. There is no well-theorized conceptualization of oral rehearsal in these policy documents and indeed its precise meaning shifts from document to document. However, one view of oral rehearsal represented in the policies is that oral rehearsal gives writers an opportunity to rehearse their written sentence aloud before writing it down so they can hear what it sounds like. This has the benefit of reducing cognitive load as writers are not simultaneously generating ideas and translating into text. More significantly, though, it might allow writers to manipulate a sentence and review effects before committing it to paper or screen and potentially would allow a teacher to draw attention to some of the differences between the spoken utterance and the orally rehearsed written sentence.

Finally, if, as this study argues, one key marker of writing development in the secondary phase is the acquisition of a linguistic repertoire which is not an oral repertoire, it is important for teaching strategies to acknowledge the differential position of speakers in the classroom in accessing this repertoire. Perera (1984) noted that 'although all children have to alter their language significantly as they move from casual speech to formal writing, those whose oral language differs markedly from Standard English will have a particularly demanding adjustment to make' (p. 213). Students for whom English is not their first language and who are orally fluent may have writing needs masked by this oral fluency. Likewise, in England at least, socio-economic differences in speech patterns also have an effect. The talk patterns of the more privileged middle classes are closer to the patterns of writing with the result that 'the difference between the syntax of speech and that of writing is far less for such groups than it is for groups whose dialects are little if at all influenced by the structure of writing' (Kress, 1994, p. 3).

References

Alamargot, D., & Chanquoy, L. (2001). *Through the models of writing*. New York: Kluwer Academic Publishers.

Allison, P., Beard, R., & Willcocks, J. (2002). Subordination in children's writing. *Language in Education, 16*(2), 97–111.

Badecker, W., & Kuminiak, F. (2007). Morphology, agreement, and working memory retrieval in sentence production: Evidence from gender and case in Slovak. *Journal of Memory and Language, 56*, 65–85.

Bereiter, C., & Scardamalia, M. (1982). From conversation to composition: The role of instruction in a developmental process. In R. Glaser (Ed.), *Advances in instructional psychology* (Vol. 2, pp. 1–64). Hillsdale, NJ: Erlbaum.

Bereiter, C., & Scardamalia, M. (1987). *The psychology of written composition*. Hillsdale, NJ: Erlbaum.

Bock, K. (1995). Sentence production: From mind to mouth. In J. L. Miller & P. D. Eimas (Eds.), *Handbook of perception and cognition: Speech, language, and communication* (Vol. 11, pp. 181–216). Orlando, FL: Academic Press.

Bock, K., & Levelt, W. J. M. (1994). Language production: Grammatical encoding. In M. Gernsbacher (Ed.), *Handbook of psycholinguistics* (pp. 945–984). New York: Academic Press.

Brown, G., & Yule, G. (1983). *Discourse analysis*. Cambridge: Cambridge University Press.

Chafe, W. L. (1982). Integration and involvement in speaking, writing, and oral literature. In D. Tannen (Ed.), *Spoken and written language: Exploring orality and literacy* (pp. 35–54). Norwood, NJ: Able.

Cleland, A. A., & Pickering, M. J. (2006). Do writing and speaking employ the same syntactic representations? *Journal of Memory and Language, 54*, 185–198.

Collins, A., & Gentner, D. A. (1980). A framework for a cognitive theory of writing. In L. W. Gregg & E. R. Steinberg (Eds.), *Cognitive processes in writing* (pp. 51–72). Hillsdale, NJ: Erlbaum.

Crowhurst, M., & Piche, G. (1979). Audience and mode of discourse effects on syntactic complexity in writing at two grade levels. *Research in the Teaching of English, 13*(2), 101-109.

Crystal, D. (1995). *The Cambridge encyclopedia of the English language*. Cambridge: Cambridge University Press.

Czerniewska, P. (1992). *Learning about writing*. Oxford: Blackwell.

Drieman, G. H. J. (1962). Differences between written and spoken language. *Acta Psychologica, 20*, 36-57.

English and Media Centre (1984). *Making stories*. London: EMC.

Flower, L. (1979). Writer-based prose: A cognitive basis for problems in writing. *College English, 41*(1), 19-37.

Harpin, W. (1986). Writing counts. In A. Wilkinson (Ed.), *The writing of writing* (pp. 158-176). Milton Keynes: OUP.

Hartsuiker, R. J., & Westenberg, C. (2000). Word order priming in written and spoken sentence production. *Cognition, 75*(2), 27-39.

Haswell, R. H. (2000). Documenting improvement in college writing. *Written Communication, 17*(3), 307-352.

Hayes, J. R., & Flower, L. S. (1980). Identifying the organisation of writing processes. In L. W. Gregg & E. R. Steinberg (Eds.), *Cognitive processes in writing* (pp. 3-30). Hillsdale, NJ: Erlbaum.

Hunt, K. W. (1965). *Grammatical structures written at three grade levels*. Champaign, IL: NCTE.

Jones, S. M., & Myhill, D. A. (2007). Discourses of difference? Examining gender difference in linguistic characteristics of writing. *Canadian Journal of Education, 30*(2), 456-482.

Kress, G. (1994). *Learning to write*. London: Routledge.

Kroll, B. M. (1978). Cognitive egocentrism and the problem of audience awareness in written discourse. *Research in the Teaching of English, 12*(2), 269-281.

Kuhn, D. (2006). The development of learning. *Journal of Cognition and Development, 7*(3), 309-312.

Loban, W. (1976). *Language development: Kindergarten through grade twelve*. Urbana, IL: National Council of Teachers of English, (Research Report 18).

Macarthur, C., Graham, S., & Fitzgerald, J. (2006). *Handbook of writing research*. New York: Guilford Press.

Massey, A. J., Elliott, G. L., & Johnson, N. K. (2005). *Variations in aspects of writing in 16 + english examinations between 1980 and 2004: Vocabulary, spelling, punctuation, sentence structure, non-standard english research matters: Special issue 1*. Cambridge: University of Cambridge Local Examinations Syndicate.

McCutchen, A. (1996). A capacity theory of writing: Working memory in composition. *Educational Psychology Review, 8*(3), 299-325.

Micciche, L. (2004). Making a case for rhetorical grammar. *College Composition and Communication, 55*(4), 716-737.

Myhill, D. A. (2008). Towards a linguistic model of sentence development in writing. *Language and Education, 22*(5), 271-288.

Myhill, D. A. (2009). Children's patterns of composition and their reflections on their composing processes. *British Educational Research Journal, 35*(1), 47-64.

Myhill, D. A., & Jones, S. (2007). More than just error correction: Children's reflections on their revision processes. *Written Communication, 24*(4), 323-343.

Negro, I., & Chanquoy, L. (2005). The effect of psycholinguistic research on the teaching of writing. *L1 Studies in Language and Literature, 5*(2), 105-111.

Nystrand, M. (2006). The social and historical context for writing research. In C. Macarthur, S. Graham, & J. Fitzgerald (Eds.), *Handbook of writing research* (pp. 11-27). New York: Guilford Press.

O'Donnell, R. C. (1974). Syntactic differences between speech and writing. *American Speech, 49*(1/2), 102-110.

Paraskevas, C. (2006). Grammar apprenticeship. *English Journal, 95*(5), 65-69.

Pea, R., & Kurland, D. (1987). Cognitive technologies for writing. *Review of Research in Education, 14,* 277–326.

Perera, K. (1984). *Children's writing and reading: Analysing classroom language.* Oxford: Blackwell.

Perera, K. (1986). Grammatical differentiation between speech and writing in children aged 8–12. In A. Wilkinson (Ed.), *The writing of writing* (pp. 90–108). Milton Keynes: OUP.

Perera, K. (1987). *Understanding language.* Sheffield: NAAE.

Prior, P. A. (2006). Socio-cultural theory of writing. In C. Macarthur, S. Graham, & J. Fitzgerald (Eds.), *Handbook of writing research* (pp. 54–66). New York: Guilford Press.

Stallings, L. M., MacDonald, M. C., & O'Seaghda, P. G. (1998). Phrasal ordering constraints in sentence production: Phrase length and verb disposition in heavy-NP shift. *Journal of Memory and Language, 39,* 392–417.

Verhoeven, L., Aparici, M., Cahana-Amitay, M., van Hell, J. V., Kriz, S., & Viguie-Simon, A. (2002). Clause packaging in writing and speech: A cross-linguistic developmental analysis. *Written Language and Literacy, 5*(2), 135–161.

Wells, G., & Chang, G. L. (1986). From speech to writing: Some evidence on the relationship between oracy and literacy. In A. Wilkinson (Ed.), *The writing of writing* (pp. 109–131). Milton Keynes: OUP.

Teaching and Learning Writing, 45–62
BJEP Monograph Series II, 6
© 2009 The British Psychological Society

The
British
Psychological
Society

www.bpsjournals.co.uk

The impact of oral language skills on the production of written text

Julie E. Dockrell[1]* and Vincent Connelly[2]

[1]School of Psychology and Human Development, Institute of Education, University of London, London, UK
[2]Department of Psychology, Oxford Brookes University, Oxford, UK

Background. While oral language seems crucial to written language development there has been relatively little research on explicit links between the two.

Aims. This paper reviews and explores the links between oral language skills and the development of writing with particular reference to children with specific language impairment (SLI).

Arguments. Children with SLI are poor at writing and we review evidence from our own and others work showing how oral language and oral vocabulary skills, in particular, are closely associated with written language production in this population. We detail a set of longitudinal analyses showing close relationships between oral language, writing, and other literacy related skills.

Conclusions. We conclude that oral language skill does constrain the development of writing. Children with SLI are very poor at writing. Whether this is due to their general language level or a problem in a specific area such as vocabulary, grammar, or spelling remains to be seen.

We discuss the implications for educational provision of this set of research findings.

The impact of oral language skills on the production of written text

It is well established that oral language competence underpins the development of literacy (Bishop & Snowling, 2004; Catts, Fey, & Tomblin, 1997) and later educational achievements. Children whose oral language skills are compromised often struggle with learning to read and their overall academic achievement is reduced in comparison with their peers. Surprisingly, few studies have attempted to elucidate the ways in which components of the oral language system can enhance or limit the production of written text. This chapter explores the barriers that language learning difficulties in children pose for developing competence in producing written texts and proceeds to explore

*Correspondence should be addressed to Dr Julie E. Dockrell, Psychology and Human Development, Institute of Education, 20 Bedford Way, London WC1H 0AL, UK (e-mail: j.dockrell@ioe.ac.uk).

DOI:10.1348/000709909X421919

whether language difficulties result in delayed or different profiles of text production. The implications of the reported studies for research and practice are explored.

Learning to write successfully is dependent on a number of basic perceptual, cognitive, and language processes (Kellogg, 1994) and, not surprisingly, poor performance in writing tasks can therefore be the behavioural manifestation of a wide range of developmental difficulties (Dockrell, in press). Although text generation shares many components with oral language production, including lexical retrieval and syntactical formulation, writing places additional demands on the developing cognitive system. For example, children find producing a written narrative significantly more difficult than producing an oral narrative (Gillam & Johnston, 1992) and the written mode takes up more cognitive resource (Bourdin & Fayol, 2000). To understand the nature of the relationship between oral and written language, it is necessary to consider both the subcomponents of the oral language system and the ways in which these components may directly or indirectly impact on the processing of written text (Bishop & Snowling, 2004). It is also necessary to investigate how oral language may be mediated by other skills which are prerequisites for the production of written text.

Oral and written language

The four language systems (speaking, listening, writing, and reading) develop in synchrony (Shanahan, 2006); however, models of writing development do not specifically identify oral language as central to the writing process. Careful consideration of the subcomponents of the language system; phonology, the lexicon, grammar, and pragmatics (Hirsh-Pasek, Kochanoff, Newcombe, & de Villiers, 2005), leads to the clear prediction that these components will all impact on the production of written texts and could do so at different developmental phases. Increased oral language facility is associated with increased written language proficiency (McCutchen, 1986), although to date no thresholds of oral language competence to support writing have been identified (Shanahan, 2006). While oral language competencies and verbal reasoning contribute to composition in the intermediate grades the relationships between these skills are difficult to specify because of high covariance between reading and oral language (Abbott & Berninger, 1993). There is some evidence that children's compositional quality is influenced by oral language skills at several levels including subword, word, sentence, and text levels (Abbott & Berninger, 1993; Berninger, Mizokawa, Bragg, Cartwright, & Yates, 1994). For example, at the single word level, phonological processes impact directly on children's spelling development, the mastery of which is a prerequisite to extended text generation (Graham, Berninger, Abbott, Abbott, & Whitaker, 1997). In the early school years, there are parallels between oral and written modalities in writing (Hidi & Hidyard, 1984). At this point in development, oral language can be viewed as leading the production of written text (Shanahan, 2006). Over time these processes diverge. The focus of oral language is on elaboration whereas the focus in writing is the development of cohesion (Gillam & Johnston, 1992; McCutchen, 1986) and knowledge transformation. Despite the differentiation of the two processes, as children become more skilled in writing and speaking, there are continual links between them. Over time as writing develops it too influences the other language systems.

By corollary, poor oral language skills are associated with difficulties in fluently producing words and clauses in text and are more generally associated with reduced compositional quality (Berninger & Fuller, 1992; Berninger *et al.*, 1992). Limitations with oral vocabulary (Bishop & Clarkson, 2003; Dockrell, Lindsay, Connelly, & Mackie, 2007) and oral narrative performance (Cragg & Nation, 2006) are related to poor written text production. A recent comparative study of dyslexic, language impaired, and typically developing matched children demonstrated the ways in which different profiles of skills can impact on writing performance (Puranik *et al.*, 2007). Language-impaired participants, but not dyslexic participants, produced fewer words and numbers of ideas than typically developing matched peers. In contrast, both dyslexic pupils and language-impaired pupils produced more spelling and grammar errors than typically developing matched peers. These authors argued that the differences between the language-impaired group and dyslexic group rested in the non-phonological dimensions of text production that were impaired in the children with oral language difficulties. Even when early language problems are overcome, written language continues to suffer in children (Naucler & Magnusson, 2002). Difficulties appear to be particularly marked in the production of expository texts (Scott & Windsor, 2000) where production may be constrained by the additional cognitive demands in developing these texts. Studying both typical and atypical development in the same tasks, and with the same methodology, can be both mutually informative, and can help reveal underlying mechanisms of developmental change.

Children with specific language difficulties

Writing poses a number of challenges for children with language learning difficulties. Practitioners, policy makers, and researchers use a range of different terms to describe this population (see Lindsay, Dockrell, Mackie, & Letchford, 2002). Moreover, a range of terms is used in Europe (dysphagia) and North America (USA: specific language impairment (SLI), or in parts of Canada: dysphagia) and more recently primary language disorder (Tomblin *et al.*, 2003). The specific characteristic of the children's development are difficulties with the acquisition and processing of oral language skills. The most commonly used core criterion to identify children is that their language problems cannot be explained in terms of other cognitive, neurological, or perceptual deficits (Bishop, 1997; Leonard, 1998). These children typically have non-verbal skills within the average range and language problems are evident by a protracted rate of language development as well as difficulties with subcomponents of the language system (Leonard, 1998). Therefore, the high cognitive demands placed on the individual when learning to write may overload a language system that is reduced in processing capacity (Ellis Weismer, Evans, & Hesketh, 1999; Montgomery, 2000; Windsor & Hwang, 1999) and lead to problems with text production. Such difficulties lead to reduced length of texts and higher levels of errors than children of a similar age, and possibly language level.

There are also reasons to predict particular patterns of errors in the written text of these children at both the word and sentence level. For example, the reduced lexical knowledge experienced by some children with language difficulties may impact directly on the children's written outputs. More advanced writing is associated with a greater number of different words (Beard, 2000), increases in the number of adjectives (Wells & Chang, 1986), and an increased number of adverbs and adverbial phrases (Perera, 1984). Thus, limits in vocabulary are likely to influence both the length and content of the written texts of children. In contrast, the grammatical complexity of the written outputs produced by the children may be influenced by their morphological (Leonard, Eyer, Bedore, & Grela, 1997) and syntactic skills (van der Lely & Christian, 2000; van der Lely

& Ullman, 2001). The writing profile of children with difficulties with morphology and syntax will arguably lead to quite different patterns of problem than the difficulties experienced by children with phonological difficulties.

Morphology and syntactic difficulties may manifest themselves in writing through the construction of simple rather than complex sentences and the omission of prepositions, articles, and verbs. Many children with SLIs have particular difficulties in acquiring inflectional morphemes which represent tense and agreement in the underlying syntactic structure of sentences (Leonard, McGregor, & Allen, 1992; Rice & Oetting, 1993). Together, these difficulties would predict problems in producing coherent written texts. The texts are, therefore, expected to contain high levels of grammatical errors and reflect immature sentence constructions. These grammatical limitations will reduce the children's ability to express semantic content.

A significant proportion of children with SLI also experience phonological difficulties (Bishop, North, & Donlan, 1996; Briscoe, Bishop, & Norbury, 2001; Gathercole & Baddeley, 1990) and thus have spelling difficulties (xxx) which will influence written text both directly and indirectly. Problems with phonology may impact on writing through increased numbers of spelling errors (Clarke-Klein, 1994; Lewis & Freebairn, 1992; Treiman, 1993). In fact, children with SLI do indeed produce a high number of spelling errors (Bishop & Clarkson, 2003; Lewis & Freebairn, 1992; Treiman, 1993) particularly phonological errors (Clarke-Klein, 1994; Mackie & Dockrell, 2004) and there are suggestions that error patterns can deviate from both chronological and language matched peers (Mackie & Dockrell, 2004).

Given the range of problems related to the oral language system it is not surprising that the children also experience problems with reading in general (Bishop, 1997; Gallagher, Frith, & Snowling, 2000; McArthur, Hogben, Edwards, Heath, & Mengler, 2000) and so this is another potential barrier to producing fluent and coherent written texts. Early experience and developmental competence in reading increases children's ability to produce coherent written texts. Reading can assist in the development of vocabulary meaning and meaning gained through connected text (Anglin, 1993). Reading also provides knowledge of letter shapes and an introduction to morphological awareness (Fitzgerald & Shanahan, 2000). Early literacy experience increases awareness of sentence structures and text organization. Thus, it is important to consider to what extent the writing problems experienced by children with SLI are mediated by their difficulties in reading (Bishop, 1997; Gallagher *et al.*, 2000; McArthur *et al.*, 2000).

Recent research on the writing of children with SLI

Despite the substantial indirect evidence that children with SLI will have difficulties with written language, there have been limited attempts to specify the nature and extent of the children's problems beyond the single word level and we now know that there is a substantial variation in written narrative skill of children with SLI that is not captured by single word spelling alone (Bishop & Clarkson, 2003). In general, studies have supported the view that children's difficulties in producing written text reflect a particular vulnerability in linguistic form, as evidenced by their grammatical errors (Gillam & Johnston, 1992; Mackie & Dockrell, 2004; Scott & Windsor, 2000; Windsor, Scott, & Street, 2000). These errors include both the percentage of written utterances containing grammatical errors (Gillam & Johnston, 1992; Mackie & Dockrell, 2004; Scott & Windsor, 2000) and the total number of verb composite errors (Windsor *et al.*, 2000).

Errors are not simply restricted to verbs but include the omission of whole words, the omission of plural inflections, as well as the overuse of the conjunction 'and' (Mackie & Dockrell, 2004). Bishop and Clarkson (2003) confirmed the vulnerability of children with language difficulties in producing written text but found that the commonest problems were not grammatical difficulties but problems with spelling and punctuation, and poorer semantic skills. They argued that it was the children's phonological processing deficits that were central in causing the children's written language problems and that this was demonstrated by the close link with the children's difficulties in repeating non-words. Morphological errors are more prevalent in children with SLI but these errors cannot always be explained by phonology alone (Mackie & Dockrell, 2004). Morphological development, both inflectional and derivational, plays a key role in the development of typical children's written language (Green, McCutchen, Schwiebert, Quinlan, Eva-Wood, & Juelis, 2003) and it is important to consider the extent to which these dimensions relate to the written language of children with SLI.

Cross-sectional studies limit our ability to model the relationships between language and literacy difficulties and text production. Children's profiles of linguistic deficits change over time (Bishop & Adams, 1990; Conti-Ramsden & Botting, 1999) and, since written language skills are built on competencies in other tasks, examination of both longitudinal and concurrent competencies is an important component in understanding the nature and extent of the children's written language deficits. Moreover, if early predictors of later writing performance can be identified in longitudinal studies, this provides a basis for identifying appropriate comparison groups to explore delayed or different patterns of text production in cross-sectional studies. This approach will also help highlight the textural features which should be the focus of detailed analyses and provide a infrastructure to devise appropriate interventions for children with language learning disabilities.

An initial attempt to examine the longitudinal effects of oral language on writing was reported by Dockrell *et al.* (2007). This study examined the writing skills of a cohort of children from age 8 to 11 who had been identified with a specific language problem earlier in their development. Writing performance was examined in relation to both earlier and concurrent oral language skills and literacy levels. As a cohort, these children experienced significant problems in producing written text throughout the study period. Both concurrent and predictor measures of receptive vocabulary and reading showed similar patterns of strong relationships with the outcome written language measure.

However, in contrast to previous research, neither working memory nor oral grammatical competence was statistically significantly associated with writing at this point in time. This was surprising given previous research (Mackie & Dockrell, 2004; Scott & Windsor, 2000; Windsor *et al.*, 2000) but was consistent with the data from Bishop and Clarkson (2003). Importantly, a factor analysis of the subscales of the writing measure captured two different dimensions of the writing process: semantics and rules. The semantic factor was significantly related to the amount of written text produced. In contrast, the scores on the rule-based factor were negatively correlated with text production. This relationship highlights the fact, that for children with written language difficulties, the more text that is produced the greater the scope for errors of grammar and punctuation. The importance of semantic skills in underpinning the writing skills of the children was further substantiated by the significant independent contribution of the vocabulary measure in the regression analyses.

Previous studies had provided indicative evidence that vocabulary knowledge may be a relevant dimension in the writing of children with SLI. Lexical diversity was shown to be a factor in the performance of the children studied by Scott and Windsor (2000), and semantic content was associated with writing in the Bishop and Clarkson (2003) study but in both cases the researchers minimized the role of semantics as a support for writing for the participants' production of written texts. In contrast, the Dockrell *et al.* (2007) study reported that vocabulary was the only language factor to contribute significantly in regressions with the quality of written text composition. As with oral language, vocabulary appears to provide a building block for written language (see also Green *et al.*, 2003). A range of lexical items allows the child to build a text and provide the basic infrastructure of text meaning. This is consistent with work published by Berninger, Hart, Abbott, and Karovsky *et al.* (1992), where text generation skills in typically developing 5- to 9-year-olds were constrained by verbal IQ, including vocabulary development. They also noted that basic oral language skills such as word finding influenced the development of transcription skills in children's writing. The extent and nature of children's semantic representations was a central dimension in the texts produced.

The Dockrell *et al.* (2007) study also indicated that the production of written text was indeed mediated by the children's reading levels. Thus, studies of children with SLI need to address this factor prior to drawing any conclusions about the role of oral language skills. The influence of reading skills has an impact at a number of levels of writing development from a lack of familiarity with books constraining knowledge of narrative structure (Juel, 1988) to limited knowledge of spellings constraining the development of low level writing skills such as transcription and text generation (Berninger *et al.*, 1992).

At age 11, for the pupils in the Dockrell *et al.* (2007) study, their writing resembled that of much younger children. However, it is not clear to what extent their pattern of performance differs from children of a similar language age. Nor does the data speak to potential continuities in the factors that support the pupils' performance on writing texts. We now turn to these questions. In the first instance, we consider the continuity of writing performance and predictors of writing performance.

The continuity of writing performance in children with language impairments

To examine the trajectories in the pupils writing performance, we further examined the same group's language, literacy, and writing skills at the age of 16 (Dockrell, Lindsay, & Connelly, in press). At this point in development, measures of language and literacy, assessed both longitudinally and concurrently, were examined to establish their relative contribution to written text production. The pupils continued to experience specific difficulties with language and literacy and the data indicated that by the age of 16 literacy skills were a particular area of weakness. The production of written text continued to be an area of marked vulnerability for these pupils, with writing scores often being the lowest standardized score of all the language and literacy measures. Moreover, during their teenage years the pupils' writing skills decreased relative to standardized norms. Thus, this current data contrast with data in the elementary years where a relative improvement in the production of written story composition has been noted (Fey *et al.*, 2004). These differences are important to address. The decreases in pupils' performance on written measures may reflect their specific language difficulties. For typically developing children their increasing language competence supports later development;

for those with continued language difficulties these resources are not available. In conjunction, it is important to consider the specific support provided to children when developing their competencies in the written mode, an issue we return to later. This decrease in writing skills occurred at the time when, in the UK, it is expected that by the age of 11 pupils will have mastered the basic skills in reading and writing, moved towards the analysis of genres, writing with technical accuracy, and organizing text into planned and coherent sequences (Department for Children, Schools and Families, 2007, www.standards.dfes.gov.uk/keystage3/) – a major challenge for the pupils in this study.

By the age of 16, the pupils' written productions could be captured by a single dimension. This differs from the patterns at age 11 (Dockrell *et al.*, 2007) and age 14 (Dockrell & Connelly, 2007). Despite the apparent co-ordination of the two dimensions of rules and semantics identified in Dockrell *et al.* (2007), difficulties in relation to form (spelling and handwriting) and content generation was a specific area of weakness. By the age of 16, the significant concurrent predictors of text production were spelling and vocabulary. The current data add further weight to the view that vocabulary continues to provide a building block for written language for these young people.

The poor spelling skills of the participants were evident both in their written text productions and in the assessment of their single word spellings. At 11, the participants' writing levels were mediated by their reading levels. The point of fracture had moved, and on the surface appears similar to difficulties exhibited by young adults with dyslexia (Connelly, Campbell, MacLean, & Barnes, 2006) where writing was constrained by their transcription skills in the form of poor spelling and slow handwriting. This difficulty had a direct impact on the amount of words produced by the young adults with dyslexia when writing and the overall quality of composition produced by this population. However, our participants differed to those of Connelly *et al.* (2006) where participants could produce compositions that were age appropriate in terms of the ideas and development, sentence structure and organization, and unity and coherence on a standardized writing measure. The children with SLI were not producing age appropriate scores in any of these areas. Thus they had problems with spelling and transcription combined with a wider problem in language that was leading to very poor performance in all aspects of the writing process.

We examined concurrent and longitudinal predictors with path analysis. As shown in Figures 1 and 2, the best fit model for the concurrent path analysis included direct effects of vocabulary, spelling, and writing fluency, with reading fluency (a timed measure of reading decoding) having an indirect effect through spelling and writing fluency. The concurrent model confirmed both the effects of semantic factors, as measured by vocabulary, and phonological factors, as measured by spelling, and indicated that an independent contribution of writing fluency featured in the adolescents' writing. In our second model, we explored the longitudinal predictors for the pupils' writing performance at 16. This model identified direct effects of reading, spelling, and writing 2 years previously on writing at 16. These data demonstrated the ways in which literacy measures come to the fore in the writing performance of older pupils with a history of language difficulties. These measures reflected both phonological and morphological features of oral language. Non-phonological factors were also evident, and unlike the literacy measures, their impact was traced back to the age of 8. Vocabulary appears to form a semantic basis which supports both continued vocabulary growth and written text production at age 11 and oral sentence construction at age 14. Over time the impact of oral language was mediated by both the pupils' reading skills and their writing skills.

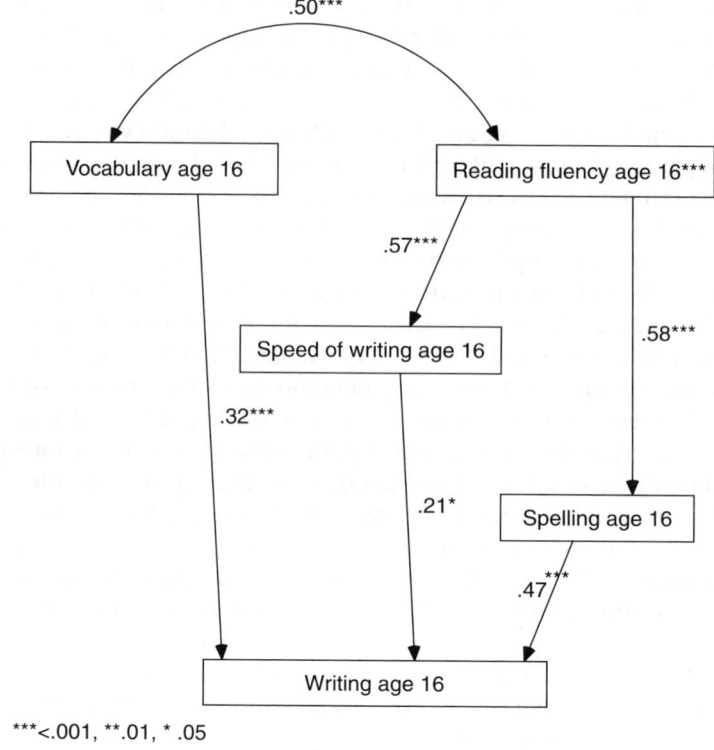

Figure 1. Path analysis examining concurrent contributions of literacy and language to writing at age 16.

As the figures demonstrate, at both time points in this longitudinal study, vocabulary played a key role in these pupil's written text productions. We now examine the extent to which this reliance on vocabulary is a compensatory mechanism for reduced performance in other areas.

Patterns of written text production in children with specific language difficulties: delayed or different?

Comparisons of the writing of children with specific language difficulties with other groups of writers are limited. Of those comparisons, there have been mixed results in specifying how the writing of children with specific language difficulties differs from that of typically developing children. Partly, this inconsistency may due to the nature of the language comparisons identified. Of particular, concern is the use of language age matches (Dockrell, 2001; McCauley & Swisher, 1984; Plante *et al.*, 1993). Age-equivalent scores are often made by extrapolation from a child's score that lies midway between two age scores on the particular test. There is, however, no reason to assume that a score mid-way equates with age-equivalent midpoint score. Moreover, age-equivalent scores do not necessarily mean that a child is performing in an equivalent fashion to a peer of a younger age. A range of factors affect performance and additional language and social experience will be one such factor (McCauley & Swisher, 1984). Finally, such scores are made up by a child's results on a number of subtests and there is no, a priori, reason to

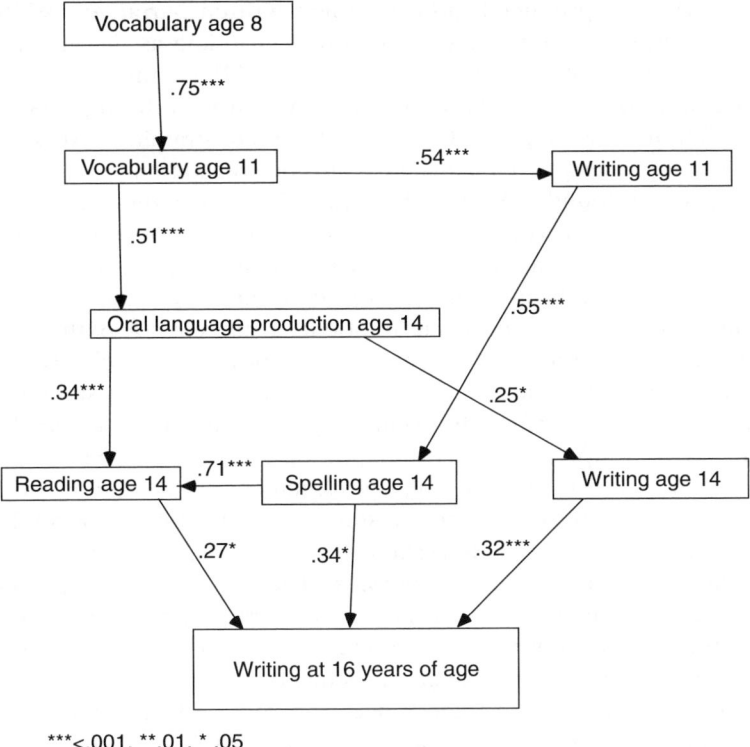

***<.001, **.01, * .05

Figure 2. Path analysis examining predictions of literacy and language to writing at age 16.

assume that the pattern of results will be the same across children of different chronological ages but with the same total score. One way to minimize these difficulties is to match language-impaired children with typically developing children on a key variable thought to underpin performance in the task (see Thomas *et al.*, in press for a discussion of alternative approaches). If children are matched on the skills that predict later writing in a language-impaired population then differences in their writing profiles from their relevant matches will allow an examination of specific areas of impairment. Moreover, profiles of weaknesses in text production over time should guide the focus of the data collected about the children's performance beyond simple standardized measures.

The writing skills of 10-year-old children with language difficulties were compared with chronological, language age, and reading age matches by Gillam and colleagues (Gillam & Johnston, 1992; McFadden & Gillam, 1996) The language-impaired children's scores on the Detroit Test of Learning Aptitude-2 was converted to an age equivalent and typically developing children within that age range were identified as language age matches. As such children were not matched on absolute performance on a language measure – either syntactic or semantic. Their results indicated that children with specific language difficulties had holistic level scores in writing texts that were at the same level as the language age match children but less than the chronologically matched peers. This would point to a general delay in writing development. However, the children with language difficulties and their reading age matches produced more complex oral narratives than written narratives, while the other children, including the language age matches, produced more complex written narratives. Writing for the children with language difficulty was also more demanding as the grammatical error rates in writing per complex utterance were higher (78%) compared to an average of 46% grammatical error rates in oral narratives. This early study suggests that it is not simply the children's oral language levels which are constraining text production but reading levels and processing demands must also be considered.

A similar result was found by Scott and Windsor (2000) who reported on comparisons on general language performance measures between groups of children of 11-year-old children and their age match and language age match comparison groups. Language matches were identified from language age equivalents on the Test of Language Development (TOLD) spoken language quotient, a measure of both expressive and receptive language (Hammill & Newcomer, 1988). They assessed children's writing on 10 general language performance measures. On nine of these measures there was no difference between the children with specific language difficulties and their language age match comparison group. There was though a difference between the language age match and the children with specific language difficulties on the number of grammatical errors produced in T-units. T-units are the shortest grammatically allowable sentences into which writing can be segmented (Hunt, 1965). T-units, which are longer and have more subordinate clauses are more complex. The children with specific language difficulties produced more of these errors in both narrative and expository writing and also across narrative and expository spoken summaries, although the effects of discourse and genre were consistent across the groups studied.

T-unit errors encompassed a wide range of errors and included 'any error that rendered a T-unit ungrammatical' (Scott & Windsor, 2000, p. 330). As such it is not possible to distinguish, for example, failures in spelling to mark tenses from difficulties with subordinate clause relationships. Therefore, while they made the claim that children with specific language difficulties had difficulties with grammar, it was uncertain if this was a general deficit or could have been due to a particular weakness in one area such as grammatical rules applied to spelling.

Windsor et al. (2000) carried out a further analysis on the same group of children and reported that the children with language difficulties made more verb and noun composite errors on both the spoken and written narratives than either their chronological or language age matched peers. Verb composite errors included errors with the regular past tense, third person singular, and copula and auxiliary forms of be while noun composite errors included the regular plural, articles, and the possessive. The rate of errors on the written narratives was very much higher than that found in the spoken narratives for the children with language difficulties but not for the language and chronological age matches. They also made three times as many verb as noun errors in the written narratives while there was no difference between rate of errors in the spoken narratives. Further analysis found that most of this difference was accounted for by verb composite errors on the past tense '-ed' ending in verbs and article errors in noun composites but there was substantial variability in the children's performance, Zero marking of '-ed' in writing was claimed by Windsor et al. (2000) as a clinical marker of the writing of children with language impairment since typical children do not show difficulties with '-ed' beyond the age of 8 or 9 years (Carlisle, 1996, Nunes, Bryant, & Bindman, 1997). However, while omitting '-ed' may be a failure of grammatical awareness, it may also be a failure to spell orthographically. When children are slow in processing language they may experience difficulties in processing sounds with rapid acoustic transitions and/or perceiving phonemes with low phonetic salience (for example, t/d and s/z). These difficulties can affect both the regular past tense (ed) and tense agreement (plurals, for example, 'plays'; Montgomery & Leonard, 1998). Despite an attempt to account for this complication in their ratings of spellings of words that should have contained '-ed' Windsor *et al.* were not able to draw a clear conclusion on the basis of the children's errors. No spelling skill level was reported for the children in the study and it is therefore difficult to disentangle spelling levels and language levels. Therefore, it may be that children with language impairments in this study, while matched on language levels with a comparison group may have been poorer spellers.

We could find very few studies that had a matched spelling group with children with language impairment and that also compared writing performance. No significant differences in spelling between the children with language impairment and language aged controls were found by Mackie and Dockrell (2004). However, when word length and linguistic structures are considered in greater detail, children with language difficulties are more impaired than their spelling matched peers (Silliman, Bahr, & Peters, 2006). Particular difficulties were evident with more complex phonological structures in words and more inflected and derived morphological markers were omitted compared to spelling matched peers (Silliman *et al.*, 2006). Both studies are small-scale (Mackie & Dockrell, 2004, *N* = 11; Silliman *et al.*, 2006, *N* = 8). Nonetheless, these studies in conjunction with our longitudinal data indicate that children with language impairments may differ in how they deal with the orthographic and grammatical aspects of spelling during writing.

Vocabulary and spellings as indicators of writing problems for children with language impairment

Based on the evidence of our longitudinal study, and the inconsistent results in the literature about the nature of the writing difficulties experienced by children with language difficulties, we examined the differences in written text between children in the longitudinal sample at age 10 (Dockrell *et al.*, 2007) and typically developing children matched for vocabulary skills and spelling level. Language age and chronological age matches were identified for 23 of the original language-impaired population. The language age match group was aged 7.11. All children also completed a standardized spelling measure. This showed that the language age match group was no different to the children with language impairment in overall spelling ability. All the children completed a standardized writing assessment, the Wechsler objective language dimensions (WOLD; Rust, 1996), that was scored across six dimensions.

Our first step was to examine whether the two-factor solution that explained the performance of the language-impaired sample (Dockrell *et al.*, 2007; Connelly & Dockrell, 2009) was also evident in the writing of the comparison groups. We had interpreted the two-factor solution for the language-impaired sample as a failure to coordinate two components of writing – text generation and transcription. Specifically, we interpreted the first factor as relating to semantic or meaning dimensions of written language including ideas and vocabulary, while the second factor was interpreted as relating to rule-based factors including grammatical morphology and punctuation. We confirmed this two-factor solution both for the smaller subset of language-impaired children and for the language matched comparison group. Importantly, in both cases the factors accounted for similar percentages of variance (language impairment 45 and 22%; language matched 56 and 19%). However, only a one-factor solution was found for the older chronological age matched children that accounted for 60% of the variance. These results suggest that by age 11 typically developing children are coordinating idea generation while these dimensions have independent influences for younger typically developing children. Moreover, these data suggest that the difficulty in coordinating the two dimensions by the language-impaired group reflects their language level rather than specific cognitive impairments.

To further examine the produced by the three cohorts, we used a systematic analysis of language transcripts to compare key linguistic features. As with previous studies, the majority of these measures showed no difference with their language age controls while underperforming relative to their chronological age match comparison group. This analysis included areas such as word count and number, types of word use frequency of error such as bound morpheme errors, verb tense errors, pronoun errors, preposition errors, article errors, or subject errors. Nor did the total percentage of grammatical errors produced by the children with language difficulties differ from their language age controls. In contrast, the children with language difficulties did differ from their language age controls in the average number of different word roots used. The restriction in number of different word roots again appears to highlight the importance of a flexible use of vocabulary for this group of children.

We also examined the spelling errors within the written narratives. We found that, again, in general terms, the children with language difficulties were producing the same amount of spelling errors as their language aged peers. However, a more detailed classification revealed a more subtle pattern of errors. Three error types were identified, errors relating to a misapplication of phonology, errors relating to a misapplication of orthography, and non-word errors where the errors aetiology was more difficult to classify. Language age matched children produced more errors that were misapplications of orthography than the children with language impairments. The children with language impairments tended to produce more non-words but the effect was not statistically significant to differentiate between the groups. This then mirrors the results from other studies that show that despite being matched generally for spelling there are subtle differences in the spelling errors displayed by children with language impairments (Mackie & Dockrell, 2004; Silliman *et al.*, 2006).

We also found differences between the SLI cohort and the children matched for language ability in their use of punctuation (see also Bishop & Clarkson, 2003). Punctuation marking throughout a text signifies that the child has grasped some of the key differences in parsing between spoken and written language. Full stops and capital letters are indicative of children who have grasped this knowledge. Correct use of these sentence boundary markers is established quite early on in writing by typical children at about age 9. However, we found that the children with language impairment produced more errors relating to full stops and capital letters than their language age peers.

Implications for educational provision

Children and young people with a history of language learning difficulties will need additional support and instruction to master the production of written text. A systematic and sensitive approach to intervention is required if both writing difficulties and motivational factors are to be addressed. There is evidence overall that teachers' adaptations for children struggling to learn to write are limited (Graham, Harris, & Fink-Chorzempa, 2002). Even teachers who are well prepared to meet the needs of children with writing difficulties transfer of their knowledge and attitudes into classroom practice can be limited (Moni *et al.*, 2007).

Overall, there is a paucity of studies investigating writing in the classroom (Hooper *et al.*, 1994) and we know of no studies that have focused on children with language learning needs. Nor is it known what the contribution of teaching is to the long-term writing strategies of developing writers, although there is some evidence that the differences in strategy use found in older writers may have arisen from how they were initially taught writing (Torrance *et al.*, 1999; Whitaker *et al.*, 1994). The importance of the curricular/instructional explanation for the differences in the writing skills of children with learning difficulties, both within and across genres, has gathered a vocal and growing number of proponents (Scott, 1999).

For children with language learning difficulties even the best classroom support may not be enough; more intensive and explicit instruction will be required (Troia, 2006). This review has identified the key instructional components that should be evaluated and can subsequently be supported through targeted intervention. As long as translating continues to place heavy demands on writing the management of planning will be impaired. Approaches to supporting translation skills are therefore a basic prerequisite to any intervention program. An analysis of spelling errors can provide reliable cues for spelling instruction (see Berninger & Amtmann, 2003). Handwriting (or word processing) and spelling need to be, at least, partly automated to open the way up for pupils to develop text production. Once some automaticity is established pupils can move from word and sentence level to the development of text structures and planning and revision. As we see/have seen in other chapters in this volume, a number of effective strategies have been identified. The appropriate mix for children with language learning needs yet to be established.

Summary and conclusions

This review points to some general conclusions about the writing ability of children with language impairments. Their writing level is generally commensurate with that of their language age controls when such controls are used on most general measures of writing ability. Vocabulary level is a good indicator of writing level and is highly associated with skill at writing in children of all ages.

Controversy still remains over whether there are markers of difference in the writing of children with language impairments over and above the general low level of their writing. The writing of children in our sample of 11-year-olds with language impairments showed children who had not yet been able to blend aspects of the writing system, transcription and text generation. This would seem to indicate an immaturity with the construction of written language. However, it also appears to be related to language level and does not necessarily show children with language impairment develop writing differently, albeit more slowly, than their peers.

There is some evidence that the incidence of grammatical errors in children with language impairments is higher than would be expected for their language age. However, the precise natures of these difficulties have been difficult to establish and is complicated by spelling skills. Those studies that have matched for spelling as well as writing have generally found less difference than others in terms of grammatical markers (but see Silliman *et al.*, 2006, for a study that focuses solely on spelling and not writing per se). However, spelling does appear to be a clearly difficult area for children with language impairment. More investigation of this area would allow us to see if spelling development is disproportionately affected by SLI.

There is evidence that children with language impairment also struggle more with the rules of writing such as punctuation. Again, this seems to indicate more clearly an immaturity with written language than any clear marker of difference in this population.

Kroll (1981) described how oral and written language interacts in a complex manner by proposing four stages of spoken/written form relationships. In the early stages of writing, texts are less complex and not as sophisticated as oral language (the preparation stage). In the consolidation phase, writing begins to be as complex as oral language. During the differentiation phase, a distinct written style of grammar develops using structures only found in written language. Elements of oral language grammar may still be used inter-changeably in texts. In the final, integration phase, children can differentiate between oral and written forms and grammars and can consciously use them interchangeably. Scott (1999) concludes that children with language impairment may be stuck at the Kroll (1981) preparation or consolidation phase in their writing. Some of our more recent evidence on the 11-year-old children with language impairments may well fit this description. What is needed though is a more specific understanding of why they are not progressing forward to the differentiation stage.

References

Abbott, R. D., & Berninger, V. W. (1993). Structural equation modeling of relationships among developmental skills and writing skills in primary and intermediate grade writers. *Journal of Educational Psychology, 85,* 478–508.

Anglin, J. M. (1993). Vocabulary development: A morphological analysis. *Monographs for the Society for Research in Child Development, 58.*

Beard, R. (2000). *Developing writing* (pp. 3–13). London: Hodder & Stoughton.

Berninger, V. W., & Amtmann, D. (2003). Preventing written expression disabilities through early and continuing assessment and intervention for handwriting and/or spelling problems: Research into practice. In H. L. Swanson, K. Harris, & S. Graham (Eds.), *Handbook of learning difficulties.* New York & London: Guildford Press.

Berninger, V., & Fuller, F. (1992). Gender differences in orthographic, verbal, and compositional fluency: Implications for diagnosis of writing disabilities in primary grade children. *Journal of School Psychology, 30,* 363–382.

Berninger, V., Hart, T., Abbott, R., & Karovsky, P. (1992). Defining reading and writing disabilities with and without IQ: A flexible developmental perspective. *Learning Disabilities Quarterly, 15,* 103–118.

Berninger, V., Mizokawa, D., Bragg, R., Cartwright, A., & Yates, C. (1994). Intraindividual differences in levels of written language. *Reading and Writing Quarterly, 10,* 259–275.

Berninger, V., Yates, C., Cartwright, A., Rutberg, J., Remy, E., & Abbott, R. (1992). Lower-level developmental skills in beginning writing. *Reading and Writing. An Interdisciplinary Journal, 4,* 257–280.

Bishop, D. V. M. (1997). *Uncommon understanding: Development and disorders of language comprehension in children.* Hove: Psychology Press.

Bishop, D. V. M., & Adams, C. (1990). A prospective study of the relationship between specific language impairment, phonological disorders and reading retardation. *Journal of Child Psychology and Child Psychiatry, 31,* 1027–1050.

Bishop, D. V. M., & Clarkson, B. (2003). Written language as a window into residual language deficits: A study of children with persistent and residual speech and language impairments. *Cortex, 39*(2), 215–237.

Bishop, D. V. M., North, T., & Dolan, C. (1996). Nonword repetition as a behavioural marker for inherited language impairment: Evidence from a twin study. *Journal of Child Psychology and Psychiatry, 37,* 391–403.

Bishop, D. V. M., & Snowling, M. J. (2004). Developmental dyslexia and specific language impairment: Same or different? *Psychological Bulletin, 130*(6), 858–886.

Bourdin, B., & Fayol, M. (2000). Is graphic activity cognitively costly? A developmental approach. *Reading and Writing: An Interdisciplinary Journal, 13,* 183–196.

Briscoe, J., Bishop, D. V. M., & Norbury, C. F. (2001). Phonological processing, language and literacy: A comparison of children with mild-to-moderate sensorineural hearing loss and those with specific language impairment. *Journal of Child Psychology and Psychiatry, 42,* 329–340.

Carlisle, J. F. (1996). An exploratory study of morphological errors in children's written stories. *Reading and Writing, 8,* 61–72.

Catts, H. W., Fey, M., & Tomblin, B. (1997). Language basis of reading disabilities. Paper presented at the Society for the Scientific Study of Reading, Chicago, IL.

Clarke-Klein, S. M. (1994). Expressive phonological deficiencies: Impact on spelling development. *Topics in Language Disorders, 14,* 40–55.

Connelly, V., Campbell, S., MacLean, M., & Barnes, J. (2006). Contribution of lower-order letter and word fluency skills to written composition of college students with and without dyslexia. *Developmental Neuropsychology, 29*(1), 175–196.

Connelly, V., & Dockrell, J. E. (2009). The role of vocabulary in the production of written text: Development and delay. Manuscript in preparation.

Conti-Ramsden, G., & Botting, N. (1999). Classification of children with specific language impairment: Longitudinal considerations. *Journal of Speech, Language and Hearing Research, 42,* 1195–1204.

Cragg, L., & Nation, K. (2006). Exploring written narrative in children with poor reading comprehension. *Educational Psychology, 26,* 55–72.

Department for Children, Schools and Families (n.d.). *English Curriculum Standards.* Retrieved September 10, 2007, from www.standards.dfes.gov.uk/keystage3/

Dockrell, J. E. (2001). Assessing language skills in preschool children. *Child Psychology and Psychiatry Review, 6,* 74–85.

Dockrell, J. E. (in press). Causes of delays and difficulties in writing development. In R. Beard, D. Myhill, M. Nystrand, & J. Riley (Eds.) *Sage Handbook of Writing Development.*

Dockrell, J. E., & Connelly, V. (2007). SLI, language skills and writing. *Paper presented at Learning & Teaching Writing British Journal of Educational Psychology Current Trends Conference* 28–29 June, 2007. Oxford: Oxford Brookes University.

Dockrell, J. E., Lindsay, G. A., & Connelly, V. (in press). The impact of a history of specific language impairment on the production of written text during adolescence. *Exceptional Children.*

Dockrell, J. E., Lindsay, G. A., Connelly, V., & Mackie, C. (2007). Constraints in the production of written text in children with specific language impairments. *Exceptional Children, 73,* 147–164.

Ellis Weismer, S., Evans, J., & Hesketh, L. (1999). An examination of verbal working memory capacity in children with specific language impairment. *Journal of Speech, Language, and Hearing Research, 42,* 1249–1260.

Fey, M. E., Catts, H. W., Proctor-Williams, K., Tomblin, J., & Zhang, X. Y. (2004). Oral and written story composition skills of children with language impairment. *Journal of Speech Language and Hearing Research, 47*(6), 1301–1318.

Fitzgerald, J., & Shanahan, T. (2000). Reading and writing relations and their development. *Educational Psychologist, 35,* 39–51.

Gallagher, A., Frith, U., & Snowling, M. (2000). Precursors of literacy delay among children at genetic risk of dyslexia. *Journal of Child Psychology and Psychiatry, 41,* 203–213.

Gathercole, S. E., & Baddeley, A. D. (1990). Phonological memory deficits in language disordered children: Is there a causal connection? *Journal of Memory and Language, 29,* 336–360.

Gillam, R., & Johnston, J. (1992). Spoken and written language relationships in language learning impaired and normally achieving school-age children. *Journal of Speech and Hearing Research*, *35*, 1303–1315.

Graham, S., Berninger, V., Abbott, R., Abbott, S., & Whitaker, D. (1997). The role of mechanics in composing of elementary school students: A new methodological approach. *Journal of Educational Psychology*, *89*(1), 170–182.

Graham, S., Harris, K. R., & Fink-Chorzempa, B. (2002). Contributions of spelling instruction to the spelling, writing, and reading of poor spellers. *Journal of Educational Psychology*, *94*, 669–686.

Green, L., McCutchen, D., Schwiebert, C., Quinlan, T., Eva-Wood, A., & Juelis, J. (2003). Morphological development in children's writing. *Journal of Educational Psychology*, *95*, 752–761.

Hammill, D. D., & Newcomer, P. L. (1988). *Test of Language Development-2, Intermediate*. Austin, TX: Pro-Ed.

Hidi, S., & Hilyard, A. (1984). The comparison of oral and written productions in two discourse modes. *Discourse Processes*, *6*(2), 91–105.

Hirsh-Pasek, K. Kochanoff, A., Newcombe, N., & de Villiers, J. (2005). Using scientific knowledge to inform preschool assessment: Making the case for 'empirical validity', Social Policy Report, *9*(1), 3–19, Society for Research in Child Development.

Hooper, S. R., Montogomery, J., Swartz, C., Reed, M. S., Sandler, A. D., Levine, M. D., *et al.* (1994). Measurement of written language expression. In G. R. Lyon (Ed.), *Frames of reference for the assessment of learning disabilities: New views on measurement issues* (pp. 375–417). Baltimore, MD: Paul H. Brooks.

Hunt, K. (1965). *Grammatical structures written at three grade levels*. Champaign, IL: National Council of Teachers of English.

Juel, C. (1988). Learning to read and write: A longitudinal study of 54 children from first through fourth grades. *Journal of Educational Psychology*, *80*, 437–447.

Kellogg, R. T. (1994). *The psychology of writing*. New York: Oxford University Press.

Kroll, B. M. (1981). Developmental relationship between speaking and writing. In B. M. Kroll & R. J. Vann (Eds.), *Exploring speaking-writing relationships: Connections and contrasts* (pp. 32–54). Urbana, IL: National Council of Teachers of English.

Leonard, L. B. (1998). *Children with SLI*. Cambridge, MA: MIT Press.

Leonard, L. B., Eyer, J., Bedore, L., & Grela, B. (1997). Three accounts of the grammatical morpheme difficulties of English-speaking children with specific language impairment. *Journal of Speech, Language and Hearing Research*, *40*, 741–753.

Leonard, L. B., McGregor, K. K., & Allen, G. D. (1992). Grammatical morphology and speech perception in children with specific language impairment. *Journal of Speech and Hearing Research*, *35*, 1076–1085.

Lewis, B., & Freebairn, L. (1992). Residential effects of pre-school phonology disorder in grade school, adolescence and adulthood. *Journal of Speech and Hearing Research*, *35*, 819–831.

Lindsay, G., Dockrell, J., Letchford, B., & Mackie, C. (2002). Self-esteem of children with specific speech and language difficulties, *Child Language Teaching and Therapy*, 125–143. Retrieved 2008 from ProQuest Education Journals database.

Mackie, C., & Dockrell, J. E. (2004). The nature of written language deficits in children with SLI. *Journal of Speech Language and Hearing Research*, *47*(6), 1469–1483.

McArthur, G. M., Hogben, J. H., Edwards, V. T., Heath, S. M., & Mengler, E. D. (2000). On the 'specifics' of specific reading disability and specific language impairment. *Journal of Child Psychology and Psychiatry*, *41*, 869–874.

McCauley, R. J., & Swisher, L. (1984). Psychometric review of language and articulation tests for preschool children. *Journal of Speech and Hearing Disorders*, *49*, 34–42.

McCutchen, D. (1986). Domain knowledge and linguistic knowledge in the development of writing ability. *Journal of Memory and Language*, *25*, 431–444.

McCutchen, D. (2000). Knowledge, processing and working memory: Implications for a theory of writing. *Educational Psychologist, 35*, 13-23.

McFadden, T., & Gillam, R. (1996). An examination of the quality of narratives produced by children with language disorders. *Language, Speech and Hearing Services in Schools, 27*, 48-56.

Moni, K., Jobling, A., van Kraayenoord, C., Elkins, J., Miller, R., & Koppenhaven, D. (2007). Teachers' knowledge attitudes and the implementation of practices around the teaching of writing in inclusive middle years' classrooms: No quick fix. *Education and Child Psychology, 24*, 18-35.

Montgomery, J. (2000). Verbal working memory and sentence comprehension in children with specific language impairment. The role of phonological working memory. *Journal of Speech Language and Hearing Research, 43*, 293-308.

Montgomery, J., & Leonard, L. (1998). Real-time inflectional processing by children with specific language impairment: Effects of phonetic substance. *Journal of Speech, Language and Hearing Research, 41*, 1432-1443.

Naucler, K., & Magnusson, E. (2002). How do preschool language problems affect language abilities in adolescence. In F. Windsor & M. L. Kelly (Eds.), *Investigations in clinical phonetics and linguistics* (pp. 243-269). Mahwah, NJ: Erlbaum.

Nunes, T., Bryant, P., & Bindman, M. (1997). Spelling and grammar. The NECECSED move. In C. Perfetti, L. Rieben, & M. Fayol (Eds.), *Learning to spell: Research, theory and practice across languages* (pp. 151-170). Mahwah, NJ: Erlbaum.

Perera, K. (1984). *Children's writing and reading: Analyzing classroom language*. Oxford: Basil Blackwell.

Plante, E., Swisher, L., Kiernan, B., & Restrepo, M. (1993). Language matches: Illuminating or confounding? *Journal of Speech and Hearing Research, 36*, 772-775.

Puranik, C., Lombardino, L., & Altman, L. (2007). Writing through retellings: An exploratory study of language impaired and dyslexic populations. *Reading and Writing, 20*, 251-272.

Rice, M., & Oetting, J. (1993). Morphological deficits of children with SLI: Evaluation of number marking and agreement. *Journal of Speech and Hearing Research, 36*, 1254-1262.

Rust, J. (1996). *The manual of the Wechsler objective language dimensions (WOLD)* (UK Edition). London: The Psychological Corporation.

Scott, C. M. (1999). Learning to write. In H. W. Catts & A. G. Kahmi (Eds.), *Language and reading disabilities* (pp. 224-259). Boston: Allyn & Bacon.

Scott, C. M., & Windsor, J. (2000). General language performance measures in spoken and written narrative and expository discourse of school-age children with language learning disabilities. *Journal of Speech, Language, and Hearing Research, 43*, 324-339.

Shanahan, T. (2006). Relations among oral language, reading and writing development. In C. MacArthur, S. Graham, & J. Fitzgerald (Eds.), *Handbook of writing research* (pp. 171-183). New York: Guilford Press.

Silliman, E., Bahr, R., & Peters, M. (2006). Spelling patterns in preadolescents with atypical language skills: Phonological, morphological, and orthographic factors. *Developmental Neuropsychology, 29*, 93.

Thomas, M. S. C., Annaz, D., Ansari, D., Serif, G., Jarrold, C., & Karmiloff-Smith, A. (in press). The use of developmental trajectories in studying developmental disorders. *Journal of Speech, Language, and Hearing Research*.

Tomblin, J. B., Zhang, X. Y., Buckwalter, P., & O'Brien, M. (2003). The stability of language disorder: Four years after kindergarten diagnosis. *Journal of Speech, Language, and Hearing Research, 46*, 1283-1296.

Torrance, M., Thomas, G. V., & Robinson, E. J. (1999). Individual differences in the writing behaviour of undergraduate students. *British Journal of Educational Psychology, 69*, 189-199.

Treiman, R. (1993). Phonology and spelling: The case of syllabic consonants. *Journal of Experimental Psychology, 56*, 267-290.

Troia, G. A. (2006). Writing instruction for students with learning disabilities. In C. A. MacArthur, S. Graham, & J. Fitzgerald (Eds.), *Handbook of writing research* (pp. 324–336). New York: Guilford Press.

van der Lely, H. K. J., & Christian, V. (2000). Lexical word formation in children with grammatical SLI: A grammar-specific versus an input-processing deficit? *Cognition*, *75*, 33–63.

van der Lely, H. K. J., & Ullman, M. T. (2001). Past tense morphology in specifically language impaired and normally developing children. *Language and Cognitive Processes*, *16*, 177–217.

Wells, G., & Chang, G. L. (1986). From speech to writing: Some evidence on the relationship between oracy and literacy. In A. Wilkinson (Ed.), *The writing of writing* (pp. 109–131). Milton Keynes, UK: Open University Press.

Whitaker, D., Berninger, V., Johnston, J., & Swanson, H. L. (1994). Intraindividual differences in levels of language in intermediate grade writers: Implications for the translating process. *Learning and Individual Differences*, *6*, 107–130.

Windsor, J., & Hwang, M. (1999). Children's auditory lexical decisions: A limited processing capacity account of language impairment. *Journal of Speech, Language and Hearing Research*, *42*, 990–1002.

Windsor, J., Scott, C. M., & Street, C. K. (2000). Verb and noun morphology the spoken and written language of children with language learning disabilities. *Journal of Speech, Language and Hearing Research*, *43*, 1322–1336.

Teaching and Learning Writing, 63–75
BJEP Monograph Series II, 6
© 2009 The British Psychological Society

The
British
Psychological
Society

www.bpsjournals.co.uk

Associations and dissociations in reading and spelling French: Unexpectedly poor and good spellers

Michel Fayol[1]*, Michel Zorman[2] and Bernard Lété[3]

[1]Université Blaise Pascal & CNRS, Clermont-Ferrand, France
[2]Université Pierre Mendes France, Grenoble, France
[3]INRP & Université de Lyon 2, Lyon, France

Background and aims. The relationship between reading and spelling is generally considered to be very close, with good readers (R+) also being good spellers (S+) and poor readers (R−) being poor spellers (S−). We investigated both associations (R+ S+ and R− S−) and dissociations (R+ S− and R− S+) between reading and spelling words in French in order to identify the underlying mechanisms leading to patterns of dissociation.

Sample. One thousand four hundred and fifty-three fifth graders (10-year-olds) were given a phonological task, and had to read and to spell regular and irregular words and pseudowords.

Method. Reading level and reading performance (accuracy and speed) were tested individually. The spelling performance (accuracy) was tested in groups. Four groups of children were distinguished as a function of their reading and spelling scores (R+ S+, R− S−, R+ S−, and R− S+).

Results. Most good readers were good spellers and most poor readers were poor spellers. Two small groups of pupils exhibited the double dissociation: some read fast and accurately, but had poor spelling scores, and exhibited a slight phonological deficit; others were accurate but slow readers with adequate spelling.

Conclusion. Reading and spelling scores are usually closely associated (R+ S+ and R− S−). However, they can dissociate. When slight phonological deficits are associated with fast processing, children read accurately and quickly but their spelling performance is impaired (R+ S−). In other cases (R− S+), accurate but slow readers are good spellers. Longitudinal studies are required to confirm these observations and to better understand the genesis of these different profiles.

*Correspondence should be addressed to Michel Fayol, Université Blaise Pascal & CNRS, UMR 6024, 34 Avenue Carnot, 63000 Clermont-Ferrand, France (e-mail: Michel.fayol@univ-bpclermont.fr).

DOI:10.1348/000709909X421973

At first sight, the relationships between reading and spelling appear to be quite simple. Generally, good readers (hereafter R+) are good spellers (S+) while poor readers (R−) are poor spellers (S−). Most investigators believe that the relationships between the two skills are very close (Adams, 1990; Treiman, 1993). Correlational findings from various studies in different orthographic systems reported that word reading performance is related to word spelling performance. Most of the correlations ranged from .60 to .80 (Bosman & Van Orden, 1997; Ehri, 1997; Fitzgerald & Shanahan, 2000; Juel, Griffith, & Gough, 1986; Morris & Perney, 1984; Shanahan, 1984). However, two observations conflict with such a simple view, and show that reading and spelling can dissociate although such dissociations are exceptional and difficult to explain.

The first dissociation (R+ S−) indicates, consistent with Treiman (1993)'s observation that some children who experience difficulties with spelling read quite well, that 12-year-old good readers are sometimes poor spellers. Frith (1980) described a group of 12-year-old unexpectedly poor spellers (atrocious spellers) whose reading performance was far better than their spelling performance. The spelling errors of those R+ S− were compared to that of two other groups: R+ S+ and R− S−. Results showed that R+ S− spelled phonetically, that is, they preserved the sounds of the target words and performed well on pseudoword spelling tasks, but could not recall the exact letters of specific words. Several studies have confirmed Frith's (1980) observation in child and adult English speakers: at least in English, many adults who have a good grasp of phoneme–grapheme correspondences have difficulties remembering word-specific information (Burden, 1992; Holmes & Carruthers, 1998; Holmes & Castles, 2001; Holmes & Ng, 1993). The second dissociation (R− S+) has been reported only twice and many believe that it does not even exist. Lovett (1987) described a group of 10-year-old English-speaking Canadian children who were slow readers but as accurate in their spelling as normal fluent readers. Wimmer and Mayringer (2002) found a number of slow readers with no reliable spelling deficit (R− S+) and some good (accurate and fast) readers but poor spellers (R+ S−) in a group of German-speaking fourth graders. Some children (42 out of 826) presented a single reading fluency deficit defined as a slow reading rate associated with a better spelling score (R− S+) whereas another group (33) exhibited the reverse pattern: a close to normal reading rate associated with poor spelling performance (R+ S−). Again, as with Frith's unexpectedly poor spellers, almost all of the R+ S−'s misspellings were phonologically plausible.

These observations raise two questions, one about the mechanisms underlying the two dissociations (Berninger, Abbott, Abbott, Graham, & Richards, 2002), and the other about the possible role of orthographic systems (Jaffré & Fayol, 2005; Sprenger-Charolles, 2003).

As far as the first question is concerned, some researchers assume that reading and spelling would rely on two different lexicons: an input lexicon and an output lexicon (Hanley, Hastie, & Kay, 1992). However, most researchers consider that there is only one lexicon (Bosman & Van Orden, 1997; Perfetti, 1992). How is it possible that people perform differently in reading and spelling although they refer to the same underlying lexicon?

Two complementary hypotheses have been put forward to explain the reading–spelling gap (Tainturier & Rapp, 2001): one posits that orthographic representations are incomplete or even erroneous; the other that access to orthographic representations is difficult (e.g. slow). The first hypothesis accounts well for the R+ S− dissociation. The acquisition of the orthographic lexicon depends on phonological recoding. Because phonological recoding relies on knowledge of phoneme–grapheme correspondences, any phonological deficit should lead some children to acquire only partial orthographic information (e.g. T_W_R for tower). When they reach fifth grade, they are able to read quickly and efficiently because such knowledge is precise enough to distinguish one word from the others (Frith, 1980; Seymour & McGregor, 1984) and because they have practiced reading. However, it is not sufficient to spell words because spelling requires precise knowledge about the letters and their positions in words. Such a hypothesis predicts that R+ S− children have mild phonological deficits which are difficult to detect (Bruck & Waters, 1988, 1990; Waters, Bruck, & Seidenberg, 1985) but interfere with learning phoneme–grapheme correspondences. Consequently, they are somewhat less accurate in reading than R+ S+, they produce more phonologically inappropriate misspellings of words and pseudowords (as R− S−), and they perform at a lower level than R+ S+ children in phonological tasks.

The second of these hypotheses corresponds to the (R− S+) dissociation. Some children are accurate but slow readers (Lovett, 1987). The low speed of access hinders their reading performance (R−), at least in standard tests which take account of both accuracy and speed. Their good phonological abilities enable them to form the precise orthographic representations used for reading and spelling. As a consequence, their spelling performance is better than their reading performance (R− S+). Such a hypothesis predicts that R− S+ children should exhibit good phonological and accurate reading performances, produce correct pseudoword spellings and phonetically appropriate misspellings, and have no difficulties with specific orthographic configurations, in the same way as R+ S+ children. They are just slow readers. In addition, some children exhibit both inaccurate and slow reading and poor spelling (R− S−).

Concerning the second question, the R+ S− dissociation has been frequently described in English. In contrast, R− S+ has been rarely reported in English despite numerous studies exploring reading–spelling relations (Ehri, 1997). The clearest description was reported with German speaking pupils (Wimmer & Mayringer, 2002). The English orthographic system is both extremely inconsistent from graphemes to phonemes (i.e. reading) and from phonemes to graphemes (i.e. spelling). As good reading but poor spelling is possible with incomplete orthographic representations, the R+ S− profile is (relatively) easy to find and has frequently been described. In contrast, R− S+ subjects are probably very rare (but see Lovett, 1987), and large populations are required to find them. The German orthographic system is highly consistent in reading but less consistent in spelling, thus favouring R+ S− profiles. Accurate reading is the norm, and reading impairment manifests itself through dysfluent reading. Provided that it is not associated with a phonological impairment, the speed deficit does not prevent the building up of the orthographic lexicon. As a consequence, when reading tests take both accuracy and speed into account, it is possible to find R− S+ profiles (Wimmer & Mayringer, 2002). The French orthographic system is fairly consistent for reading. In contrast, the system is strongly inconsistent for spelling. R+ S− profiles are thus expected. However, the R− S+ subjects are probably as rare as in English, again necessitating the study of large populations.

The present paper is intended, first, to show that associations and dissociations between reading and spelling performance also occur in French and, second, to identify the mechanisms leading to this dissociation. French fifth graders (10-year-olds) were asked to read and spell words and pseudowords and to complete phonological tasks. The performance of four groups (R+ S+, R+ S−, R− S+, and R− S) was compared on several tasks.

EXPERIMENT

Method

Participants

One thousand four hundred and fifty-three (726 females and 727 males) 5th graders (*M* age = 10 years 6 months, *SD* = 5 years 4 months) coming from 104 different classrooms randomly selected among the 2,179 classrooms (37,000 pupils) of the Grenoble school area participated in the study.

Material

The children were given a series of tests.

The reading level used to select the four groups of children was assessed via a standardized test: 'l'Alouette' (Lefavrais, 1965). The children read a 265-word text as rapidly and as accurately as possible. The text includes rare words and some spelling traps: items with silent letters (temps/tã/, nids/ni/), contextual graphemes (gai–geai), and items which are phonologically similar (Annie–amie). The test also tracks contextual anticipation which characterizes the youngest and least skilled readers (Stanovich, 1984). The text contains fixed expressions which are modified ('au clair de lune' instead of the usual 'au clair de la lune') or words similar to those that would be predicted by the context: e.g. 'poison' rather than 'poisson' (fish) after 'lac' (lake). The reading level is calculated by taking speed and number of errors into account. This level is then converted into a lexical age (from 6 to 14 years).

The reading performance was assessed using a specially devised test aimed at testing decoding abilities (pseudoword reading), and word reading (frequent vs. rare words). Word frequencies were extracted from the *Manulex* database which is specifically devoted to assessing word frequencies for first to fifth grades (Lété, Sprenger-Charolles, & Colé, 2004). Word-consistency values were extracted from *Manulex-infra* to estimate word regularity (Peereman, Lété, & Sprenger-Charolles, 2007). The test comprised 40 regular words that could be read by using grapheme–phoneme correspondences (e.g. fuite, montagne) (consistency from 80 to 89; 20 frequent and 20 rare: mean log frequencies = 2.01 and 1.20, respectively), 40 irregular items (e.g. août, chorale) (consistency from 66 to 69; 20 frequent and 20 rare: mean log frequencies = 2.04 and 0.95, respectively), and 40 pseudowords (e.g. toir, gental) (20 bi- and 20 tri-syllabic). Two scores were calculated: a speed score (in seconds) based on time taken to read the items, and an accuracy score based on the number of correct responses (one point for each correct response). Each score was calculated for all 120 items (global score) and for each of the six subcategories.

The spelling performance test took the form of a dictation task consisting of 50 items divided into three word classes: regular items (e.g. frite) (20 items, consistency = 85), irregular items (e.g. peinture) (12 items, consistency = 69), and 18 pseudowords (e.g. datoir, verdulin). The regular items and pseudowords could be spelled by referring only to phoneme–grapheme correspondences whereas irregular items could not. One point was given for each correct answer, leading to four scores, one for each of the three categories of items and one global score (out of 50).

The phonological test included several tasks (39 items): initial phoneme suppression (15 items), phonemic segmentation (12 items), and phonemic blending (12 items).

Again, one point was given for each correct answer, thus resulting in four scores (three categories plus one global score out of 39).

Procedure

The children were tested in their school. Reading level, reading performance, and phonological awareness were assessed individually. The children were instructed to read quickly and accurately. The spelling test was administrated collectively in the classrooms. The children were instructed to spell the words correctly and the pseudowords in a phonologically plausible manner.

Results

One thousand four hundred and fifty-three children completed the protocols. Four groups of children were distinguished as a function of their scores on the reading-level test and their global scores on the spelling performance test. We used percentile ranks instead of the 1 *SD* cutoff because they are commonly used with the standardized scores of the tests that we selected (percentages of subjects who scored at or below the score of interest). A good reader (R+) was defined by a reading score above the 70th percentile; a good speller (S+) by a spelling score above the 70th percentile. A poor reader (R−) was defined by a reading score below the 30th percentile, and a poor speller (S−) by a spelling score below the 30th percentile. Thus, four groups were distinguished: an R+ S+ group (*n* = 304; 21%); an R− S− group (*n* = 251; 17.6%); an R+ S− group (*n* = 58; 4%); and an R− S+ group (*n* = 58; 4%). Two reasons led us to use the 30th percentile instead of the usual 1 *SD* cutoff for S− and the 70th percentile for S+. Firstly, the 30th percentile corresponds roughly to the mean minus 1/3 *SD*. The 30th percentile adds only 6% of the subjects in the abnormal range and results in a larger number of participants in each group, especially in the R+ S− and R− S+ groups than if we had used the 1 *SD* cutoff. Secondly, in training studies, when children reach a score corresponding to the 70th percentile they are considered to have overcome their difficulties (Vellutino, Fletcher, Snowling, & Scanlon, 2004).

The mean scores and standard deviations for the main dependent variables are displayed in Table 1. Due to the number of different tests performed, we set the criterion for all reported effects at .01. The most frequently used criterion of significance in behavioural research is the .05 criterion, which keeps the chances of a Type II error (missing out on a new finding) lower than for the .01 criterion. Given that we want to avoid accepting a dissociation falsely, we choose to minimize Type I error instead of Type II error and we set the criterion to .01. The precise significance levels of all pairwise comparisons and the effect sizes measured by Cohen's *d* (Cohen, 1988) are displayed on Table 2.

Note that we used a series of *t* tests instead of ANOVA *post hoc* pairwise comparisons. Indeed, our data did not meet the assumptions required for applying ANOVA: for most variables, the within-group distributions did not pass .05 normality tests; the within-group variances were significantly heterogeneous at the .01 level; the effects of variance heterogeneity were worsened by the large differences between the sample sizes of the groups (58 R− S+, 58 R+ S−, 304 R+ S+, and 251 R− S−). We focused exclusively on two groups at a time, and tested *a priori* hypotheses based on previous observations of similar variables. For each variable and each pair

Table 1. Means and SD of the four reading and spelling groups

	R− S+		R+ S−		R+ S+		R− S−	
	M	SD	M	SD	M	SD	M	SD
Reading level (months)	104	5	138	10	148	13	100	6
Reading performance (120)	106	6	109	5	114	4	97	10
Reading time (120)	150	28	101	19	95	18	173	54
Phonological performance (39)	28	7	28	7	31	6	26	6
Spelling regular words (20)	20	1	18	11	20	1	17	2
Spelling pseudowords (18)	18	1	15	2	18	1	15	3
Spelling irregular words (12)	11	1	8	2	11	1	7	2
Spelling performance (50)	48	1	41	3	48	1	39	4

Note. R− S+, poor readers good spellers; R + S−, good readers poor spellers; R + S+, good readers good spellers, R− S−, poor readers poor spellers.

of groups, we ran four tests under SPSS: Levene's test for equality of the two variances, two Student tests (respectively with and without the assumption of equal variances), and the non-parametric Mann & Whitney test; the two t-statistics and the four p-values were pasted in an XL sheet, in order to select the right t-statistic according to the p-value of the Levene's test; the p-value of the surviving t was then compared with the p-value of the M–W test. In the few cases where these two p-values disagreed by more than .01, displaying the needle plots of the two distributions helped to decide whether t or M–W should be trusted more than the other because its own specific application conditions were mistreated less.

Reading level
t Tests revealed that all the pairwise comparisons between the four groups on the reading-level test were significant. However, the differences between the two good-reader groups (R+ S+: 148; R+ S−: 138; difference = 10) and between the two poor-reader groups (R− S+: 104; R− S−: 100; difference = 4) were small, whereas they were higher between the good and poor-reader groups. This result validates the selection of the four groups.

Reading performance
Considering first the global accuracy score, t *tests* showed that the R+ S+ group was significantly better (114) and that the R− S− group was worse (97) than the other two groups. Interestingly, R+ S− was only slightly better than R− S+ (109 vs. 106, $p < .05$). The global speed scores provide a quite different picture: R+ S+ was the fastest (95s) and R− S− the slowest (173s). However, R+ S− was significantly faster (101) than R− S− (150) and the difference was large (49).

Phonological performance
R+ S+ achieved the best performance (31) and R− S− the worst (26). The other two groups were significantly worse than R+ S+ and significantly better than R− S−. Again, R+ S− (28) and R− S+ (28) did not differ.

Table 2. Effect sizes measured by Cohen's d and significance levels of the t-statistic for between-groups comparisons

	R − S+ vs. R + S−		R − S+ vs. R + S+		R − S+ vs. R − S−		R + S− vs. R + S+		R + S− vs. R − S−		R + S+ vs. R − S−	
	d	p-value	d	p-value	d	p-value	d	p-value	d	p-value	d	p-value
Reading level (months)	4.51	1×10^{-38}	6.61	1×10^{-125}	0.71	4×10^{-06}	0.96	1×10^{-09}	4.10	6×10^{-39}	4.82	1×10^{-205}
Reading performance (120)	0.45	2×10^{-02}	1.46	4×10^{-15}	1.33	6×10^{-16}	1.14	3×10^{-11}	1.82	2×10^{-25}	2.24	2×10^{-80}
Reading time (s)	2.10	4×10^{-20}	2.10	2×10^{-22}	0.65	1×10^{-05}	0.31	3×10^{-02}	2.47	1×10^{-43}	1.85	6×10^{-63}
Phonological performance (39)	0.06	7×10^{-01}	0.45	2×10^{-03}	0.28	5×10^{-02}	0.56	2×10^{-04}	0.22	1×10^{-01}	0.85	1×10^{-21}
Spelling regular words (20)	1.32	7×10^{-10}	0.09	5×10^{-01}	2.60	2×10^{-48}	1.12	9×10^{-11}	0.67	7×10^{-06}	1.76	4×10^{-58}
Spelling pseudowords (18)	1.94	4×10^{-16}	0.02	9×10^{-01}	1.96	2×10^{-32}	1.57	5×10^{-16}	0.03	8×10^{-01}	1.26	7×10^{-37}
Spelling irregular words (12)	2.14	3×10^{-18}	0.52	3×10^{-04}	3.51	2×10^{-62}	1.99	2×10^{-20}	0.38	9×10^{-03}	2.84	1×10^{-106}
Spelling performance (50)	3.67	6×10^{-31}	0.43	3×10^{-03}	4.44	2×10^{-94}	3.16	1×10^{-30}	0.71	3×10^{-06}	2.94	6×10^{-102}

Spelling performance

On a score out of 50, the R+ S+ group (48) were significantly better and the R− S− group significantly worse (39) than the other two groups: R+ S− (41) and R− S+ (48). The results for regular items (20) were similar to those for the global performance: R+ S+ (20), R− S+ (20), and R+ S− (18) performed significantly better than R− S− (17). When we consider the pseudowords (18), R+ S+ (18) and R− S+ (18) did not differ, and were significantly better than R+ S− (15) and R− S− (15), which also did not differ from each other. Lastly, in the case of irregular words (12), R+ S+ (11) was slightly but significantly better than R− S+ (11) and these two groups were better than the other two groups: R+ S− (8) which, in turn, was significantly better than R− S− (7).

To summarize, R+ S+ and R− S− exhibited an association between reading and spelling - both were either good or poor. The R+ S+ children read accurately and quickly, and succeeded in the phonological and spelling tests. By contrast, the R− S− children exhibited poor accurate reading and spelling performances and were slow readers. They were poor at resolving phonological tasks.

The unexpectedly poor speller group (R+ S−) read almost as accurately and fast as R+ S+ but was phonologically less efficient than the R+ S+ group. In the spelling tasks, this group was worse than R+ S+ and R− S+, especially when spelling pseudowords. Its performance did not differ from that of R− S−, which suggests a phonological deficit. R+ S− was almost as efficient as R+ S+ and R− S+ when spelling regular words, probably because these children had recourse to both phonology and lexical knowledge. However, the R+ S− group was very poor at spelling irregular words, a task that cannot be successfully completed using phoneme–grapheme associations or simple orthographic knowledge.

The results for the R− S+ group were quite different. These children were accurate but very slow readers. This explains why they scored poorly in the reading test, which takes both accuracy and speed of processing into account. Their performance was equivalent to R+ S+ in spelling pseudowords but slightly weaker in terms of phonological abilities. They probably had no phonological deficit. Accordingly, their performance in spelling regular and irregular words was good.

Discussion

As expected, comparing the reading and spelling scores of a large sample of French fifth graders enabled us to show that these two activities are usually associated but may become dissociated. Most of the good readers were good spellers and most of the poor readers were poor spellers. However, two small groups of pupils (each representing about 2% of the sample) exhibited the expected double dissociation: some read fast and accurately but failed in spelling (R+ S−); others read slowly but had good spelling scores (R− S+). Thus, it is possible to provide evidence of a double dissociation between reading and spelling in French.

Two main hypotheses might explain the reading-spelling dissociation. The first hypothesis suggests that readers with slight phonological deficits can overcome their initial difficulties in learning to read and become proficient readers. However, their spelling performance lags behind their reading performance. This hypothesis predicts that reading is better than spelling, a fact that has been systematically described for many years whatever the orthographic system studied. It also predicts that unexpectedly poor spellers (R+ S−) should exhibit long-lasting phonological deficits. Such deficits are difficult to detect in older children, especially with classical tasks (e.g. the phoneme deletion task) but they manifest themselves in more complex tasks (e.g. pseudoword spelling; Bruck & Waters, 1988, 1990; Treiman, 1998).

The second hypothesis is that some difficulties in the learning of reading are due to slow processing. Some children have an age-appropriate word recognition accuracy and are deficient only in reading speed.

The results of the present study suggest that the two aforementioned hypotheses are relevant in explaining the performances of our R+ S− and R− S+ groups. The unexpectedly poor spellers (R+ S−) were almost as good readers as R+ S+ but their spelling performance was as bad as that of the worst spellers (R− S−). The phonological task we used was probably not sufficiently sensitive to detect a possible phonological deficit: the phonological score of the R+ S− group did not suggest the existence of a phonological deficit even though this group had poor scores in the pseudoword spelling task which is well known to tap phonological knowledge (Treiman, 1998). Indeed, Mann (1993) reported that a spelling task provided a good measure of the phonological capacity. The score obtained by the R+ S− group (15.2) was as low as that of the R− S− group (15.2). This result suggests that R+ S− did indeed suffer from a phonological deficit. This deficit hindered their pseudoword spelling performance more than their spelling of regular words, probably because the latter benefited from reading practice (i.e. exposure to print, Cunningham & Stanovich, 1997). However, their experience of reading was not enough to overcome their difficulties in the spelling of irregular words. To summarize, the performance of the R+ S− group is compatible with the first hypothesis. These children exhibited a slight phonological deficit which could be observed mainly in the pseudoword spelling task. This deficit had been overcome in reading but continued to be observed in spelling, probably because spelling requires more precise representations of words (Perfetti, 1992). Their good reading level enabled these children to practice reading and thus to memorize at least some regular words that they were then able to spell better than pseudowords.

The R− S+ group read accurately but slowly. The main question raised by the R− S+ group is how it is possible to be good at spelling while being a slow reader. An attention-based interpretation can be put forward. R− S+ children had no phonological deficit, so they performed well in pseudoword spelling. In addition, they were accurate in reading, albeit slowly. It is well known that learning depends on attention (Logan & Etherton, 1994), and that attention is time-dependent. Given that R− S+ children are accurate but slow readers, they invest enough time (and thus attention) in accomplishing efficient orthographic and phonological mappings of a word while they decode it to be able to store complete and precise representations of words.

Several conclusions can be drawn. First, reading and spelling are usually closely associated. Good spellers are both fast and accurate readers: presumably, they are able to decode words precisely and quickly. As a consequence, they memorize the correct orthographic forms of the words (Share, 1995, 1999), even when these words are irregular. Poor readers who are also poor spellers exhibit the reverse pattern. Because they exhibit both phonological deficits and a slow reading rate, their reading is both slow and not very accurate. Recoding is not an efficient self-teaching device for them as it is for good readers. The direct effect of their phonological deficit is their poor spelling performance on both pseudowords and regular words; the indirect effect is the incomplete and possibly erroneous representation of stored word forms (if any), especially in the case of rare irregular words. Therefore, R− S− children (and adults) have great difficulties in improving their spelling performance.

Second, reading and spelling can dissociate. In some cases, when slight phonological deficits are associated with fast processing, children can read accurately and quickly. They can rely on incomplete orthographic representations which are mostly sufficient to distinguish between words. However, due to the poor quality of decoding and the high speed of processing, it is possible that they do not allocate enough time (and thus attention) to the orthographic forms of words. They might thus memorize incomplete representations that impair their spelling performance, thus making them bad spellers. In other cases, rarely described and studied and whose existence has sometimes been denied, accurate but slow readers are good spellers. The efficiency of their phonological abilities and the slowness of their processing combine and enable them to store precise orthographic representations. These representations support both their accurate reading and spelling performance.

One important question concerns the nature and quality of orthographic representations that support reading and spelling and make possible the reported associations and dissociations. Most researchers consider that reading and spelling are both supported by a common lexical and/or sublexical representation, a highly probable possibility. Two different complementary conceptions exist. The first assumes that people memorize whole word representations whose precision increases with school level (i.e. reading) level (Perfetti, 1992; Share, 1995). According to this conception, children move from initial fuzzy to highly precise orthographic representations (Ehri, 2005). A strong argument favouring such a conception is that the priming of written words (e.g. play) in recognition tasks becomes more and more restrictive as a function of school level: young children's lexical items are primed by both exact spellings (play: the repetition effect) and by approximative wordforms (e.g. rlay, lpay). By contrast, adults' priming only occurs with items similar to the target item (play) (Castles, Davis, Cavalot, & Forster, 2007). It is thus possible that some children (i.e. R+ S−) learn only partially the letters and the sequential organisation they have in a given word. As a consequence, they could read successfully but would have difficulties in spelling the same words, despite referring to the same orthographic lexicon (Frith, 1980). The second possibility considers that people learn letter sequences (i.e. graphotactic regularities) that are the components of words in both reading and spelling: when reading, these components are combined in the stimulus and deciphered. When spelling, people have to retrieve from memory both the components and their order of occurrence in the target words, which is much more complicated and more open to errors than in reading, especially in inconsistent orthographic systems (Lété, Peereman, & Fayol, 2008). Accordingly, Delattre, Bonin, and Barry (2006) provided evidence through a spelling to dictation task that adults remain sensitive to the inconsistency of words: the latencies were longer and writing slower with inconsistent items than with consistent ones. Unfortunately, no corresponding study is available with children. The two conceptions, lexical or sublexical, can explain both the associations and the dissociations described in this experiment. R+ S+ children have good performance in reading and spelling because both would rely on the same precise representations. The reverse is true for R− S− children: reading and spelling would rest on fuzzy representations. R+ S− children would process words with precise enough representations in reading, guided by the forms of the stimuli. The greater load associated with retrieving wordforms or word fragments from memory and combining them (Bourdin & Fayol, 1994, 2002) would increase the frequency of errors in spelling, but not in reading, despite referring to the same representations. Finally, R− S+ children do not raise any representation problem: they read accurately (and slowly) and thus can memorize word forms or fragments. They are only impaired regarding speed of reading, for reasons that our study cannot determine. Longitudinal studies are required to confirm the relevance of these observations and to come to a better understanding of the origins of these different profiles, and more specifically the two atypical developmental patterns (R+ S− and R− S+).

One question raised by our results comes from the fact that no measure of spelling speed was available in the present study. As a consequence, reading performance relied on both accuracy and speed whereas spelling performance only rested on accuracy. Could taking into account writing speed modify the pattern of results that was depicted in this study? More specifically, could we find both slow and accurate and/or fast and accurate spellers among R − S+ children? No clear answer is possible at the moment. Very few studies have analysed writing speed in children (Chanquoy, Foulin, & Fayol, 1990), especially in conjunction with spelling performance. When it was done, spelling accuracy and handwriting accuracy and speed were used as predictors and accuracy and rate of written composing as the outcome (Graham, Berninger, Abbott, Abbott, & Whitaker, 1997) but such analyses have not been conducted with spelling speed as one of the predictors.

The results reported here largely confirm those coming from previous studies in English (Lovett, 1987) and in German (Wimmer & Mayringer, 2002). They suggest that phonological decoding plays an essential role in learning both to read and to spell: R+ S+ and R− S+ children have good scores on the phonological task (i.e. the spelling of pseudowords); by contrast, R− S+ and R− S− children have poor performance on this task. As a consequence, it seems clear that the teaching of decoding is very important to establish the foundations of reading and spelling. It is widely acknowledged that decoding a word, that is, translating it from print to sound, would incidentally lead to the learning of the detailed orthographic representation of this word. However, the efficiency of this incidental learning varies as a function of word frequency and of the consistency of the orthographic systems. Accordingly, the reported data show that the learning of English words depends on the number of encounters of these words and of the interval between exposures and tests (Nation, Angell, & Castles, 2007). By contrast, Share (2004, Experiment 1) found no effect of the number of exposures and delay in third graders reading Hebrew. These results suggest that the consistency of the orthographic system has an impact on the relative difficulty of acquiring through self-teaching and securing in memory the detailed orthographic representation of words (Perfetti, 1992). Children having to acquire low-consistent orthographies must pay greater attention to word-specific orthographic information. The question is to determine how children can learn the orthographic form of low consistent words (e.g. words having silent letters). At the moment, little is known on this topic and few experiments are available. Is self-teaching efficient enough to enable children to acquire words such as *théatre* (theatre) in French? Or is it necessary to teach explicitly the orthography of those words? Experimental studies are required to answer this question.

References

Adams, M. J. (1990). *Beginning to read*. Cambridge, MA: The MIT Press.

Berninger, V. W., Abbott, R. D., Abbott, S. P., Graham, S., & Richards, T. (2002). Writing and reading: Connections between language by hand and language by eye. *Journal of Learning Disabilities, 35*, 39-56.

Bosman, A. M. T., & Van Orden, G. C. (1997). Why spelling is more difficult than reading. In C. A. Perfetti, L. Rieben, & M. Fayol (Eds.), *Learning to spell* (pp. 173-194). Mahwah, NJ: Erlbaum.

Bourdin, B., & Fayol, M. (1994). Is written language production really more difficult than oral language production? *International Journal of Psychology, 29*, 591-620.

Bourdin, B., & Fayol, M. (2002). Even in adults, written production is still more costly than oral production. *International Journal of Psychology, 37*, 219-222.

Bruck, M., & Waters, G. (1988). An analysis of the spelling errors of children who differ in their reading and spelling skills. *Applied Psycholinguistics, 9*, 77-92.

Bruck, M., & Waters, G. (1990). Analysis of the component spelling skills of good readers poor spellers. *Applied Psycholinguistics, 11*, 425-437.

Burden, V. (1992). Why are some 'normal' readers such poor spellers? In C. M. Sterling & C. Robson (Eds.), *Psychology: Spelling and education* (pp. 200-214). Clevedon, UK: Multilingual Matters.

Castles, A., Davis, C., Cavalot, P., & Forster, K. (2007). Tracking the acquisition of orthographic skills in developing readers: Masked form priming. *Journal of Experimental Child Psychology, 97*, 165-182.

Chanquoy, L., Foulin, J.-N., & Fayol, M. (1990). The temporal management of short text writing by children and adults. *European Bulletin of Cognitive Psychology, 10*, 513-540.

Cohen, J. (1988). *Statistical power analysis for the behavioral sciences* (2nd ed.). Mahwah, NJ: Erlbaum.

Cunningham, A. E., & Stanovich, K. E. (1997). Early reading acquisition and its relation to reading experience and ability 10 years later. *Developmental Psychology, 33*, 934-994.

Delattre, M., Bonin, P., & Barry, C. (2006). Written spelling to dictation: Sound-to-spelling regularity affects both writng latencies and durations. *Journal of Experimental Psychology: Learning, Memory, and Cognition, 32*, 1330-1340.

Ehri, L. (1997). Learning to read and learning to spell are one and the same, almost. In C. A. Perfetti, L. Rieben, & M. Fayol (Eds.), *Learning to spell* (pp. 237-269). Mahwah, NJ: Erlbaum.

Ehri, L. C. (2005). Learning to read words: Theory, findings, and issues. *Scientific Studies of Reading, 9*, 167-188.

Fitzgerald, J., & Shanahan, T. (2000). Reading and writing relations and their development. *Educational Psychologist, 35*, 39-50.

Frith, U. (1980). Unexpected spelling problems. In U. Frith (Ed.), *Cognitive processes in spelling* (pp. 495-515). London: Academic Press.

Graham, S., Berninger, V., Abbott, R., Abbott, S., & Whitaker, D. (1997). The role of mechanics in composing of elementary school students: A new methodological approach. *Journal of Educational Psychology, 89*, 170-182.

Hanley, J. R., Hastie, K., & Kay, J. (1992). Developmental surface dyslexia and dysgraphia: An orthographic processing impairment. *Quarterly Journal of Experimental Psychology, 44A*, 285-320.

Holmes, V. M., & Carruthers, J. (1998). The relation between reading and spelling in skilled adult readers. *Journal of Memory and Language, 39*, 264-289.

Holmes, V. M., & Castles, A. E. (2001). Unexpectedly poor spelling in university students. *Scientific Studies of Reading, 5*, 319-350.

Holmes, V. M., & Ng, E. C. (1993). Word specific knowledge, word-recognition strategies, and spelling abilities. *Journal of Memory and Language, 32*, 230-257.

Jaffré, J.-P., & Fayol, P. (2005). Orthography and literacy in French. In R. M. Joshi & P. G. Aaron (Eds.), *Handbook of orthography and literacy* (pp. 81-103). Mahwah, NJ: Erlabaum.

Juel, C., Griffith, P. L., & Gough, P. B. (1986). Acquisition of literacy: A longitudinal study of children in first and second grade. *Journal of Educational Psychology, 78*, 243-255.

Lefavrais, P. (1965). Description, définition et mesure de la dyslexie. Utilisation du test 'L'Alouette'. *Revue de Psychologie Appliquée, 15*, 33-44.

Lété, B., Peereman, R., & Fayol, M. (2008). Phoneme-to-Grapheme consistency and word-frequency effects on spelling among first- to fifth-grade French children: A regression-based study. *Journal of Memory and Language, 58*, 952-977.

Lété, B., Sprenger-Charolles, L., & Colé, P. (2004). MANULEX: A grade-level lexical database from French elementary-school readers. *Behavior Research Methods, Instruments, & Computers, 36*, 156–166.

Logan, G. D., & Etherton, J. L. (1994). What is learned during automatization? The role of attention in constructing an instance. *Journal of Experimental Psychology: Learning, Memory, and Cognition, 20*, 1022–1050.

Lovett, M. W. (1987). A developmental approach to reading disability: Accuracy and speed criteria of normal and deficient reading skill. *Child Development, 58*, 234–260.

Mann, V. (1993). Phoneme awareness and future reading ability. *Journal of Learning Disabilities, 26*, 259–269.

Morris, D., & Perney, J. (1984). Developmental spelling as a predictor of first-grade reading achievement. *Elementary School Journal, 84*, 440–457.

Nation, K., Angell, P., & Castles, A. (2007). Orthographic learning via self-teaching in children learning to read: Effects of exposure, durability, and context. *Journal of Experimental Child Psychology, 96*, 71–84.

Peereman, R., Lété, B., & Sprenger-Charolles, L. (2007). Manulex-infra: Distributional characteristics of grapheme–phoneme mappings, infra-lexical and lexical units in child-directed written material. *Behavior Research Methods, 39*, 593–603.

Perfetti, C. A. (1992). The representation problem in reading acquisition. In P. B. Gough, L. C. Ehri, & R. Treiman (Eds.), *Reading acquisition* (pp. 145–174). Hillsdale, NJ: Erlbaum.

Seymour, P. H. K., & McGregor, J. (1984). Developmental dyslexia: A cognitive experimental analysis of phonological, morphemic and visual impairments. *Cognitive Neuropsychology, 1*, 43–82.

Shanahan, T. (1984). Nature of the reading–writing relation: An exploratory multivariate analysis. *Journal of Educational Psychology, 76*, 466–477.

Share, D. L. (1995). Phonological recoding and self-teaching: Sine qua non of reading acquisition. *Cognition, 55*, 151–218.

Share, D. L. (1999). Phonological recoding and orthographic learning: A direct test of the self-teaching hypothesis. *Journal of Experimental Child Psychology, 72*, 95–129.

Share, D. L. (2004). Orthographic learning at a glance: On the time course and developmental onset of self-teaching. *Journal of Experimental Child Psychology, 87*, 267–298.

Sprenger-Charolles, L. (2003). Linguistic processes in reading and spelling: The case of alphabetic writing systems: English, French, German and Spanish. In T. Nunes & P. Bryant (Eds.), *Handbook of children's literacy* (pp. 43–65). Dordrecht: Kluwer.

Stanovich, K. E. (1984). The interactive copenstory model of reading: A confluence of developmental, experimental, and educational psychology. *Remedial and Special Education, 5*, 11–19.

Tainturier, M. J., & Rapp, B. (2001). The spelling process. In B. Rapp (Ed.), *The handbook of cognitive neuropsychology*. Hove, UK: Psychology Press.

Treiman, R. (1993). *Beginning to spell*. New York: Oxford University Press.

Treiman, R. (1998). Why spelling? The benefits of incorporating spelling into beginning reading instruction. In J. L. Metsala & L. C. Ehri (Eds.), *Word recognition in beginning literacy* (pp. 289–313). Mahwah, NJ: Erlbaum.

Vellutino, F. R., Fletcher, J. M., Snowling, M. J., & Scanlon, D. M. (2004). Specific reading disability (dyslexia). What have we learned in the past four decades? *Journal of Child Psychology and Psychiatry, 45*, 2–40.

Waters, G., Bruck, M., & Seidenberg, M. (1985). Do children use similar cognitive processes to read and spell words? *Journal of Experimental Child Psychology, 39*, 511–530.

Wimmer, H., & Mayringer, H. (2002). Dysfluent reading in the absence of spelling difficulties: A specific disability in regular orthographies. *Journal of Educational Psychology, 94*, 272–277.

Teaching and Learning Writing, 77–93
BJEP Monograph Series II, 6
© 2009 The British Psychological Society

The
British
Psychological
Society

www.bpsjournals.co.uk

fMRI activation related to nature of ideas generated and differences between good and poor writers during idea generation

Virginia W. Berninger[1]*, Todd L. Richards[1], Patricia S. Stock[1], Robert D. Abbott[1], Pamala A. Trivedi[1], Leah E. Altemeier[1] and John R. Hayes[2]

[1]Department of Educational Psychology, University of Washington, Seattle, Washington, USA
[2]Department of Psychology, Carnegie Mellon University, Pittsburgh, Pennsylvania, USA

Background and aims. Idea generation is fundamental to writing, but has received scant research attention compared to the other cognitive processes of writing. Transcribed oral production protocols were categorized for nature of the ideas generated. Based on these categories, hypotheses were formulated and tested about which brain regions would differentiate good and poor writers during idea generation.

Sample. Oral idea generation protocols were collected when children were 7 ($N = 124$) and 9 ($N = 119$ remaining in a longitudinal study). When they were 10, right-handed good writers ($N = 12$) and poor writers ($N = 8$) from the larger study underwent functional magnetic resonance imaging (fMRI) scanning.

Method. Two independent raters read all the oral idea generation protocols and categorized responses. During brain scanning, children rested (no task control condition) or generated ideas on a topic they wrote about after leaving the fMRI scanner.

Results. Categories of ideas reflected cognitive ($N = 10$), metacognitive ($N = 4$), or language ($N = 2$) processes and included self-reference ($N = 2$), behavioural demonstrations ($N = 1$), or break-downs in the idea generation process ($N = 5$). On the fMRI idea generation/rest contrast, good writers activated more than poor writers in brain regions associated with cognition, language, and executive functions, consistent with predictions, and also in working memory, motor planning, and timing. Poor writers activated more than good writers in a brain region associated with working memory but on the opposite side of the brain.

Correspondence should be addressed to Virginia W. Berninger, 322 Miller, Box 353600, University of Washington, Seattle, WA 98195-3600, USA (e-mail: vwb@u.washington.edu).

DOI:10.1348/978185409X421949

Conclusions.   Brain activation of good and poor writers may differ during the idea generation process of writing because the good writers are more efficient than poor writers in engaging working memory while generating thoughts.

Although all the major cognitive models of writing include idea generation (e.g. Alamargot & Chanquoy, 2001; Hayes, 1996; Hayes & Flower, 1980; Kellogg, 1994), idea generation has not been well studied, at either the behavioural or brain levels, compared to other cognitive processes such as translation, transcription, review, and revision. The current study is the first in a programmatic line of research on the nature of ideas, the idea generation process, and translation of ideas into written language (i.e. composition which is the written expression of ideas).

This initial study combined two research methods, each assessing idea generation at different levels of analysis – behavioural and brain. First, we examined the nature of ideas generated at the behavioural level in written transcriptions of oral protocols. Independent raters read all the written transcriptions of oral idea generation protocols and decided which category described each response and overall which set of categories characterized the overall nature of ideas produced. Because we were also interested in the source of idea generation within the brain, we used these categories of behavioural response to predict, based on current understanding of brain–behaviour relationships, where blood oxygen level dependent (BOLD) activation during functional magnetic resonance imaging (fMRI) might differentiate children who were good or poor writers. We compared these good and poor writers on an fMRI contrast between idea generation on a topic about which they wrote after leaving the brain scanner and a rest (control) condition during which they did not perform any task.

We compared the brain activation of the good and poor writers on this contrast for two reasons. On the one hand, considerable research has shown that good and poor writers differ on transcription skills (for review, see Berninger & Amtmann, 2003; Connelly, Campbell, MacLean, & Barnes, 2006; Graham, 1990) but the assumption has been that they do not differ on idea generation. For example, if children dictate orally, thus bypassing transcription skills, the quality of content, that is, ideas generated, is often comparable across good and poor writers. Thus, the prediction was that the good and poor writers would not differ on the fMRI contrast between idea generation and baseline resting. On the other hand, because writing researchers have noted that sometimes children experience problems in accessing information in long-term memory (e.g. Bereiter & Scardamalia 1987; Boscolo, 1990), we also examined whether the good and poor writers might differ in brain activation associated with the executive functions involved in searching long-term memory for ideas. In addition, because Kellogg (1994) proposed that planning, which includes idea generation, is qualitatively different from other cognitive processes in writing because it involves visual/spatial rather than verbal memory, we also explored the possibility that the good and poor writers might differ in brain regions associated with visual memory.

That is, brain activation was expected in the regions associated with categories of orally generated ideas. We were not expecting major overall differences between the good and poor writers during idea generation. However, we expected that good and poor writers might possibly differ in regions associated with executive functions in memory access and in visual spatial processing.

Method

Participants

Behavioural idea generation study

Participants were from a 5-year longitudinal study. They were recruited by sending letters, which announced the opportunity to participate, to every parent of a kindergartener (age 5) who would be entering first grade the following year in a large urban school district near a major research university in the Northwest United States. Interested parents contacted the research staff who provided more information about the study that was approved by the Institutional Review Board for Human Subjects. Children were excluded who had a developmental or medical history indicating that they might not be normally developing writers and readers. Overall, attrition was low. Of the 128 children who began the longitudinal study in Grade 1 (age 6), 124 participated in Grade 2 (age 7), and 119 in Grade 4 (age 9).

These children came to the university annually during the second, third, or fourth month of the school year for a half day of writing and other activities until they completed fifth grade (age 10). This study focused on the oral idea generation protocols collected when children were in second and fourth grades. The children were instructed to generate ideas orally first about computers and then about robots. They were audiotaped as they generated their ideas for 5 min on each topic. Then the audiotapes were transcribed and the written transcriptions were read to determine the categories of ideas generated. Idea generation protocols on the topic of computers were available for 109 second graders in year 2 (age 7) and 119 fourth graders in year 4 (age 9). Idea generation protocols on the topic of robots were available for 103 second graders in year 2 (age 7) and 119 fourth graders (age 9) in year 4. Their mean standard score for age on the *Wechsler Individual Achievement Test*, 2nd ed. (WIAT II; Psychological Corporation, 2002) Written Expression subtest ranged from average range (second graders, $M = 101.89$, $SD = 13.91$) to high average range (fourth graders, $M = 112.33$, $SD = 15.95$). The increase from an average of $SD = 0.07$ above the population mean in year 2 to about $SD = 0.8$ above the population mean in year 4 may reflect the increasing emphasis on writing in the curriculum for upper elementary compared to early elementary students in our community. This added writing instruction is designed to help students perform optimally on the state mandated tests, which require considerable writing. These tests are used for accountability of schools in most states in the USA as a result of the school reform movement.

The sample of children completing oral idea generation protocols was diverse in ethnicity and parents' level of education (one indicator of socio-economic background) and the diversity was representative of the community from which the children were recruited. At the time of initial enrolment in Grade 1, parent-reported ethnicity was as follows: Asian-American (23.4%), African-American (6.3%), European-American (64.8%), Hispanic (1.6%), Native American (1.6%), and other (2.3%). About 10% of the parents had less than a high school education or graduated from high school (7% mothers and 12.5% fathers). About 9% of the parents had more than a high school education but less than a college education (11.7% mothers and 7.8% fathers). About 42% of the parents had an undergraduate education (45.3% mothers and 39.8% fathers). About 33% of the parents had completed graduate degrees (33.6% mothers and 32.0% fathers). Information on parental level of education was missing for 2.4% of the mothers and 7.9% of the fathers.

fMRI study

At completion of the study when children had just finished fifth grade (10–11 years of age), a subsample of good and poor writers was identified who were equivalent in verbal intelligence and whose parents gave permission to participate in an fMRI study. Only right-handers who did not wear metal braces or other non-removable metal and met research inclusion criteria could be invited to participate. Inclusion criteria for good writers were at or above age or grade level for handwriting, spelling, and composition ($N = 12$). Inclusion criteria for poor writers were below the mean and at least 1 SD below their verbal IQ in handwriting, spelling, and/or composition ($N = 8$). These poor writers did not necessarily have reading problems and were not necessarily learning disabled; most did not qualify for special education in their school. However, the poor writers showed reliable weaknesses in their writing skills.

The good ($M = 119.25, SD = 17.00$) and poor ($M = 116.63, SD = 8.23$) writers did not differ significantly in Wechsler Individual Intelligence Test 4th Edition (WISC IV) Verbal IQ [$F(1, 18) = 0.16, p = .69$], on which both good and poor writers fell in the above average range. They did differ significantly in all writing skills and working memory skills, which are based on standard scores ($M = 100, SD = 15$) or z scores ($M = 0, SD = 1$). The good and poor writers differed significantly on Process Assessment of the Learner (PAL; Berninger, 2007) alphabet writing (automatic letter writing on this handwriting task; good, $M = 0.45$ z, $SD = 0.74$; poor $M = -0.44$ z; $SD = 0.93$; $F(1, 18) = 5.66$, $p = .029$, WIAT II spelling (good, $M = 114.00$, $SD = 9.59$; poor $M = 93$, $SD = 6.46$; $F(1, 18) = 29.22$, $p = .001$), WIAT II written composition ($M = 113.25$, $SD = 8.78$; poor $M = 96.25$, $SD = 10.74$; $F(1, 18) = 15.08$, $p = .001$), Woodcock Johnson Revised (WJ-R, Woodcock & Johnson, 1990) phonological working memory measure for digits backwards (good, $M = 124.17$, $SD = 24.99$; poor, $M = 104.13$, $SD = 10.45$; $F(18) = 4.78$, $p = .042$), and PAL orthographic working memory – words (good, $M = 0.20$, $SD = 0.66$; poor, $M = -1.14$, $SD = 1.78$; $F(18) = 9.61, p = .006$). On each of these measures, the good and poor writers differed by at least 1 SD despite comparable verbal IQs. With the exception of phonological working memory, even when the poor writers' writing or orthographic working memory scores were in the average range (± 0.67 SD), the scores were on average below the population mean and typically less than would be expected based on verbal IQ.

Procedures

Behavioural study of idea generation

For the behavioural study, a university-approved protocol was used in which parents gave informed consent and children gave oral assent when the protocol was read to them. Children were asked to think aloud and tell all the ideas they could about computers and then all the ideas they could about robots. Their oral idea generation was audiotaped and later transcribed into written transcripts by the student assistant who was giving the assessment measures in the study. The time limit for think aloud was 5 min. We examined the transcribed oral idea generation protocols because we were interested in the kinds of ideas children could generate apart from their ability to express them in full syntactic structures during text generation or transcription processes of translation. The transcribed protocols were coded for categories of ideas by two independent coders who then discussed where they agreed and differed and discussed any differences (for about 15% of the responses on the transcripts) until consensus was reached. Although the coders did not always agree initially on how specific items should be coded, they could resolve these differences and reached 100% agreement on what categories occurred in the protocols overall, which was the only research aim for this study. The purpose of coding categories of ideas was to generate testable predictions of regions of probable activation for the brain imaging study. These are explained at the end of the results for coded categories for the nature of ideas. These are also being used in related programmatic research comparing different ways of coding idea expression (e.g. Hayes & Berninger, 2009) or facilitating idea expression (e.g. Dunn, Clayton, Scattergood, & Tudor, 2008; Dunn & Finley, 2008).

Imaging study

A university-approved protocol was used for the imaging study. Parents gave informed consent and children gave oral assent when the protocol was read to them. Outside the scanner, children were told that, after they finished their tasks (related to another study), at the end of the imaging session, they would have a chance to rest in the scanner after all their hard work. Then they would hear, through the earphones, a topic for which they would be asked to generate ideas. They were also told that when they got out of the scanner, they would write a composition about that topic. Because they heard the topic for the first time at the end of scanning session, they could not engage in idea generation until then. They did know that they were generating ideas for the purpose of composing later.

The scanning protocol was one 5-min resting period (off-task) followed by one 5-min idea generation period (on-task) rather than the usual alternation of an on- and an off-task.

Instructions for these tasks were as follows:

Off (control) task. Now you have some time to rest. We do not have a task for you. Just rest. You have worked hard.

On-task. Think about what you learned this summer that you never learned in school. In a little while, you will leave the scanner and write about this topic.

On–off contrast. Comparison of mean BOLD in the on and off conditions identified brain regions where the two conditions were significantly different. Regions that are significantly different in BOLD activation are uniquely associated with effortful, task-driven idea generation as opposed to spontaneous cognition that is known to occur when the brain is at rest rather than engaged in a specific task (Fox *et al.*, 2005). The living brain, unlike electronic devices that are turned off, is never totally inactive when not being used for explicit cognitive tasks in conscious awareness – although it may shift to another state of mind.

Imaging protocol for acquisition

Structural MR scans and fMRI scans for group maps were acquired on a Philips Achieva 3-T scanner (version 2.1, Philips Medical Systems, Best, The Netherlands) with dual Quasar gradients (80 mT/m with a slew rate of 110 mT/m per s or 40 mT/m at a slew rate of 220 mT/m per s) using an 8-channel SENSE Head coil. An MPRAGE localizer was acquired in the sagittal plane for structural analysis and fMRI co-registration of anatomy with parameters: TR/TE 7.0/3.2 ms, SENSE factor = 1.5 in RL direction, 160 slices, 3D acquisition resolution matrix $224 \times 221 \times 160$ with reconstructed resolution of $0.94 \times 0.94 \times 1.0$ mm, flip angle = 8°, field of view $240 \times 240 \times 160$ mm, scan duration 449 s. Functional MRIs were acquired using these parameters: gradient echo (single shot) echo-planar pulse sequence (called epi field echo by Philips), TR/TE 3000/30 ms, FOV 240 mm, slice thickness/gap 4.0/1.0, 32 slices covering the entire brain, 2D matrix 64 × 64, epifactor 63, SENSE factor = 1, number of dynamics 212, scan duration 636 s. A B0 map (Fast Field Echo, TR/TE 935/20 ms, echo difference time of 4 msec for B0map calculation, scan duration 123 s, 32 slices, 64 × 64 reconstructed matrix, FOV 240 mm) was also acquired at exactly the same slice positions as the fMRI image with a B0 correction using FSL software.

fMRI data analysis

Pre-processing

FSL (FEAT Expert Analysis Tool Version 5.4 in FMRIB's Software Library, www.fmrib.ox.ac.uk/fsl) was used for motion correction using MCFLIRT (Jenkinson, Bannister, Brady, & Smith, 2002); non-brain removal using BET (Smith, 2002); spatial smoothing using a Gaussian kernel of FWHM 5 mm; and mean-based intensity normalization of all volumes by the same factor; highpass temporal filtering (Gaussian-weighted LSF straight line fitting, with σ = 50.0s). FEAT's feature for B0 correction was used for B0 phase and magnitude maps that Philips automatically produces as part of the B0 map image reconstruction (TE difference 4 ms, dwell time = 0.655 μs, +y polarity, input parameters).

First level

Time-series statistical analysis was carried out using FMRIB's improved linear model (FILM; Woolrich, Ripley, Brady, & Smith, 2001) in a block design with local autocorrelation correction. z (Gaussianised T/F) statistic images were thresholded using clusters determined by $z > 2.3$ and a corrected cluster significance threshold of $p = .01$ (Worsley, Evans, Marrett, & Neelin, 1992). Registration to high resolution and/or standard images was carried out using FLIRT (Jenkinson & Smith, 2001; Jenkinson *et al.*, 2002). ICA-based exploratory data analysis using multivariate exploratory linear optimized decomposition into independent components (MELODIC; Beckmann & Smith 2004) was used to investigate possible presence of unexpected artefacts or activation. The individual ICA/MELODIC output components were analysed by custom software to find out which components had large amounts of activation rimness (>0.65), which is activation at boundaries of the brain surface or the ventricular walls. These ICA components may be 'artefact' from subject motion. The MELODIC filter option filtered out the 'artefact' components identified in the previous step. The output 4D fMRI data were then rerun through FEAT individual-level analyses to find valid activation. Effects at each voxel were estimated; regionally specific effects were compared using linear contrasts.

Group level

Contrasts for individual subjects were aggregated for the group in a random effects analysis carried out using FSL's FLAME (FMRIB's local analysis of mixed effects) for stage 1 only (i.e. without the final MCMC-based stage; Beckmann, Jenkinson, & Smith, 2003; Woolrich *et al.*, 2001). z (Gaussianised T/F) statistic images were thresholded using clusters determined by $z > 2.3$, $p = .01$ uncorrected (Worsley *et al.*, 1992). Effects at each voxel were estimated; regionally specific effects were compared using linear contrasts.

Results

Behavioural study of idea generation

We first summarize each of the 24 categories observed when the V. W. Berninger and P. S. Stock read all the oral idea generation protocols, independently coded the nature of the ideas expressed, and discussed any discrepancies until they reached agreement. We provide in Table 1 an example of each category observed in the oral protocols. The purpose was not to determine how many of each category each child produced but rather to identify all the possible categories in the responses for the purposes of (a) characterizing the nature of generated ideas at this stage of writing development; and (b) generating predictions, to test during fMRI imaging, where brain activation might occur and differentiate good and poor writers during idea generation.

Table 1. Twenty-four categories in oral idea generation protocols

Categories	Examples
1. Descriptors	Computers are smart
2. Actions	They can move. . .pick up stuff and talk
3. Function	Robots are good for cleaning your room
4. Definitions	Robots are metal creatures
5. Qualifications	They cannot do things without people telling them to
6. Examples	Some robots are featured in movies like Star Wars
7. Comparisons	They are supposed to be like humans
8. Explanations	They're probably voice activated or heat activated
9. Conditional statements (facts)	If it bumps into a wall, it just turns around
10. Conditional statements (imagination)	It would be cool if you could control siblings that way with an on/off switch and tell them what to do
11. Topic elaborations	I like computers. . .*because I know how to do games and get them started*
12. New topic	Don't play it too long or you will waste electricity
13. Personal sharing	I used to think that computers would turn you into a unicorn
14. Opinions	I think that in the future they might talk to you
15. Editorial comments	Just kidding
16. Summary	That is pretty much what a computer is
17. Ending statements	Now I am done
18. Metacognitive reflections	I don't know which one it is
19. Fragmented output	So, a computer is a −com −a −device thingy. . .
20. Filled pause	Well um and ahhhh. . .
21. Tangential to topic	I'm sleepy
22. Repetition of words	You can. . . .. And *you can*. . .
23. Repetition of thought	Do not have minds of their own. . .*they really don't have minds*
24. Pantomime	They go like this − ⟨child moved around the room⟩

Two categories reflected language: adjectives and verbs. However, 10 reflected cognitive processes: (a) functions, (b) definitions, (c) qualifications, (d) examples, (e) comparisons and analogies, (f) explanations, (g) factual conditional relationships, (h) imaginative conditional relationships, (i) elaborations, and (j) adding new information. Two categories referenced self: (a) sharing personal experience and perspectives, and (b) opinions. Four categories were metacomments on the idea generation process: (a) editorial comments, (b) summaries, (c) ending statements, or (d) self-reflections about thought processes. One involved pantomime. Five reflected breakdowns in idea generation and probably executive functions guiding the idea generation process: (a) false starts, interruptions, and hesitations, (b) filled pauses, (c) word repetitions, (d) thought repetitions, and (e) tangential comments.

Thus, we predicted, based on current understanding of brain–behaviour relationships in writing (e.g. see Berninger & Richards, 2002, chap. 6) that brain regions associated with language (in temporal, parietal, and frontal regions), cognition (in frontal regions), metacognition (in frontal regions), executive functions (in frontal regions), and visual imagery (in parietal and occipital regions) might activate during fMRI idea generation in good writers. Because most of the 24 categories reflected cognitive, metacognitive, or executive functions, we expected the most significant BOLD activation in frontal regions. Altemeier, Abbott, and Berninger (2008) reported evidence that typically developing writers show substantial individual differences in executive functions that predict their achievement in a variety of writing and reading skills. However, because no transcription tasks were involved, we predicted that the good and poor writers would not differ in posterior regions associated with letter writing or spelling or frontal regions associated with motor function.

Brain imaging results

Significant activation in good writers
Initial analyses identified regions of significant BOLD activation in the good writers. These results, which are available from T. L. Richards, showed that good writers activated significantly in regions associated with higher order cognition and working memory (left middle frontal gyrus), language (left inferior frontal gyrus), non-verbal cognition (right superior and middle temporal gyri), executive functions (left anterior cingulate) and affect (left posterior cingulate), and visual imagery (left occipital gyrus). However, in the current study we focus on the comparisons between good and poor writers to identify regions where BOLD activation was greater in good than poor writers and conversely where brain activation was greater in poor than good writers.

Comparisons of good and poor writers
Quantitative values for analyses of where good writers showed significantly more BOLD activation than poor writers on the on–off contrast for idea generation versus baseline resting are shown in Table 2. Quantitative values for analyses where poor writers showed significantly more BOLD activation than the good writers on the same contrast are reported in Table 3. For readers not familiar with the cognitive/behavioural functions associated with specific brain regions, the most common functions associated with specific regions are indicated in parentheses. However, keep in mind that these local regions are typically part of distributed neural networks (see Berninger & Richards, 2002, chap. 6, for brain regions and neural networks involved in writing).

Good writers activated more than poor writers in nine brain regions (see Figures 1 and 2): left and right superior frontal gyrus and left medial region of superior frontal gyrus (associated with access to concepts and higher order cognitive functions); left inferior frontal – operculum and triangularis (language and executive functions related to language), right middle frontal orbital gyrus (working memory area), left and right supplementary motor area (planning for motor output), and right cerebellum (timing

Table 2. Group map fMRI quantitation for idea generation contrast for good writers greater than poor writers

| Brain region | Average z score | MNI coordinate | | | Brodmann | Number of pixels |
		X	Y	Z		
Frontal_Sup_L	2.541	− 10	36	48	9	35
Frontal_Sup_R	2.431	32	− 8	58	6	13
Frontal_Mid_Orb_R	2.544	22	58	− 12	11	23
Frontal_Inf_Oper_L	2.643	− 42	10	28	44	14
Frontal_Inf_Tri_L	2.653	− 42	10	26	48	44
Supp_Motor_Area_L	2.674	2	24	60	8	19
Supp_Motor_Area_R	2.709	2	22	60	0	15
Frontal_Sup_Medial_L	2.548	− 10	52	40	9	44
Cerebelum_8_R	2.603	16	− 72	− 58	0	56

Note. Sup, superior; L, left; R, right; Mid, middle; Orb, orbital; Inf, inferior; Oper, Operculum; Tri, triangularis; Supp, supplementary.

Table 3. Group map fMRI quantitation for idea generation contrast for poor writers greater than good writers

| Brain region | Average z score | MNI coordinate | | | Brodmann | Number of pixels |
		X	Y	Z		
Frontal_Mid_L	2.47	− 34	30	30	46	14

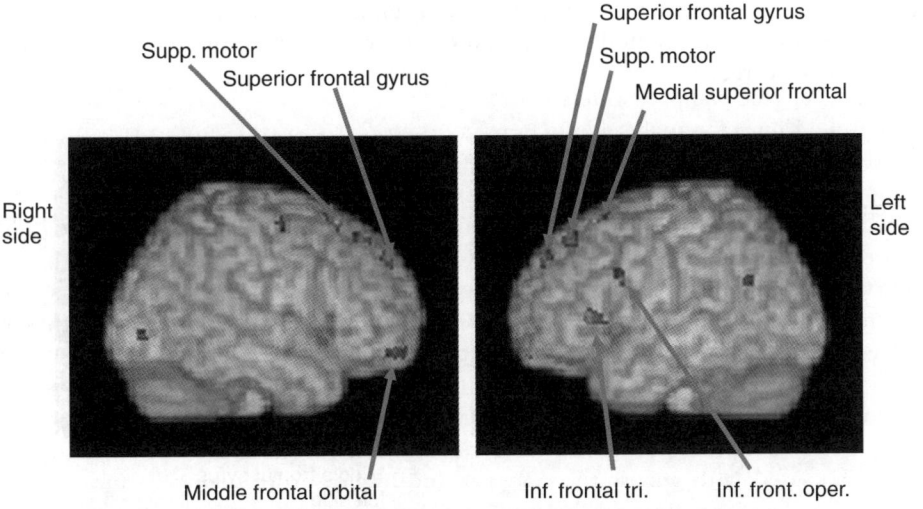

Figure 1. Group comparison fMRI activation for the idea generation task for good writers greater than poor writers. Cross hairs are positioned on the activation in specific brain regions.

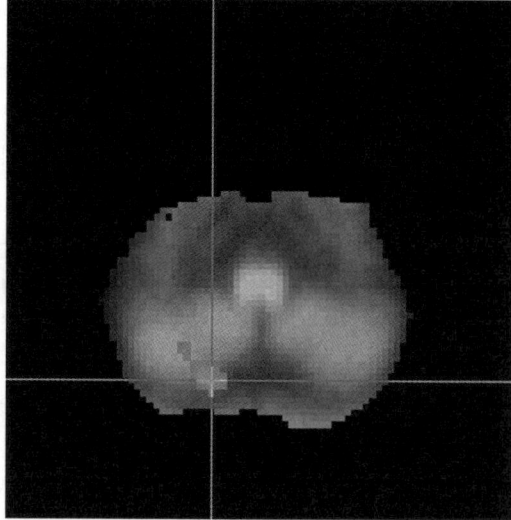

Figure 2. Group comparison fMRI activation for the idea generation task for good writers greater than poor writers. Cross hairs are positioned on the activation in the cerebellum.

and coordination). Poor writers activated more than good writers in one brain region: left middle frontal gyrus (working memory; see Figure 3).

As reported in the Method section (see Participants), the good and poor writers differed significantly on working memory measures, with poor writers having significantly lower mean working memory scores than good writers. These behavioural results converge with brain imaging results showing that poor writers and good writers differ in working memory.

We also examined quality of writing samples in first and fifth grades in the good and poor writers. The Appendix contains these for two representative good writers and two representative poor writers. Qualitative differences in their writing were evident at the beginning of learning to compose in written language and persisted 5 years later at the time they participated in the fMRI study. The quantitative and qualitative differences converge.

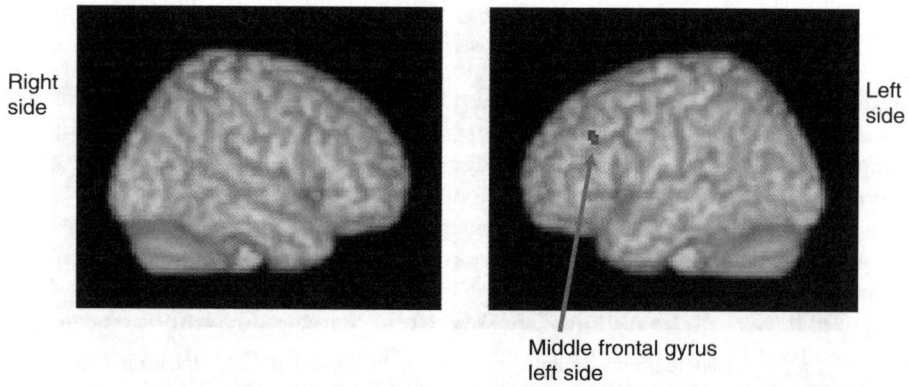

Figure 3. Group comparison fMRI activation for the idea generation task for poor writers greater than good writers. Cross hairs are positioned on the activation in the left middle frontal gyrus.

We repeated each of the behavioural analyses of categories of ideas for the whole sample of second and fourth graders as described earlier for the subsample who participated in the brain imaging study at the end of fifth grade. The goal was to evaluate whether the results for the whole sample earlier in development generalized to individuals in the smaller sample at a later time in writing development. Year 4 Oral Idea Generation protocols collected at age 9 were transcribed and inspected to evaluate whether the categories on the coding scheme in Table 1 accounted for the observed productions in the children who later had their brains scanned at age 10–11 during idea generation. The same categories that were observed in the total sample (see Table 1) were also observed in the subsample who participated in the fMRI study.

Discussion

New findings

The hypothesis that poor writers and good writers are comparable in brain activation associated with idea generation was not supported. Poor writers activated a brain region (left middle frontal gyrus) associated with working memory to a greater degree than good writers, suggesting that the poor writers are inefficient in engaging working memory during idea generation. This finding is of interest because although good writers showed significant BOLD activation in this same left middle frontal gyrus, when they were compared to poor writers, the good writers showed significantly more activation in right middle frontal gyrus. This result suggests that both right and left middle frontal gyrus are part of a network in working memory and the over-activation of poor writers relative to good writers in left middle frontal gyrus may be due to their under-activation compared to good writers in right middle frontal gyrus, the homologous structure on the other side of the brain. These findings are of interest for the field of writing research because they indicate that poor writers may not engage working memory normally from the beginning of the writing process during idea generation prior to the translation of ideas into written language.

Good writers, in contrast to poor writers, activated bilateral superior frontal gyrus, including regions that may be involved in executive support for access to cognitive representations or operations, to a greater extent. See du Boisgueheneuc *et al.* (2006) for evidence that superior frontal gyrus may be a brain region where cognition occurs with guidance from the higher level executive functions of working memory. In addition, good writers activated Broca's area and regions in it associated with the executive functions of language, consistent with idea generation involving a translation of cognitions into language with executive function support. Both of these results are consistent with the observation that poor writers may have difficulty in accessing verbal information in long-term memory (Bereiter & Scardamalia, 1987; Boscolo, 1990). The good writers also activated more than the poor writers in brain regions associated with planning motor output (supplementary motor areas) and temporal coordination (cerebellum). Planning and temporal coordination are also executive functions that contribute to self-regulation of the writing process.

Taken together, these findings are consistent with good writers engaging brain regions involved in executive functions more than poor writers for purposes of self-regulation of writing processes. It is well established in the research literature that poor writers have difficulty with self-regulation of the writing process (e.g. Graham & Harris, 2003). This self-regulation difficulty may occur as early in the writing process as idea generation, at least in children. Research on the behavioural and brain bases of idea generation in adult writers is also needed.

The preponderance of categories of ideas related to cognition, metacognition, and executive functions led us to predict significant activation in frontal brain regions. Not all predictions generated from behavioural idea generation protocols were confirmed. Although activation was observed in left occipital gyrus (associated with visual imagery) in good writers, the good and poor writers did not differ in this region. Thus, idea generation may draw upon visual imagery but good and poor writers did not differ in activation in the brain region associated with that cognitive function. Also, although frontal regions associated with language differentiated the good and poor writers, the posterior temporal regions associated with language did not differentiate them. The analyses for significant BOLD activation in good writers mentioned at the beginning of the results section did find significant activation in these posterior temporal and occipital regions during idea generation, but these were not the regions where the good and poor writers differed significantly.

Contribution of brain research to writing research

Some psychologists and educators remain skeptical about the value of brain imaging research in general and for writing in particular. The combination of a behavioural and brain study on the same sample illustrates how research can benefit from combining multiple levels of analysis in study of writing. As explained next, the analyses at the brain level often converge with those at the behavioural level.

Cognitive studies at the behavioural level of analysis have shown that working memory supports the writing process (Alamargot & Chanquoy, 2001), especially translation (e.g. Alamargot & Chanquoy, 2001; Chenoweth & Hayes, 2001, 2003) and transcription (Alamargot & Chanquoy, 2001; Hayes & Chenoweth, 2006) in children (Bourdin & Fayol, 1994; Swanson & Berninger, 1996) and adults (Hayes & Chenoweth, 2006). Lower order executive functions such as rapid automatic switching of mental set, which is relevant during idea generation, were unique predictors of writing achievement during the elementary grades, but lower order executive functions contributed more to word-level writing (spelling transcription) and reading skills than to text-level composition and reading comprehension, which require higher order executive functions (Altemeier *et al.*, 2008). Berninger and Richards (2002) proposed that the cognitive processes in the Hayes and Flower (1980) model are those higher order executive functions that guide the cognitive planning (including idea generation), translating (including text generation), and reviewing and revising.

Brain imaging studies have shown that middle frontal gyrus is involved in working memory (e.g. see Crosson *et al.*, 1999; for review with application to writing, see Berninger & Winn, 2006). The significant new finding from the present study's brain perspective was that poor writing is related to how working memory is engaged during idea generation. Poor writers, who scored lower on the phonological and orthographic working memory measures, engaged left middle frontal gyrus, associated with working memory, more than the good writers, who engaged the same region more than did the poor writers but on the right side of the brain. The middle frontal gyrus contains Brodmann area 8, which is Exner's area, which Exner (1881) proposed as a writing centre in the brain. More recently, supportive evidence has been reported by Anderson, Damasio, and Damasio (1990) for Exner's area being a writing centre in the brain, but most likely not the only one.

Thus, the current study, which showed differences in BOLD activation in this region between good and poor writers during idea generation, provides converging evidence consistent with prior behavioural findings that good and poor writers differ in working memory. This finding does not rule out transcription as a contributing factor to poor writing, but future research should address whether transcription and working memory factors contribute independently to poor writing or an underlying working memory problem may underlie the transcription problems that many poor writers display.

The results should not be interpreted to mean that only idea generation draws on working memory. Most likely many aspects of writing draw on working memory – not only idea generation but also executive processes for translation of thought into written language that guide text generation and transcription. Thus, observed brain activation may not reflect a single cognitive process but rather a mechanism that supports several cognitive processes contributing to writing.

Moreover, the current study shows that brain imaging studies yield interesting information about higher order cognitive functions such as idea generation and not only lower order processes such as motor processes or transcription skills on which many brain imaging studies related to writing have focused. We hope that the current study will stimulate many more studies on the higher order cognitive processes in writing that combine behavioural and brain levels of analysis.

Conclusions

This study has contributed two kinds of new knowledge. First, we showed that nature of ideas generated can be studied at the behavioural level. The majority of observed categories were non-language in nature. More were cognitive or metacognitive. The prediction based on the initial behavioural studies that not only language areas of brain but also areas of brain associated with cognition and executive functions (metacognitive or self-regulation) would activate during idea generation was confirmed. Second, this study of child writers may be the first brain imaging study to investigate idea generation for writing. We identified the brain regions where good writers activated more than poor writers and poor writers activated more than good writers during the idea generation/resting baseline contrast prior to written composition.

Acknowledgements

This paper is based on invited presentations by Virginia W. Berninger at the Learning and Teaching Writing, *British Journal of Educational Psychology*, Psychological Aspects of Education Current Trends Conference at Oxford Brookes University, Oxford, England, June 28, 2007, and the Italian Psychological Association on 21 September, 2008, Padua, Italy. Virginia W. Berninger thanks Barbara Arfé for helpful feedback on the contribution of fMRI research to the study of higher-order cognitive processes in writing. National Institute of Child Health and Human Development (NICHD) supported this research (Grant no. HD25858).

References

Alamargot, D., & Chanquoy, L. (2001). Through the models of writing. In Gert Rijlaarsdam (Series ed.). *Studies in writing series*. Dordrecht: Kluwer Academic Publishers.

Altemeier, L., Abbott, R., & Berninger, V. (2008). Executive functions for reading and writing in typical literacy development and dyslexia. *Journal of Clinical and Experimental Neuropsychology, 30*, 588–606.

Anderson, S., Damasio, A., & Damasio, H. (1990). Troubled letters but not numbers. Domain specific cognitive impairments following focal damage in frontal cortex. *Brain, 113*, 749–760.

Beckmann, C., Jenkinson, M., & Smith, S. (2003). General multi-level linear modelling for group analysis in FMRI. *Neuroimage, 20*, 1052–1063.

Beckmann, C., & Smith, S. (2004). Probabilistic independent component analysis for functional magnetic resonance imaging. *IEEE Transactions on Medical Imaging, 23*, 137–152.

Bereiter, C., & Scardamalia, M. (1987). *The psychology of written composition*. Hillsdale, NJ: Erlbaum.

Berninger, V. (2007). *Process assessment of the learner-II (PAL II). Diagnostic for reading and writing*. San Antonio, TX: The Psychological Corporation.

Berninger, V., & Amtmann, D. (2003). Preventing written expression disabilities through early and continuing assessment and intervention for handwriting and/or spelling problems: Research into practice. In H. L. Swanson, K. Harris, & S. Graham (Eds.), *Handbook of research on learning disabilities* (pp. 345–363). New York: Guilford Press.

Berninger, V., & Richards, T. (2002). *Brain literacy for educators and psychologists*. New York: Academic Press.

Berninger, V., & Winn, W. (2006). Implications of advancements in brain research and technology for writing development, writing instruction, and educational evolution. In C. MacArthur, S. Graham, & J. Fitzgerald (Eds.), *Handbook of writing research* (pp. 96–114). New York: Guilford Press.

Boscolo, P. (1990). The construction of expository text. *First Language, 10*, 217–230.

Bourdin, B., & Fayol, M. (1994). Is written language production more difficult than oral language production – a working-memory approach. *International Journal Psychology, 29*, 591–620.

Chenoweth, N., & Hayes, J. R. (2001). Fluency in writing. Generating text in L1 and L2. *Written Communication, 18*, 80–98.

Chenoweth, N. A., & Hayes, J. R. (2003). The inner voice in writing. *Written Communication, 20*(1), 99–118.

Connelly, V., Campbell, S., MacLean, M., & Barnes, J. (2006). Contribution of lower order skills to the written composition of college students with and without dyslexia. *Developmental Neuropsychology, 29*, 175–196.

Crosson, B., Rao, S., Woodley, S., Rosen, A., Bobholz, J., Mayer, A., *et al.* (1999). Mapping of semantic, phonological, and orthographic verbal working memory in normal adults with functional magnetic resonance imaging. *Neuropsychology, 13*, 171–187.

du Boisgueheneuc, F., Levy, R., Volle, E., Seassau, M., Duffau, H., Kinkingnehun, S., *et al.* (2006). Functions of the left superior frontal gyrus in humans: A lesion study. *Brain, 129*, 3315–3328.

Dunn, M. W., Clayton, S., Scattergood, C., & Tudor, D. (2008). Ask, reflect, text: ART as a narrative story-writing strategy. Manuscript submitted for publication.

Dunn, M., & Finley, S. (2008). Thirsty thinkers: A workshop for artists and writers. *Journal of Reading Education, 33*(2), 28–36.

Exner, S. (1881). *Untersuchungen über die lokalisation der funktionen in der grossshirnrinde des menschen*. Vienna: Wilhelm Braumuller.

Fox, M., Snyder, A, Vincent, J., Corbetta, M., van Essen, D., & Raichle, M. (2005). The human brain is intrinsically organized into dynamic, anticorrelated functional networks. *Proceedings National Academy Sciences, 102*, 9673–9678.

Graham, S. (1990). The role of production factors in learning disabled students' compositions. *Journal of Educational Psychology, 82*, 781–791.

Graham, S., & Harris, K. (2003). Students with learning disabilities and the process of writing: A meta-analysis of SRSD studies. In H. L. Swanson, K. Harris, & S. Graham (Eds.), *Handbook of learning disabilities* (p. 203) New York: Guilford Press.

Hayes, J. R. (1996). A new framework for understanding cognition and affect in writing. In C. M. Levy, & S. Randall (Eds.), *The science of writing: Theories, methods, individual differences, and applications* (pp. 1–27). Mahwah, NJ, Lawrence Erlbaum Associates.

Hayes, J. R., & Berninger, V. (2009). Relationships between idea generation and transcription: How act of writing shapes what children write. In C. Braverman, R. Krut, K. Lunsford, S. McLeod, S. Null, P. Rogers, & A. Stansell (Eds.), *Traditions of writing research*. New York: Routledge.

Hayes, J. R., & Chenoweth, N. (2006). Is working memory involved in the transcribing and editing of texts? *Written Communication, 23,* 135-149.

Hayes, J. R., & Flower, L. S. (1980). Identifying the organization of writing processes. In L. W. Gregg & E. R. Steinbert (Eds.), *Cognitive processes in writing* (pp. 3-30). Hillsdale, NJ: Erlbaum.

Jenkinson, M., Bannister, P., Brady, M., & Smith, S. (2002). Improved optimisation for the robust and accurate linear registration and motion correction of brain images. *Neuroimage, 17,* 825-841.

Jenkinson, M., & Smith, S. (2001). A global optimisation method for robust affine registration of brain images. *Medical Image Analysis, 5,* 143-156.

Kellogg, R. T. (1994) *The Psychology of Writing.* New York: Oxford University Press.

Psychological Corporation (2002). *Wechsler Individual Achievement Test* (2nd ed.). San Antonio, TX: Psychological Corporation.

Smith, S. M. (2002). Fast robust automated brain extraction. *Human Brain Mapping, 17,* 143-155.

Swanson, H. L., & Berninger, V. (1996). Individual differences in children's writing: A function of working memory or reading or both processes? *Reading and Writing. An Interdisciplinary Journal, 8,* 357-383.

Wechsler, D. (2004). *Wechsler Individual Intelligence Test (WISC IV)* (4th ed.). San Antonio, TX: The Psychological Corporation.

Woodcock, R., & Johnson, B. (1990). *Woodcock-Johnson Revised Tests of Cognitive Ability - Standard and supplemental batteries: Examiner's manual.* Allen, TX: DLM Teaching Resources.

Woolrich, M. W., Ripley, B. D., Brady, J. M., & Smith, S. M. (2001). Temporal autocorrelation in univariate linear modeling of FMRI data. *Neuroimage, 14,* 1370-1386.

Worsley, K. J., Evans, A. C., Marrett, S., & Neelin, P. (1992). A three-dimensional statistical analysis for CBF activation studies in human brain. *Journal of Cerebral Blood Flow and Metabolism, 12,* 900-918.

Appendix. Composition samples in Grade 5 (after fMRI scanning) and in Grade 1 for two good writers and two poor writers

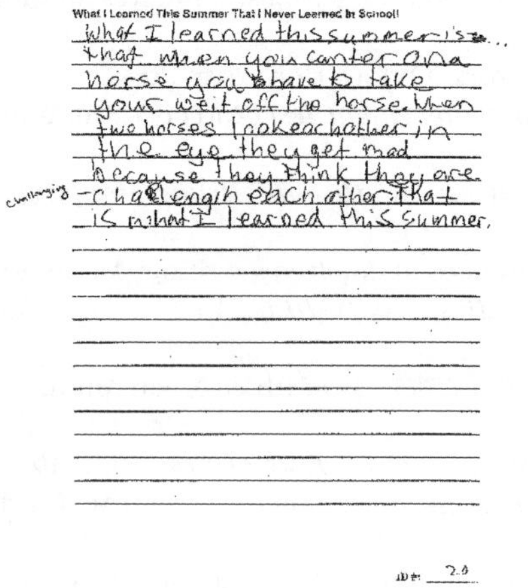

Figure A1. Poor writer 1 – Grade 5.

Figure A2. Poor writer 1 – Grade 1.

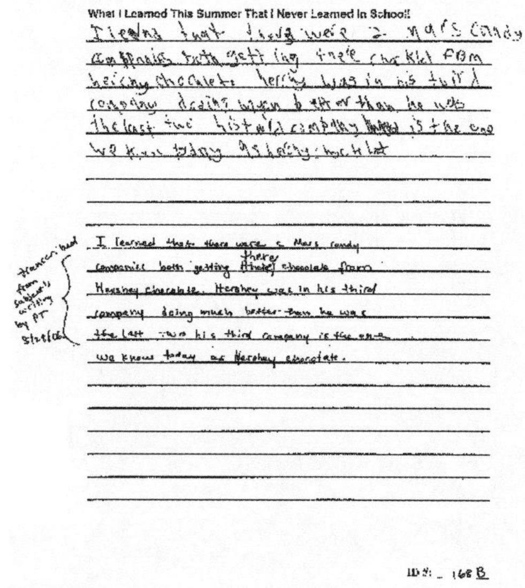

Figure A3. Poor writer 2 – Grade 5.

Figure A4. Poor writer 2 – Grade 1.

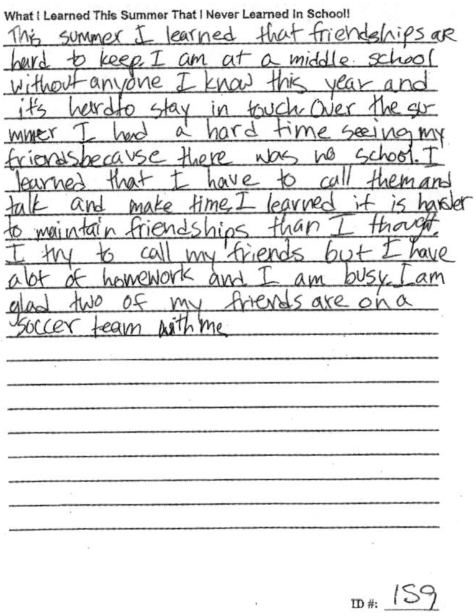

What I Learned This Summer That I Never Learned In School!

This summer I learned that friendships are hard to keep I am at a middle school without anyone I know this year and it's hard to stay in touch Over the summer I had a hard time seeing my friends because there was no school. I learned that I have to call them and talk and make time I learned it is harder to maintain friendships than I thought. I try to call my friends but I have a lot of homework and I am busy. I am glad two of my friends are on a soccer team with me

ID #: 159

Figure A5. Good writer 1 – Grade 5.

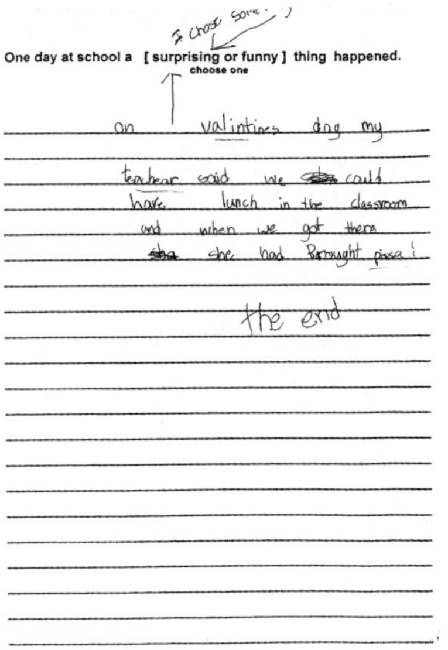

One day at school a [surprising or funny] thing happened.
choose one

on valintines day my teacher said we could have lunch in the classroom and when we got there she had brought pizza!

the end

Figure A6. Good writer 1 – Grade 1.

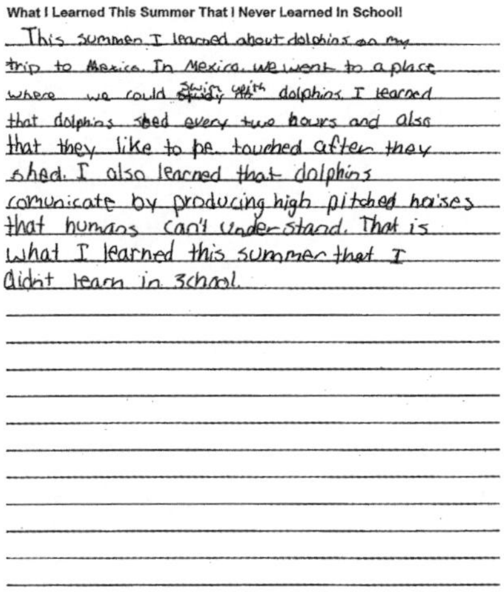

What I Learned This Summer That I Never Learned In School!

This summer I learned about dolphins on my trip to Mexico. In Mexico, we went to a place where we could swim with dolphins I learned that dolphins shed every two hours and also that they like to be touched after they shed. I also learned that dolphins communicate by producing high pitched noises that humans can't understand. That is what I learned this summer that I didn't learn in school.

211
ID #:

Figure A7. Good writer 2 – Grade 5.

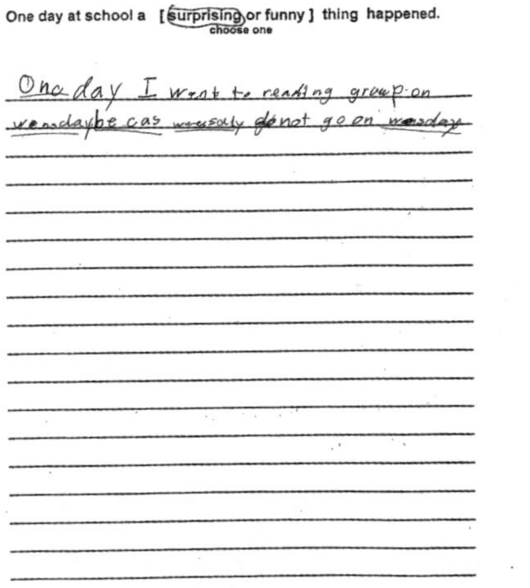

One day at school a [surprising or funny] thing happened.
choose one

One day I went to reading group on mondaybecas wesusly donot go on monday

211

Figure A8. Good writer 2 – Grade 1.

Teaching and Learning Writing, 95–111
BJEP Monograph Series II, 6
© 2009 The British Psychological Society

The
British
Psychological
Society

www.bpsjournals.co.uk

Evidence-based writing practices: Drawing recommendations from multiple sources

Steve Graham* and Karen R. Harris

Department of Special Education, Vanderbilt University, Nashville, Tennessee, USA

Background. Many youngsters find writing difficult. One possible reason for why the writing of youngsters in contemporary society is not what it needs to be is that writing instruction is not what it should be.

Aims. This paper presents 13 evidence-based recommendations for teaching writing to youngsters in grades 4–12 (ages 10–18 years).

Arguments. The recommendations were formed by drawing on three sources: a meta-analysis of experimental and quasi-experimental writing intervention studies, a meta-analysis of single-subject design studies, and a meta-synthesis of reoccurring writing instructional practices from qualitative studies examining effective schools and teachers.

Conclusions. Issues and caveats in implementing these recommendations are explored, as are recommendations for additional research.

Writing is a complex and demanding task. Even those who write for a living complain about the exacting nature of writing. For instance, the noted sportswriters, Red Smith, grumbled: 'Writing is easy. All you have to do is set down at a typewriter and open a vein' (Winokur, 1999, p. 24). Likewise, the Canadian humorist, Stephen Leacock, claimed: 'Writing is no trouble, just jot down ideas as they occur to you. The jotting is simplicity itself – it is the occurring which is difficult' (Philips, 1993, p. 338).

Why is writing so demanding? First, it is a goal directed and self-sustained activity requiring the skilful use of a variety of mental operations in order to satisfy the writer's goals. Second, the writer must deal with many demands at once. This involves intelligently managing the writing environment; the constraints imposed by the writing topic; and the processes, knowledge, and skills involved in composing (Graham, 2006; Zimmerman & Reisemberg, 1997). As Hayes and Flower (1980) noted almost 30 years ago, a skilled writer caught in the act looks very much like a busy switchboard operator, trying to juggle a number of demands on their attention simultaneously (e.g. making plans, drawing ideas from memory, developing concepts, or creating an image of the reader).

Correspondence should be addressed to Steve Graham, Department of Special Education, Vanderbilt University, Peabody College Box 228, Nashville, TN 37023, USA (e-mail: steve.graham@vanderbilt.edu).

DOI:10.1348/000709909X421928

According to Kellogg (1993), writing does 'not simply unfold automatically and effortlessly in the manner of a well learned motor skill . . . writing anything but the most routine and brief piece is the mental equivalent of digging ditches' (p. 17).

Writing entails much more than this however. It is a social activity involving either an implicit or explicit dialogue between writer(s) and reader(s). The act of writing is further shaped by the community in which it takes place. For instance, the shape and tone of writing differs considerably amongst a group of friends sharing ideas via email versus texts written by psychologists (Nystrand, 2006). Competence in one writing community also does not ensure competence in another. A youngster who is adept at using text messaging to communicate with friends, for example, may have difficulty writing a well organized, thoughtful, and informative paper for a biology class. What and how people write is further influenced by larger forces involving the cultures, society, institutions, and history in which the writer is situated (Schultz & Fecho, 2000). To illustrate, a youngster's concept of writing is likely moulded by institutional decisions about how to teach writing. If schools place a heavy emphasis on correct form, then students are likely to place considerable emphasis on correcting errors when revising (Graham & Olinghouse, in press). In contrast, if form is de-emphasized by schools, but meaning and process are stressed, a different approach to revising is likely.

Given its complexities, it is not surprising that many youngsters find writing difficult. In the USA, for example, an unacceptable number of students do not write well enough to meet grade level demands. The findings from the most recent national assessment of writing (Salahu-Din, Persky, & Miller, 2008) showed that over one-half of students in grades 8 (age 14) and 12 (age 18) obtained only partial mastery of the writing skills needed at their respective grade levels. Moreover, college teachers in the USA estimate that 50% of high school graduates are not prepared for college-level writing (Achieve Inc., 2005). Concerns about writing are not just limited to the USA, but involve other industrialized nations, such as Great Britan (Wyse, 2003).

One possible reason for why the writing of youngsters in contemporary society is not what it needs to be is that writing instruction is not what it should be. While many countries, school districts, and schools have relatively clear goals for what students need to learn in writing, there is no consensus on how to teach this complex skill (Graham & Olinghouse, in press). This is illustrated in the satirical remarks of the author, Somerset Maugham: 'There are three rules for writing the novel. Unfortunately, no one knows what they are' (Winokur, 1999, p. 146).

There are three primary sources for developing teaching practices in writing (Graham, in press). One involves advice provided by professional writers (see King, 2000), who draw on their own writing experiences and insights to make recommendations. A second source comes from teachers of writing, either directly or indirectly. For example, in a highly influential book by Atwell (1987), teachers promoted the use of instructional procedures they judge to be effective in their classroom. Likewise, those who observe writing teachers in action may recommend the use of teacher practices they view as worthwhile (Graves, 1983). A third source involves scientific studies examining the effectiveness of specific writing intervention techniques.

A central problem with the first two sources (professional writers and teacher practices) is that it is difficult to separate the 'wheat from the shaft' (Graham, in press). Most often, there is no direct evidence that a suggested instructional procedure actually produces the desired effects. When evidence is presented, it usually involves testimonials or the presentation of selected students' writing. This makes it impossible to determine if the evidence is representative. Moreover, there is no way to predict if a recommendation based on the experiences of a single teacher or professional writer (or even a few of each) will be effective for other teachers. As a result, developing a writing program solely on the basis of these first two sources is a risky proposition, as the validity, generalizability, and reliability of suggested teaching practices are usually unknown.

While the third source, drawing recommendations from experimental scientific studies, has its own set of limitations (which are addressed later), it provides a more trustworthy approach for identifying effective practices for teaching writing than the first two sources. Experimental treatment studies provide evidence on whether the instructional procedure produced the desired impact (validity), the observed effects are representative (generalizability), and how much confidence can be placed in them (reliability). Such studies quantify the observed impact of an intervention on writing performance, making it possible to take the findings from individual studies and converting them into a common metric (i.e. effect size). This allows us to determine the strength of an intervention's impact across investigations.

Purpose of this paper

In this paper, we draw on the scientific literature to develop recommendations for teaching writing to students in grades 4–12 (ages 10–18). For the most part, we draw on the third source described above – scientific studies where the effectiveness of an intervention was systematically tested. This includes true- and quasi-experimental studies, where the mean performance of a group of students receiving a specific treatment is compared to the mean performance of a group of students receiving an alternative treatment or no treatment. In true-experimental studies, students are randomly assigned to conditions, whereas they are not randomly assigned in quasi-experimental studies.

These scientific studies also included single-subject design investigations. With this type of research, the focus is on the effectiveness of an intervention at the individual level (such studies typically include more than a single student, however). This involves repeatedly measuring a student's performance before as well as during and/or after instruction to establish a stable baseline and treatment effects (assuming treatment has an impact on performance). The researcher controls when the treatment is presented to a student or across students to rule out counter explanations for the findings. This is illustrated in the following example. After establishing a stable baseline of writing performance for participating students, instruction is implemented with one student, and the researcher repeatedly measures the impact of this instruction, while simultaneously assessing the writing performance of other study participants who have not yet received the treatment. If the instructed student demonstrates a stable improvement in their writing performance, while uninstructed students demonstrate a stable lack of improvement, this provides evidence that the treatment caused the positive change in writing behaviour. If this same pattern is repeated successively across multiple students, the claim that the treatment is effective is strengthened (Horner *et al.*, 2005).

To develop these evidence-based recommendations, we draw on two recent reviews of the writing intervention literature, one involving true- and quasi-experimental treatment studies (Graham & Perin, 2007a,b) and the other focusing on single-subject design investigations (Rogers & Graham, 2008). In both of these papers, considerable effort was devoted to locating all available studies, including published articles, dissertations, thesis, book chapters, and conference presentations. Additionally, both reviews quantified the impact of specific writing treatments by conducting a meta-analysis. With meta-analysis, the effects of each individual study is converted to a common metric (i.e. effect size) that provides information on the direction (positive, neutral, or negative) and magnitude of the observed effects (Lipsey & Wilson, 2001).

For the true- and quasi-experimental studies in Graham and Perin (2007a,b), effect sizes were calculated, as Cohen's d or the standardized mean difference. This involved subtracting the mean performance of the control/comparison group from the mean performance of the treatment group following treatment and dividing by the pooled standard deviation of the two groups. For each specific treatment, a weighted average effect size was computed (i.e. effect sizes were averaged across studies, but each effect size was weighted by study size). Although it is best to interpret the magnitude of an effect size for a specific writing treatment in relation to the distribution of other average effect sizes for all other writing treatments, a widely used rule of thumb is that an effect size of 0.20 is small, 0.50 is medium, and 0.80 is large (Lipsey & Wilson, 2001).

For the single-subject design studies included in Rogers and Graham (2008), the effect size was calculated as percentage of non-overlapping data (PND; the percent of data points for a given treatment condition that exceeds the most positive value obtained during baseline). For each specific treatment, an average PND was computed (no correction for number of participants in a study were made, as such statistical procedures are not currently available). Average PND of 90% or greater is considered large, 70–90% PND is medium, and 50–70% PND is small (Scruggs, Mastropieri, & Casto 1987).

It should be noted that effect size metrics from group studies and PND from single-subject design studies are not directly comparable. Each of these metrics provides a standardized measure for assessing if a treatment has a meaningful impact on writing performance, but PND does not actually measure magnitude of improvement (as it is just concerned with the percentage of treatment data points that represent an improvement over the strongest baseline score), whereas Cohen's d does.

Another important difference between the effect size computed for the true- and quasi-experimental studies in Graham and Perin (2007a,b) and the single-subject design studies in Rogers and Graham (2008) involves the outcome measure. For the former (true- and quasi-experimental studies), effects sizes were computed for overall quality of writing only. With single-subject design studies, PND can only be calculated for variables where the score for each data point is provided during baseline and treatment (usually in the form of a graph). Single-subject design researchers typically graph the variable that is most directly associated with the intervention, and this is not typically a measure of writing quality. Thus, the outcome measures that were converted to effect sizes for the single-subject design and the group studies typically differed, but this was not always the case, as writing quality was graphed for some studies.

In the meta-analyses conducted by Graham and his colleagues (Graham & Perin, 2007a,b; Rogers & Graham, 2008), four criteria were put into place to enhance the validity of each recommendation that was offered. One, a recommendation was not made in any of these reviews unless there were at least four studies that investigated the effectiveness of the treatment (providing evidence that the findings could be reasonably replicated). Two, a summary effect size was not calculated for a treatment unless the measure in each included study was conceptually similar. Three, there was evidence that writing was measured reliably in each included study (limiting the role of error in assessing the impact of the treatment). Four, the instruction provided to students in each study assessing a given treatment was reasonably similar. We applied the same criteria in this paper, and only used effect sizes from studies involving youngsters from grades 4 to 12 (ages 10–18; this eliminated some studies from Rogers and Graham (2008), as they looked at students from grades 1 to 12).

Any scientifically-based recommendation for teaching writing is only as good as the evidence supporting it. In the reviews described above, each study was assessed in terms of study quality, providing information on the quality of the supporting evidence. For true- and quasi-experimental design studies (Graham & Perin, 2007b), nine quality indicators were assessed: assignment of subjects, mortality equivalence, no ceiling or floor effects, pre-test equivalence, instructor training described, alternative treatment control condition provided, Hawthorne effect controlled, treatment fidelity established, and teacher effects controlled. For single-subject design studies (Rogers & Graham, 2008), there were 11 quality indicators. These involved how adequately the following were described: participants, subject-selection procedures, physical description of treatment setting, testing procedures, and treatment. Other quality measures included operationally defining the outcome measures, establishing reliability of outcome measures, collecting multiple data points during baseline as well as treatment, establishing fidelity of treatment, and obtaining social validity data.

For the single-subject design studies, Rogers and Graham (2008) further established which investigations established experimental control (stable baseline and treatment data as well as patterns of data increases or decreases at treatment and baseline consistent with experimental control). This information is critical in determining the validity of the data from a single-subject design study.

In addition to drawing recommendations based on quantitative scientific studies where the effectiveness of a specific intervention has been systematically tested, we also offer recommendations based on the findings from qualitative studies where the writing practices of highly effective teachers or schools were observed. This involved a meta-synthesis of the writing practices commonly observed in qualitative studies of exceptional literacy teachers and schools (Graham & Perin, 2007c). A basic tenet in this review was that writing practices that are idiosyncratic to a specific teacher or school are potentially less important than those that are employed across all or most studies. Thus, recommendations were only drawn when a practice was observed across a majority of the available studies. These recommendations must be viewed as tenuous, as such an analysis cannot establish that a particular writing practice is responsible for students' writing performance. Nevertheless, this alternative lens for identifying potentially effective practices allowed us to extend the scope of the recommendations we were able to offer.

There are several advantages to using multiple approaches for establishing recommendations for teaching writing to students in grades 4–12 (ages 10–18). At the present time, neither the experimental nor the single-subject design writing intervention research is especially broad or deep (Graham & Perin, 2007c). Basing recommendations on all three types of research (experimental, single subject, and qualitative analysis of effective teachers and schools) makes it possible to draw a more comprehensive set of recommendations. Furthermore, we believe that the validity of a recommendation is strengthened, if it is supported by evidence from multiple methodologies. For instance, the conclusion that a specific treatment is useful is enhanced if it produced a positive impact in both experimental and single-subject design research, and it is used by effective teachers and schools.

Recommendations for teaching writing (grades 4–12)

We ordered our writing recommendations using four criteria. First recommendations were ordered into three categories based on convergence of evidence from the three sources presented above: meta-analysis of true- and quasi-experimental research (Graham & Perin, 2007a,b), meta-analysis of single-subject design research (Rogers & Graham, 2008), and meta-syntheses of qualitative studies examining effective schools and teachers (Graham & Perin, 2007c). We contend that a recommendation is more likely to be valid if all of the available evidence supports it. Recommendations that met all three of these conditions were placed in our top category. This was followed by a second category where two sources of evidence supported each recommendation, and a third category where there was only one source of support.

Second, within each of these three categories, evidence from true- and quasi-experimental studies was privileged over evidence from single-subject design and evidence from qualitative studies. Likewise, evidence from single-subject design studies was privileged over qualitative evidence. Why did we privilege group experimental evidence over single-subject design evidence? As noted earlier, effect sizes from true- and quasi-experimental research measures the magnitude of an effect, whereas PND from single-subject design studies do not. Findings from group experimental studies are also based on more participants than those from single-subject design investigations. Moreover, the meta-analysis examining true- and quasi-experimental studies focused on improvements in overall writing quality (Graham & Perin, 2007a,b), whereas PND in the single-subject design meta-analysis typically involved calculating average PND for more discrete measures of writing performance, such as amount written or number of genre elements included (Rogers & Graham, 2008). The reason why we favoured evidence from group experimental and single-subject design studies over evidence from the qualitative meta-syntheses (Graham & Perin, 2007a,b,c) is that the latter does not establish that the practice under consideration is responsible for students' writing performance.

Third, a recommendation that was based on research of higher quality was privileged over a recommendation based on research of poorer quality. In essence, more confidence can be placed in recommendations derived from studies with fewer flaws. We did not make this our primary criteria, because there was little relation between study quality and effect sizes in the meta-analyses that we draw upon in this paper (Graham & Perin, 2007b; Rogers & Graham, 2008). It should be noted that the quality of research was not examined in the meta-synthesis of qualitative studies (Graham & Perin, 2007c).

Fourth, if the evidence for two recommendations was comparable within a category, the recommendation that was based on the larger number of studies was privileged. We assumed that a recommendation based on more studies, when everything else was roughly equal, was more reliable than a recommendation based on fewer investigations.

Finally, it became necessary to create a fourth category for a single treatment. In this case, the treatment obtained a negative mean effect.

For each category of recommendations, we order recommendations based on the criteria described above. A brief description of the treatment each recommendation is based on is provided, along with evidence that supports the recommendation. When possible, we qualify recommendations based on the quality of the evidence on which it is based. We did not repeatedly cite the source of the evidence for each recommendation, as it was obvious if the evidence was from the meta-analysis of group experiments (Graham & Perin, 2007a,b), single-subject design studies (Rogers & Graham, 2008), or the meta-synthesis of qualitative investigations (Graham & Perin, 2007c). We also illustrate each recommendation with one or more examples of the practice.

Recommendations supported by all three sources of evidence

1. *Teach youngsters strategies for planning, revising, and editing their writing.* This involves explicitly and systematically teaching students' strategies for planning, revising, and/or editing text. Instruction is designed to teach students to use these strategies independently, and includes teacher modelling of the strategies and student practice in applying them (with teacher assistance provided as needed). Writing strategies ranged from processes such as brainstorming (which can be applied across genres) to strategies designed for specific types of writing, such as writing a persuasive essay.

The average weighted effect size for writing quality in 20 large group experimental design studies where planning, revising, and/or editing strategies were taught to youngsters in grades 4–10 (ages 10–16) was 0.82 (a large effect). This treatment was especially effective with struggling writers, as it yielded an average weighted effect size of 1.04.

The strong impact of strategy instruction was further supported by 24 single-subject design studies, mostly conducted with struggling writers. When students in grades 4–11 (ages 10–17) were taught how to plan and draft compositions, the average PND for the inclusion of basic compositional elements (e.g. story elements) in 15 studies was 95%. Mean PND for writing output (e.g. amount written) in eight of these studies with youngsters in grades 5–8 was 89%, whereas mean PND for quality in four of these studies (grades 4–8) was 99%. Similarly, the average PND for basic paragraph elements in four studies where youngsters were taught a strategy for planning and drafting specific types of paragraphs was 97%. When students were taught an editing strategy in five studies (grades 4–12), the mean PND for errors corrected was 84%.

Considerable confidence can be placed in this evidence, as single-subject design studies received an average quality score of 8.4 (out of 11 possible indicators of study quality – mean for all single-subject design studies was 7.9), and the mean quality score for large group experimental studies was 6.0 (out of a possible 9 indicators of study quality – mean for all true- and quasi-experimental studies was 5.3).

The importance of teaching writing strategies was also evident in the practices of exceptional teachers and schools. Teachers commonly taught students how to plan, draft, and revise. They also modelled, explained, and provided guided practice when teaching these processes (these are the same techniques used in the quantitative studies examining the effectiveness of strategy instruction with youngsters in grades 4–12).

In the true- and quasi-experimental design studies, the self-regulated strategy development model (SRSD; Harris & Graham, 1996) was a particularly potent approach for teaching writing strategies (mean weighted effect size = 1.14; grades 4–8). Furthermore, in the 15 single-subject design studies (grades 4–11; ages 10–17) where students were taught how to plan and draft compositions, average PND for elements (15 studies), quality (4 studies), and output (8 studies) was 95, 99, and 89%, respectively.

With SRSD, students go through five stages of instruction: develop background knowledge (students are taught any background knowledge needed to use the strategy successfully), describe it (the strategy as well as its purpose and benefits are described and discussed; a mnemonic for remembering the steps of the strategy may be introduced too), model it (the teacher models how to use the strategy), memorize it (the student memorizes the steps of the strategy and any accompanying mnemonic), support it (the teacher supports or scaffolds student mastery of the strategy), and independent use (students use the strategy with little or no supports). Instruction is also individualized and criterion-based. Students are treated as active collaborators in the learning process, and they are taught a number of self-regulation skills (including goal setting, self-monitoring, self-instructions, and self-reinforcement) designed to help them manage writing strategies, the writing process, and their writing behaviour.

We provide an example of strategy instruction, involving the SRSD model (Harris, Graham, & Mason, 2006). Instruction was delivered to small groups of second-grade children (age 7) who learned two planning/drafting strategies: one for story writing and the other for persuasive writing. They were taught a general strategy, POW, that prompted them to (P) pick a topic, (O) organize their ideas (or plan) in advance of writing, and (W) write and say more while writing (i.e. to continue to plan as they wrote). They were also taught more specific strategies for organizing their ideas (within the organizing step above) that involved generating, culling, and organizing ideas via basic genre elements. For story writing, students made notes in response to questions about the following story parts before writing: Who are the main characters? When does the story take place? Where does the story take place? *What* do the main characters of the story want to do? *What* happens when the main characters try to do it? H*ow* does the story end? H*ow* do the main characters feel? For persuasive writing, they responded to the following prompts: Tell what you believe; Provide three or more reasons why you believe it; End it or wrap it up right; and Do I have all my parts?

Story writing was taught first, followed by persuasive writing. For each genre, the first stage of instruction involved introducing the general (POW) and the genre-specific strategy and making sure that students were familiar with the basic parts of a story or persuasive essay. Next, the rationale for using the general and genre-specific strategy was established and students began memorizing a mnemonics to help them remember the genre specific strategy. Students also assessed and graphed their performance on a story or essay written before the start of instruction. This established a baseline against which to compare later performance, which was also assessed and graphed. Then, the teacher modelled how to apply the general and genre-specific strategy, making the process visible by thinking out-loud. Before writing a paper, the teacher set a goal to use all of the basic parts for a story or essay. Once the paper was completed, the teacher and students discussed what the teacher said that helped them while writing. Students then generated several self-statements to use while they wrote. The teacher and students collaboratively wrote the next composition, setting goals, using self-statements, and graphing their performance. The teacher gradually withdrew instructional support, until students could use the strategies and self-regulation procedures independently and successfully. Finally, students identified opportunities to apply what they were learning outside of their small group and evaluated and discussed their successes in doing so. This instruction improved the quality of students' stories and persuasive essays, and also resulted in improvements in two untaught genres: personal narrative and informative writing.

2. *Set clear and specific goals for what youngsters are to accomplish with their writing product.* This involves students or teachers setting specific goals for writing. This ranged from setting a goal for students to addresses both sides of an argument to establishing a goal for increasing the amount written. In five group experimental studies

with students in grades 4–8 (ages 10–14), goal setting had a moderate impact on the quality of students' writing (mean weighted effect size = 0.70). Similarly, goal setting had a moderate mean PND (78%) in six single-subject design studies (grades 4–12; ages 10–18) in terms of increasing writing output (e.g. number of words written). Considerable confidence can be placed in these findings, as the study quality score for large group experimental design studies was 7.6 (out of 9), and it was 8.2 (out of 11) for single-subject design investigations. In addition, goal setting was a common part of writing instruction in the classes of exceptional teachers and schools, as these teachers set high expectations for students and encouraged them to surpass their previous efforts and accomplishments.

Ferretti, MacArthur, and Dowdy (2000) provide an example of goal setting that with fourth- and sixth-grade students (ages 10–12). Students were asked to write a letter to persuade an audience to agree with their position on a controversial topic. In comparison to students who were provided with a general goal, students given a set of specific goals for their writing (which involved statement of beliefs, supporting reasons, and why someone may disagree with this belief) produced more persuasive papers.

3. *Teach youngsters how to write more sophisticated sentences.* Studies examining the teaching of sentence skills have primarily involved one of the two following approaches: (1) teaching youngsters how to construct more complex and sophisticated sentences through exercises where two or more basic sentences are combined into a single sentence, or (2) teaching a set of strategies or formulas for writing sentences. In five large group experimental design studies, the first approach (sentence combining) had a moderate impact on improving the writing quality of youngsters in grades 4–11 (ages 10–17; mean weighted effect size = 0.50). This finding is complimented by five single-subject design studies (one involving sentence combining and the other four the teaching of sentence strategies or formulas) that produced a moderate PND of 86% in terms of increasing the number of complete sentences written by youngsters in grades 6–12 (ages 12–18). Some caution must be placed in interpreting these summary findings, as the study quality score was 5.3 (out of 9) and 6.7 (out of 11) for larger group and single-subject design studies, respectively. However, the teaching of sentence skills was a common practice in the classrooms of exceptional teachers.

Saddler and Graham's (2005) study of the effects of sentence combining with grade four students (age 10) provides an example of how to teach youngsters to construct more complex sentences. They paired higher and lower achieving students and taught them how to combine smaller related sentences in order to: (1) create compound sentences (using the connectors *and*, *but*, and *because*); (2) embed adjectives or adverbs from one sentence into another; (3) embed an adverbial or adjectival clause from one sentence into another; and (4) make multiple embeddings involving adjectives, adverbs, adjectival clauses, and adverbial clauses. For each sentence skill, the teacher first modelled how to combine sentences to achieve the desired goal, followed by students working together to learn the skill. Students then applied the skill in revising papers they had written. This had a positive impact on students' sentence skills as well as the quality of their writing.

4. *Engage youngsters in pre-writing activities that help them gather and organize ideas for their compositions.* Pre-writing activities range from gathering possible information for a paper through reading to using graphic organizers to generate and organize possible ideas for writing. An example of a graphic organizer is a semantic web which students use to list and group major and subordinate ideas for their composition before writing (Loader, 1989). In five large group experimental design studies,

pre-writing activities had a small, but positive impact on enhancing the quality of compositions produced by students in grades 4–9 (ages 10–15; mean weighted effect size = 0.32). Similarly, prewriting had a PND of 52% (small effect) on the writing quality of students in grades 4–12 (ages 10–18) in four single-subject design studies. Some caution must be exercised in interpreting the findings for the group experimental design studies (mean study quality was 5.4 out of 9 possible points), but not for single-subject studies (mean study quality = 8.0 out of 11 possible points). Finally, in classes taught by exceptional teachers or located in exceptional schools, youngsters were commonly asked to engage in thoughtful prewriting activities, such as planning what they would write.

Recommendations supported by two sources of evidence

5. *Engage youngsters in the process writing approach.* Although there is no universally accepted definition for the writing process approach, it generally involves extended opportunities for writing; writing for real audiences; engaging in cycles of planning, translating, and reviewing; personal responsibility and ownership of writing projects; high levels of student interactions, creation of a supportive writing environment; self-reflection and evaluation; and personalized individual assistance and instruction.

In 21 experimental group studies, such instruction had a small, but positive impact on improving the writing quality of students in grades 4–12 (ages 10–18; mean weighted effect size = 0.32). The process approach to writing had a stronger impact on the quality of students' writing when teachers received professional development on how to implement it (mean weighted effect size = 0.46). Conversely, its impact was diminished when implemented by grade 4–6 teachers (students aged 10–12) who did not receive such professional development, and it had no impact when taught by similar grade 7–12 teachers (students aged 13–18; mean weighted effect size = −0.05). Considerable caution must be used to interpret these summary statistics, however, as mean score for study quality was low (4.5 out of 9 possible points).

It is interesting to note that exceptional teachers and schools applied many of the practices and principles incorporated in process writing. These included: (1) treating writing as a process, where students plan, draft, revise, edit, and share their work (i.e. cycles of writing processes); (2) creating a positive writing environment, where students are constantly encouraged to try hard, believe that the skills and strategies they are learning will permit them to write well, and attribute success to effort and the tactics they are learning (i.e. supportive writing environment); (3) adapting writing assignments and instruction to better meet the needs of individual students (i.e. personalized instruction); and providing just enough support so that students can make progress or carry out writing tasks and processes, while encouraging students to act in a self-regulated fashion, doing as much as they can on their own (i.e. personal responsibility and self-regulation).

Recommendations supported by a single source of evidence

6. *Teach youngsters strategies and procedures for summarizing reading material, as this improves their ability to concisely and accurately present this information in writing.* This includes teaching strategies for summarizing text or instructional activities designed to improve students' text summarization skills. Such instruction had a strong

impact (mean weighted effect size = 0.82) on improving the summary writing skills of students in grades 5-12 (ages 11-18) in four group experimental design studies. Confidence can be placed in this finding, as the mean study quality score was 6.5 (out of 9 possible points).

We illustrate the teaching of summary writing with a strategy taught by Nelson, Smith, and Dodd (1992) to students who were 9-13 years old. First, the teachers ensured that students understood the general components of a summary (a summary should contain only important information), cues in text that help identify the main idea (bold or underlined words, introductory sentences), and the steps in the strategy and the reasons for each step. The teacher and students then applied the summary strategy using a summary writing guide that visually illustrated the strategy steps: (1) identifying the main idea, (2) noting important things about the main idea, (3) rereading to make sure the main idea and important ideas were correct, (4) writing a topic sentence, (5) grouping ideas, (6) determining whether any important ideas were missing or unimportant ideas could be deleted, (7) writing the summary, (8) rereading the summary for unclear ideas, and (9) having a peer read the summary. After learning the strategy, students wrote summaries that included more main ideas and important details from the text.

7. *Develop instructional arrangements where youngsters work together to plan, draft, revise, and edit their compositions.* This involves providing a structure where students work together to complete one or more aspects of the writing process. Such an arrangement had a moderate impact (mean weighted effect size = 0.75) on improving the overall quality of compositions produced by students in grades 4-12 (ages 10-18). Confidence can be placed in this finding, as the mean study quality score for studies was 6.4 (out of 9 possible points).

A study by MacArthur, Schwartz, and Graham (1991) provides an example of this approach. Teachers taught struggling writers in grades 4-6 (ages 10-12) a structure for providing feedback to each other on their papers. After writing a paper, students met with a peer and read their paper aloud, followed by the two students discussing the paper (with an emphasis on pointing out the positive features of the paper). The peer then independently reread the paper and made revision notes on it, focusing on unclear sections and the need for any additional details. The pair then met again to discuss the peer's comments, and the author of the paper used this feedback to revise the composition. This same basic approach was then repeated, but the focus was now on editing (identifying and correcting incomplete sentences as well as capitalization, punctuation, and spelling errors). This structured approach to peer revising not only increased how much students' revised, but improved the quality of their writing.

8. *Make it possible for youngsters to use word processing as a tool for writing.* The 21 group experimental studies investigating this treatment ranged from word processing with and without supporting software, such as a spell checker. Word processing had a moderate impact on overall writing quality for students in grades 4-12 (ages 10-18; Mean weighted effect size = 0.55). This evidence must be interpreted with caution, however, as the mean quality score for these studies was 5.0 (out of 9).

Additional analysis on the effects of word processing and other technology for writing is provided by MacArthur in his article in this special issue. In keeping with his analysis, we provide an example of how word processing and other supporting software can work together to support the writing of children who struggle with writing (MacArthur, 1988). In his study, students who were 9 and 10 years old wrote dialogue journals via word processing to communicate with their teacher. They were then taught how to use supporting speech synthesis and word prediction software. The speech synthesis software provided auditory support for the students, who could choose to have the computer read aloud a particular word, sentence, or the entire journal entry, whereas the word prediction software suggested possible words based on letters entered to that point. The addition of these two software programs had a positive impact on both spelling and number of legible words written (words correctly decoded out of context).

9. *Involve youngsters in writing activities designed to sharpen their skills of inquiry.* Inquiry activities in writing are characterized by a clearly specified goal (e.g. describe the actions of people), analysis of concrete and immediate data (e.g. observe one or more peers during specific activities), use of specific strategies to conduct the analysis (e.g. retrospectively ask the person being observed the reason for their action), and applying what was learned (e.g. write a story where the insights from the inquiry are incorporated into the composition). Inquiry activities had a small, but positive impact on improving the quality of writing produced by students in grades 7–12 (ages 13–18; mean weighted effect size = 0.32) in five experimental group design investigations. Caution must be applied in interpreting this finding, as the average quality score for these studies was 4.8 (out of 9 possible points).

Another example of inquiry involves an activity applied by Hillocks (1982). The goal was to examine and infer the qualities of a number of objects and to describe them in writing. Concrete data and the strategy for carrying out this inquiry activity moved from students touching objects (e.g. a seashell) or experiencing specific sensations (e.g. listening to sounds or doing physical exercises) while wearing a blindfold. students' responses to these activities were elicited, and they were asked to write a description of them. They then shared these descriptions with peers, who encouraged them to provide more precise details. This helped students become increasingly aware of the writing task and the audience's reaction to what was written.

10. *Provide youngsters with good models for each type of writing that is the focus of instruction.* The study of models involves asking students to examine one or more specific types of text and emulate the patterns or forms in these examples in their own writing. In six experimental group studies, this practice had a small, but positive impact on improving the quality of compositions produced by youngsters in grades 4–12 (ages 10–12; mean weighted effect size = 0.25). Some caution must be exercised in interpreting this finding, as the mean quality score for these studies was 5.2 (out of 11 possible points). An example of studying models of good writing involves presenting students with two examples of excellent writing, such as two persuasive essays: one arguing for one point of view and the other arguing for an opposite point of view (Graham & Perin, 2007a). The class then discusses the two essays, followed by students using one of the two papers as a model for writing a persuasive essay on a different topic.

11. *Ask struggling writers to monitor their writing performance or behaviour.* This involves having students self-monitor either their on-task behaviour, writing productivity, or writing quality, and then visually displaying the results of their performance. In five single-subject design studies with struggling writers in grades 5–8, ages 11–14), these practices yielded a PND of 60% (a small effect) in terms of increasing how much students wrote. Some caution must be exercised with this finding as the mean quality score was 7.43 (out of 11 possible points).

A study by Shimabukuro, Prater, Jenkins, and Edelen-Smith (1999) provides a good example of how student monitoring can improve productivity. Struggling writers in grades 6 and 7 (ages 12–13) were asked to count and graph at the end of each work session how many practices exercises involving sentence construction they accurately completed. This simple monitoring procedure increased both the quantity and quality of their sentence construction skills.

12. *Provide time for youngsters to write.* A universal practice of exceptional teachers and schools is that they provide ample opportunities for youngsters to write. This includes dedicating time to writing and writing instruction, making writing part of content instruction (i.e. writing across the curriculum), and engaging students in various forms of writing over time.

Recommendation with a negative effect size

13. *Youngsters should not be taught grammar using traditional methods.* Traditional methods of teaching grammar involve studying parts of speech, sentence diagramming, and so forth. In 11 experimental group studies involving youngsters in grades 4–11 (ages 10–17), grammar instruction had a small, but negative impact on writing quality (mean weighted effect size = -0.32). Some caution must be exercised with this finding, as the mean quality score was 5.0 (out of 9 possible points).

We would like to offer a comment here. As Myhill's analysis (see her paper in this monograph) makes clear, we cannot simply ignore grammar. Instead, we must identify effective alternatives to traditional grammar instruction. One alternative is sentence combining, as it had a positive impact on writing quality (see recommendation number 4) and can improve the syntactic structure of students' writing (see Andrews *et al.*, 2006). Another potential option can be found in a study by Fearn and Farnan (2005). They found that teaching students to focus on the function and practical application of grammar within the context of writing (vs. defining and describing grammar) produced strong and positive effects on students' writing.

Concluding comments and caveats

The findings from the two meta-analysis of quantitative intervention studies (Graham & Perin, 2007a,b; Rogers & Graham, 2008) and the meta-synthesis of qualitative research on effective schools and teachers demonstrate that research has much to offer to the practice of teaching writing to students in grades 4–12 (ages 10–18). It is important, however, not to over state what we know, as the scientific literature provides an incomplete picture of how to teach writing to youngsters.

First, the foundation on which most of our recommendations are based is relatively slim. When experimental group studies and single-subject design investigations are considered together, there were only 7 instances where there were 10 or more studies examining the effectiveness of a particular treatment (i.e. strategy instruction, process approach to writing, word processing, grammar instruction, goal setting, pre-writing activities, and self-monitoring). Our approach here was to make the best of the available data. This is not to say that our recommendations are unreliable, as we only drew conclusions when a treatment was tested in four or more studies, but there is clearly a need for additional research examining the effectiveness of the less studied, but effective treatments identified here. Even for areas that have been studied more extensively, additional research is needed. For instance, there are few studies examining the effectiveness of strategy instruction with older high school students (see Chalk, Hagan-Burke, & Burke, 2005 for an exception), and there is still a need to develop and validate strategies that cover a broader range of genres as well as conduct component analyses to determine what aspects of strategy instruction are most crucial (Graham & Harris, 2005).

Another limitation of the meta-analytic approach taken in this article is that there are many treatments that have not been studied using experimental methods, and many of the treatments that are studied involve less than four experimental tests (Pressley, Graham, & Harris, 2006). Many of these unstudied or understudied writing interventions may be effective. For instance, several studies provide limited evidence that vocabulary instruction has a positive impact on the quality of students' writing (see Graham & Perin, 2007b). Such interventions as well as unstudied treatments need to be investigated more extensively.

Third, the recommendation (number 12) based solely on the findings from the meta-synthesis of qualitative studies need to be interpreted carefully, as such an analysis cannot establish that a particular practice is responsible for students' writing performance. This should not distract from the important role that qualitative research plays in establishing effective writing instruction for youngsters. Such research provides critical information for theory building and identifying potentially effective elements of instruction (many of which can be tested experimentally). Other types of studies also have an important role to play in the search for effective writing practices. For instance, a recent correlational study by Applebee, Langer, Nystrand, and Gamoran (2003) found that students made more writing progress in classes where greater emphasis was placed on discussion-based literacy approaches. This finding provides support for the continued testing of such approaches via more rigorous experimental designs.

Fourth, it must be noted that most of the research included in the meta-analysis of true- and quasi-experimental studies (Graham & Perin, 2007a,b) did not focus on youngsters most at risk for writing difficulties: students with disabilities, English language learners (ELL), and adolescents who are Black and Hispanic living in poverty. Although the single-subject design studies mostly involved students at risk for writing difficulties, including youngsters with disabilities in regular schools, the other two groups of at-risk students were not typically included in these investigations. Thus, we need to place more effort on identifying effective practices for the most vulnerable developing writers.

Fifth, assessing generalization and maintenance of treatment effects needs to become a common practice in writing intervention research. For example, such effects were not routinely addressed in the studies included in the meta-analysis of true- and quasi-experimental writing intervention studies we conducted previously (Graham & Perin, 2007a,b). One exception involved strategy instruction (see Graham, 2006), but even here, where generalization and maintenance are routinely assessed, we know little about the long-term effects of such instruction beyond 6 months.

Sixth, this paper does not provide guidance on how the treatments and practice contained in our recommendations are best combined, and what combination of treatments work best for which youngsters. With the exception of process writing (which is a full writing program), all of the recommendations involve practices that would ideally be included as part of a larger writing program. We did not try to indicate what amount of each recommendation or how recommendations should be combined as there is very little evidence on these issues. Nevertheless, we think that the teaching practices underlying these recommendations can be fruitfully combined. For instance, there is some limited evidence demonstrating that adding strategy instruction to the process approach is beneficial (Danoff, Harris, & Graham, 2003;

MacArthur, Schwartz, & Graham, 1991). In addition, Sadoski, Willson, and Norton (1997) found that students made larger writing gains when they were in classes that used a specific combination of instructional procedures reported as effective by Hillocks (1986) in his seminal meta-analysis of the writing intervention research.

Seventh, we did not address who should deliver these recommendations. For students in grades 4–12, writing instruction can conceivably occur in more than one place and with more than one person. This could include the English or language arts teacher, a learning specialist (e.g. special education teacher), and content teachers. We believe that the impact of writing instruction can be hightened if writing is viewed as a shared responsibility. For instance, in an excellent study by De La Paz (2005), teachers from two different content areas worked together to teach a series of strategies. In the history classroom, a historical reasoning strategy was taught using historical documents, whereas in the language arts classroom students were taught strategies for writing argumentation-essays, using the documents applied in the history class.

Eighth, the success of these recommendations rests on how they are viewed by teachers. Teachers' willingness to implement a specific recommendation is influenced by beliefs about (1) how suitable it is for students, (2) whether it is effective, (3) how hard it is to implement, (4) any negative impacts of implementing it, and (5) knowledge about how to implement it. We found that these five variables accounted for 30% of the variance in teachers' use of specific adaptations for struggling writers, after controlling for teaching experience, number of children in the classroom (including number of struggling writers and students receiving special services), and teacher efficacy (Graham, Papadopoulou, & Santoro, 2005). Too often, little or no attention is given to whether teachers view evidenced-based practices as acceptable.

Finally, we did not offer a recommendation on teaching handwriting, spelling, or typing. However, Graham (in press) identified four experimental studies that produced a moderate effect for writing quality when such skills were taught to student who were 6–13 years of age (Graham, in press). Unfortunately, the overall quality of these studies was not assessed, so the level of confidence that can be placed in these findings are unknown.

Concluding comment

In this paper, we presented a series of recommendations for teaching writing to youngsters in grades 4–12 (ages 10–18). These recommendations are evidence-based, as they were formed by examining experimental studies (true-experiments, quasi-experiments, and single-subject studies) where the impact of instruction was quantified for all students, writing was measured reliably, and the impact of instruction was replicated (in at least four or more studies). These recommendations were supported and further extended by drawing on the writing practices evident in a majority of the available qualitative studies examining how literacy is taught by teachers and schools whose students demonstrate exceptional literacy achievement.

It is important to emphasize, though, that just because a practice has a positive impact on students' writing performance in four or more intervention studies, does not insure that it will work in every classroom or with all students. When a physician provides a patient with a pill, there is no guarantee that it will work. Instead, the impact of the pill must be monitored to see if it has the desired effect. Schools and teachers need to do the same thing with evidenced-based recommendations for teaching writing.

References

Achieve, Inc. (2005). *Rising to the challenge: Are high school graduates prepared for college and work?* Washington, DC: Achieve, Inc.

Andrews, R., Torgerson, C., Beverton, S., Freeman, A., Locke, T., Low, G., *et al.* (2006). The effects of grammar teaching on writing development. *British Educational Research Journal, 32*, 39–55.

Applebee, A., Langer, J., Nystrand, M., & Gamoran, A. (2003). Discussion-based approaches to developing understanding: Classroom instruction and student performance in middle and high school English. *American Educational Research Journal, 40*, 685–730.

Atwell, N. (1987). *In the middle: Reading, writing, and learning from adolescents.* Portsmouth, NH: Heinemann.

Chalk, J. C., Hagan-Burke, S., & Burke, M. D. (2005). The effects of self-regulated strategy development on the writing process for high school students with learning disabilities. *Learning Disabilities Quarterly, 28*, 75–87.

Danoff, B., Harris, K. R., & Graham, S. (1993). Incorporating strategy instruction within the writing process in the regular classroom: Effects on the writing of students with and without learning disabilities. *Journal of Reading Behavior, 25*, 295–322.

De La Paz, S. (2005). Teaching historical reasoning and argumentative writing in culturally and academically diverse middle school classrooms. *Journal of Educational Psychology, 97*, 139–158.

Fearn, L. & Farnan, N. (2005). *An investigation of the influence of teaching grammar in writing to accomplish an influence on writing.* Paper presented at the annual meeting of the American Educational Research Association, Montreal, Canada.

Ferretti, R. P., MacArthur, C. A., & Dowdy, N. S. (2000). The effects of an elaborated goal on the persuasive writing of students with learning disabilities and their normally achieving peers. *Journal of Educational Psychology, 92*, 694–702.

Graham, S. (2006). Writing. In P. Alexander & P. Winne (Eds.), *Handbook of educational psychology* (pp. 457–478). Mahwah, NJ: Erlbaum.

Graham, S. (in press). Teaching writing. In P. Hogan (Ed.), *Cambridge encyclopedia of language sciences.* Cambridge University Press, Cambridge, UK.

Graham, S., & Harris, K. R. (2005). Improving the writing performance of young struggling writers: Theoretical and programmatic research from the Center to Accelerate Student Learning. *Journal of Special Education, 39*, 19–33.

Graham, S. & Olinghouse, N. (in press). Learning and teaching writing. In E. Anderman & L. Anderman (Eds.), *Psychology of classroom learning.* Farmington Hills, MI: Thomas Gale.

Graham, S., & Perin, D. (2007a). *Writing next: Effective strategies to improve writing of adolescent middle and high school.* Washington, DC: Alliance for Excellence in Education.

Graham, S., & Perrin, D. (2007b). A meta-analysis of writing instruction for adolescent students. *Journal of Educational Psychology, 99*, 445–476.

Graham, S., & Perrin, D. (2007c). What we know, what we still need to know: Teaching adolescents to write. *Scientific Studies in Reading, 11*, 313–336.

Graham, S., Papadopoulou, E., & Santoro, J. (2005). *Elementary teachers' views about the use and acceptability of adaptations for struggling writers.* Paper presented at the International Conference of the Council for Exceptional Children. Salt Lake City, UT, April.

Graves, D. (1983). *Writing: Teachers and children at work.* Exeter, NH: Heinemann.

Harris, K., & Graham, S. (1996). *Making the writing process work: Strategies for composition and self-regulation* (2nd ed.). Cambridge: Brookline Books.

Harris, K. R., Graham, S., & Mason, L. (2006). Improving the writing performance, knowledge, and motivation of young struggling writers in second grade. *American Educational Research Journal, 43*, 295–340.

Hayes, J., & Flower, L. (1980). Identifying the organization of writing processes. In L. Gregg & E. Steinberg (Eds.), *Cognitive processes in writing* (pp. 3–30). Hillsdale, NJ: Erlbaum.

Hillocks, G., Jr. (1982). The interaction of instruction, teacher comment, and revision in teaching the composing process. *Research in the Teaching of English, 16*, 261–278.

Hillocks, G. (1986). *Research on written composition: New directions for teaching*. Urbana, IL: National Council of Teachers of English.

Horner, R., Carr, E., Halle, J., McGee, G., Odom, S., & Wolery, M. (2005). The use of single-subject research to identify evidence-based practice in special education. *Exceptional Children, 71*, 165–180.

Kellogg, R. (1993). *The psychology of writing*. New York: Oxford University Press.

King, S. (2000). *A memoir of the craft: On writing*. New York: Pocket.

Lipsey, M., & Wilson, D. (2001). *Practical meta-analysis*. Thousand Oaks, CA: Sage.

Loader, L. M. (1989). *The effects of the semantic organizer on writing ability and motivation with fourth grade students*. Unpublished doctoral dissertation, University of Connecticut, Storrs, CT.

MacArthur, C. A. (1998). Word processing with speech synthesis and word prediction: Effects on the dialogue journal writing of students with learning disabilities. *Learning Disability Quarterly, 21*, 151–166.

MacArthur, C., Schwartz, S., & Graham, S. (1991). Effects of a reciprocal peer revision strategy in special education classrooms. *Learning Disability Research and Practice, 6*, 201–210.

Myhill, D. (2009). From talking to writing: Linguistic development in writing. *British Journal of Educational Psychology Monograph Series II*(6), 27–44.

Nelson, R., Smith, D., & Dodd, J. (1992). The effects of teaching a summary skills strategy to students identified as learning disabled on their comprehension of science text. *Education and Treatment of Children, 15*, 228–243.

Nystrand, M. (2006). The social and historical context for writing research. In S. MacArthur, S. Graham, & J. Fitzgerald (Eds.), *Handbook of writing research* (pp. 11–27). New York: Guilford.

Phillips, B. (1993). *Phillip's book of great thoughts and funny sayings* (p. 338). Wheaton, IL: Tyndal House.

Pressley, M., Graham, S., & Harris, K. R. (2006). The state of educational intervention research. *British Journal of Educational Psychology, 76*, 1–19.

Rogers, L., & Graham, S. (2008). A meta-analysis of single subject design writing intervention research. *Journal of Educational Psychology, 100*, 879–906.

Saddler, B., & Graham, S. (2005). The effects of peer-assisted sentence-combining instruction on the writing performance of more and less skilled young writers. *Journal of Educational Psychology, 97*, 43–54.

Sadoski, M., Willson, V., & Norton, D. (1997). The relative contribution of research-based composition activities to writing improvement in lower and middle grades. *Research in the Teaching of English, 31*, 120–150.

Schultz, K., & Fecho, B. (2000). Society's child: Social context and writing development. *Educational Psychology, 35*, 51–62.

Scruggs, T., Mastropieri, M., & Casto, G. (1987). The quantitative synthesis of single subject research: Methodology and validation. *Remedial and Special Education, 8*, 24–33.

Shimabukuro, S. M., Prater, M. A., Jenkins, A., & Edelen-Smith, P. (1999). The effects of self-monitoring of academic performance on students with learning disabilities and ADD/ADHD. *Education and Treatment of Children, 22*, 397–414.

Salahu-Din, D., Persky, H., & Miller, J. (2008). *The nation's report card: Writing 2007 (NCES 2008-468)*. Washington, DC: National Center for Education Statistics, Institute of Education Sciences, US Department of Education.

Winokur, J. (1999). *Advice to writers* (p. 24). New York: Pantheon Books.

Wyse, D. (2003). The national literacy strategy: A critical review of empirical evidence. *British Educational Research Journal, 29*, 903–916.

Zimmerman, B., & Reisemberg, R. (1997). Becoming a self-regulated writer: A social cognitive perspective. *Contemporary Educational Psychology, 22*, 73–101.

Teaching and Learning Writing, 113–135
BJEP Monograph Series II, 6
© 2009 The British Psychological Society

The
British
Psychological
Society

www.bpsjournals.co.uk

Self-regulated strategy development in writing: Premises, evolution, and the future

Karen R. Harris* and Steve Graham
Vanderbilt University, Nashville, Tennessee, USA

Background. Self-regulated strategy development (SRSD) is a strategies instruction approach under development since 1982. Originally developed for struggling writers and students with learning disabilities, research has shown that SRSD is effective for average and above writers as well.

Aims. In this article, we establish that the development of SRSD was grounded in multiple theoretical approaches, including theories often seen as incompatible.

Arguments. First, we look at research in writing and then turn to what research tells us about the importance and impact of writing strategies instruction. The theoretical and empirical foundations of SRSD are presented. The components, characteristics, and instructional processes of the SRSD model of strategies instruction are then discussed, followed by a summary of the research base for SRSD and limitations of the work done to date.

Conclusions. Finally, we address research that is still needed as SRSD, and the future of writing research, continue to evolve.

In this paper, we focus on the development of and research base for an intervention in development since 1982: self-regulated strategy development (SRSD). We establish that the development of SRSD was grounded in multiple theoretical approaches, including theories often seen as incompatible. In our view, good instruction does not require a forced choice between competing theories, but rather a blending of what we know from various perspectives and lines of research. Further, students' perceptions of what they are learning, how they are learning it, and why they are learning it are also important to effective instruction.

SRSD has primarily been researched in the area of writing instruction in the schools. Thus, we first take a brief look at research in writing, and then turn to what research tells us about the importance and impact of writing strategies instruction. The theoretical and empirical foundations of SRSD are presented. The components, characteristics, and instructional processes of the SRSD model of strategies instruction are then discussed, followed by a summary of the research base for SRSD and limitations

*Correspondence should be addressed to Karen Harris, Department of Special Education, Vanderbilt University, Peabody College Box 228, Nashville, TN 37023, USA (e-mail: karen.harris@vanderbilt.edu).

DOI:10.1348/978185409X422542

of the work done to date. Finally, we address research that is still needed as SRSD continues to evolve.

Writing research

As Prior (2006) noted, the history of writing and of research on writing has been narrated in varied ways. From its humble beginnings for record keeping, writing has advanced to become a critical tool for communication, learning, maintaining social connections and identities, enhancing self-exploration, and many other aspects of the human experience (Harris, Graham, Brindle, & Sandmel, in press). Approximately, 85% of the world's population now writes (Swedlow, 1999). Therefore, those who struggle with writing face considerable disadvantages in today's world and can face significant barriers in further education and employment. Clearly, studying the problems that struggling writers encounter and the development of effective interventions are critical, and many researchers have been involved in this enterprise. Researchers agree that writing is a complex activity, and that learning to write is therefore potentially even more complex (Harris, Graham, Mason, & Friedlander, 2008; Hayes, 2006; McCutchen, 2006). The writer must negotiate the rules and mechanics of writing, while maintaining a focus on factors such as organization, form and features, purposes and goals, audience perspectives and needs, and evaluation of communicative intent and efficacy (Bereiter & Scardamalia, 1987; Harris & Graham, 1992).

Thus, it is no surprise that research on writing is also complex and challenging. We briefly summarize the struggles often faced by students during the school years before turning to our examination of SRSD for writing, as SRSD was developed in response to research on struggling writers as well as research on models of writing and expert writers.

Expert, novice, and struggling writers

Five areas of competence have been identified as particularly difficult in learning to write among the general school population: (a) generation of content, (b) creating an organizing structure for compositions, (c) formulation of goals and higher level plans, (d) quickly and efficiently executing the mechanical aspects of writing, and (e) revising text and reformulating goals (Scardamalia & Bereiter, 1986). Further, students demonstrate significant difficulties with narrative, expository, and persuasive writing (Applebee, Langer, Mullis, Latham, & Gentile, 1994; Applebee, Langer, Jenkins, Mullis, & Foertsch, 1990). It is not surprising, therefore, that students frequently demonstrate a deteriorating attitude towards writing, even though most young children begin school with a positive attitude towards composing (Applebee, Langer, & Mullis, 1986).

When researchers turned their attention to the writing of students with learning disabilities (LD) or those with severe difficulties in school, they found that these students frequently have even greater problems with writing than their normally achieving peers (Curry, 1997; Harris & Graham, 1992, 1999). Generally, students with learning problems produce writing that is less polished, expansive, coherent, and effective than that of their normally achieving peers (for greater details on the research base, see Graham & Harris, 2002, 2003). Research indicates that these students lack critical knowledge of the writing process; have difficulty generating ideas and selecting topics; do little to no advance planning; engage in knowledge telling; lack important strategies for planning, producing, organizing, and revising text; have difficulties with mechanics that interfere with the writing process; emphasize mechanics over content when making revisions; and frequently overestimate their writing abilities.

The picture looks quite different when we look at skilled, or expert, writers. These writers are able to not only negotiate the rules and mechanics of writing, but also maintain a focus on important aspects of writing such as organization, form and features, purposes and goals, audience needs and perspectives, and evaluation of the communication between author and reader (Bereiter & Scardamalia, 1987). In addition, skilled writers exhibit extensive self-regulation and attention control (Graham & Harris, 1994, 1996, 2000). Among skilled writers, writing is a flexible, goal-directed activity that is scaffolded by a rich knowledge of cognitive processes and strategies for planning, text production, and revision.

Further, skilled writers engage in purposeful and active self-direction of these processes and strategies (Harris, Schmidt, & Graham, 1998). In fact, the ability to monitor and direct one's own composing processes is a large part of writing ability (Flower & Hayes, 1980). Skilled writers organize their goals and subgoals and can switch flexibly from simple to complex goals. To achieve their goals, they draw upon a rich store of cognitive processes and strategies for planning, text production, and revision. They also draw upon their knowledge of the patterns or schemas evident in different writing genres or models, and develop novel or modified frameworks as the writing text becomes more complex (cf. Isnard & Piolat, 1994; Kellogg, 1994). Skilled writers are sensitive to the functions their writing is intended to serve and use effective self-regulation strategies throughout the recursive writing process. Finally, they evidence knowledge of the topic, motivation, and persistence.

Expertise in writing, however, does not develop easily. Bereiter, Burtis, and Scardamalia (1988) proposed that writing ability develops through a series of stages. Space does not allow a detailed discussion of models of writing development here, but greater detail can be found in the literature (Graham, 2006; Harris *et al.*, 2008; Hayes, 2006). These models of writing and the research base on writing clearly demonstrate that it is important to address multiple aspects of competence when teaching struggling writers how to compose.

Considering multiple aspects of writing

Drawing on three sources that help synthesize writing research to date, including a meta-analysis of experimental and quasi-experimental writing intervention studies (Graham & Perin, 2007a,b), a meta-analysis of single-subject design studies (Rogers & Graham, 2007), and a meta-synthesis of qualitative studies examining writing instructional practices among effective teachers and schools (Graham & Perin, in press), Graham and Harris (2009), listed 12 evidence-based recommendations for improving writing among students in grades 4–12 (ages 10–18 years). These 12 recommendations, ordered based on the strength of the evidence and the impact on writing, are presented in Table 1.

In this paper, we focus on the SRSD model of strategies instruction. Strategies instruction research has addressed many, but not all, of these recommendations. Strategies instruction explicitly incorporates three of the top four evidence-based recommendations for teaching writing; writing more sophisticated sentences has not yet been a major element in strategies instruction, though it clearly should be in future research. Strategies instruction also typically includes monitoring of performance, use of

Table 1. Twelve evidence-based recommendations for writing instruction

---

1. Teach strategies for planning, revising, and editing writing
2. Set clear and specific goals for what writers are to accomplish in their writing product
3. Help writers learn to write more sophisticated sentences
4. Engage students in prewriting activities that help them gather and organize ideas for their compositions
5. Engage students in the process writing approach
6. Teach students strategies and procedures for summarizing reading material, as this improves their ability to concisely and accurately present this information in writing
7. Incorporate instructional arrangements that allow students to work together to plan, draft, revise, and edit their compositions
8. Make it possible for students to use word processing as a tool for writing
9. Involve students in writing activities designed to sharpen their inquiry skills
10. Provide good written models for each type of writing that is the focus of instruction
11. Have students monitor their writing performance or behaviour
12. Provide ample time for writing

Note. Ordered based on the strength of the available evidence and impact on writing; for greater detail on each, see Graham and Harris (2009).

good models of writing, and making time for writing (Wong, Harris, Graham, & Butler, 2003). While some researchers have begun to integrate reading and writing in strategies instruction as well as peer support (cf. Harris, Graham, & Mason, 2006; Mason, 2004), further research is clearly needed in these areas.

Further, we note that research clearly demonstrates it is important to address additional aspects of competence when teaching struggling writers how to compose. For example, research demonstrated that additional, explicit instruction in handwriting and spelling influenced the development of two other important writing processes: content generation and sentence construction (Graham, Harris, & Fink-Chorzempka, 2000, 2002). Thus, we do not argue that strategies instruction is the most important consideration in instruction in writing, but rather that it is an important component.

Harris, Graham and their colleagues, and Englert and her colleagues, have developed two frequently cited strategies instruction models for composition. Englert and her colleagues refer to their approach as the cognitive strategy instruction for writing (CSIW) Program. Harris and Graham's approach has come to be called SRSD; the first study using this model was published in 1985. Englert and her colleagues published two influential studies involving CSIW (Englert, Raphael, & Anderson, 1992; Englert *et al.*, 1991). Results of these studies indicated that both students with and without learning disabilities improved their knowledge of the writing process and their writing abilities. In the Englert *et al.* (1991) study, students with learning disabilities performed similarly to their peers without disabilities on all five post-test writing variables. In the 1992 study, Englert *et al.* found that the quality of students' metacognitive knowledge was positively related to measures of performance in both reading and writing. We turn now to the SRSD model.

SRSD and writing instruction

Since 1985, more than 40 studies using the SRSD model of instruction have been reported in the area of writing, involving students from the elementary grades through high school (Graham & Harris, 2003, 2009). In the meta-analyses of true- and quasi-experimental design studies, SRSD has had the strongest impact of any strategies instruction approach in writing (Graham & Perrin, 2007a). Results of meta-analysis of SRSD for writing in single-subject design studies are included in Rogers and Graham (2007). Here, we briefly summarize research on the effectiveness of SRSD, as details can be found in the article by Graham and Harris in this issue (Graham & Harris, 2009), followed by a discussion of the development of SRSD and important characteristics of this approach that are related to its effectiveness. We argue that the theoretically integrative nature of SRSD's initial and continuing development is important in understanding its effectiveness.

Evidence summary

Data from a relatively large number of group and single-subject design studies provide convincing evidence that SRSD is an effective method for teaching writing strategies to youngsters (both poor writers and students who represent the full range of writing ability in a typical class). SRSD research has resulted in the development of writing strategies (typically with the assistance of teachers and their students) for a variety of genres; these include personal narratives, story writing, persuasive essays, report writing, expository essays, and state writing tests. SRSD has resulted in significant and meaningful improvements in children's development of planning and revising strategies, including brainstorming, self-monitoring, reading for information and semantic webbing, generating and organizing writing content, advanced planning and dictation, revising with peers, and revising for both substance and mechanics (cf. Harris, Graham, & Mason, 2003).

SRSD has resulted in improvements in five main aspects of students' performance: genre elements included in writing, quality of writing, knowledge of writing, approach to writing, and self-efficacy. Across a variety of strategies and genres, the quality, length, and structure of students' compositions have improved. Depending on the strategy taught, improvements have been documented in planning, revising, content, and mechanics (Wong *et al.*, 2003). These improvements have been consistently maintained for the majority of students over time, with some students needing booster sessions for long-term maintenance, and students have shown generalization across settings, persons, and writing media.

Harris and Graham have emphasized from the beginning, however, that SRSD should not be thought of as a panacea; promoting students' academic competence and literacy requires a complex integration of skills, strategies, processes, and attributes (Harris, 1982; Harris & Graham, 1996; Harris *et al.*, 2003). While SRSD represents an important contribution to teachers' instructional repertoires, it does not represent a complete writing curriculum. No research to date has been conducted examining the contribution of SRSD to the larger writing curriculum; such research is clearly needed. While SRSD helps get children 'on the playing field' for writing, research has not gone on to address how to take this beginning and continue children's development of expertise in writing.

Development of SRSD

While students with learning problems are a heterogeneous group, research indicates that one commonality among these students is that the significant difficulties they face often arise from multiple problems of an affective, behavioural, and cognitive nature

(Harris, 1982; Harris & Graham, 1992, 1996). Ecological variables, including the situational, educational, cultural, and community networks the student is part of, are also critical concerns (Harris, 1982). As researchers have noted for some time, the transactional relationships among affect, behaviour, cognition, and social and ecological variables need to be carefully considered (Harris, 1982).

Further, many of these students have difficulty with self-regulation, including the self-regulation of organized, strategic behaviours (Graham, Harris, & Reid, 1992; Harris, 1986). They may have difficulty comprehending task demands, producing effective task strategies, and using strategies to mediate performance (Harris & Graham, 1992). Some may lack or fail to make use of effective verbal mediation processes or may not have developed an effective linguistic control system, and thus experience difficulties using verbalizations (often referred to as self-speech) to guide behaviour. Many of these students also experience reciprocal relationships among academic failure, self-doubts, learned helplessness, maladaptive attributions, unrealistic pre-task expectancies, low self-efficacy, and low motivation. Impulsivity, difficulties with memory or other aspects of information processing, low task engagement and persistence, devaluation of learning, and low productivity are also among the problems these students and their teachers may need to deal with.

Underlying premises

Harris and Graham began development of the SRSD approach to instruction with the underlying premise that students who face significant and often debilitating difficulties would benefit from an integrated approach to instruction that deliberately and directly addressed their affective, behavioural, and cognitive characteristics, strengths, and needs (Harris, 1982). Further, they argued that these students often require more extensive, structured, and explicit instruction to develop skills, strategies (including academic, social, and self-regulation strategies), and understandings that their peers form more easily. The level of explicitness of instruction, however, should be adjusted to meet student needs (Harris & Graham, 1996). This perspective requires that the same academic and self-regulation strategies are not necessarily targeted for all students, and that instructional components and processes need to be individualized. SRSD research indicates that as students' learning and behavioural challenges become more significant, strategy and self-regulation development becomes more complex and explicit, involving multiple learning tasks, components, and stages (Sawyer, Graham, & Harris, 1992; Sexton, Harris, & Graham, 1998).

While SRSD has been used in other academic areas, including math and reading (see Wong *et al.*, 2003), Harris and Graham began SRSD in writing with three goals (Harris *et al.*, 1998, p. 134): (1) assist students in developing knowledge about writing and powerful skills and strategies involved in the writing process, including planning, writing, revising, and editing. (2) support students in the ongoing development of the abilities needed to monitor and manage their own writing, and (3) promote children's development of positive attitudes about writing and themselves as writers.

Theoretical bases

The SRSD approach to strategies instruction views learning as a complex process that relies on changes that occur in learners' skills, abilities, self-regulation, strategic knowledge, domain-specific knowledge and abilities, and motivation. There exists to date no single theory of teaching or learning that addresses all of the challenges faced by struggling learners, their teachers, and their schools (Harris, 1982; Pressley, Graham, & Harris, 2006). Thus, a further premise evident from the beginning of Harris and Graham's work on SRSD was the need to integrate multiple lines of research from multiple theoretical perspectives in order to develop powerful interventions for students who face significant academic challenges (Harris, 1982; Harris & Alexander, 1998; Harris & Graham, 1985). A thoughtful, effective integration of diverse, validated approaches to learning, regardless of whether or not the theories and disciplines from which they originated are viewed by some as discordant (such as affective, behavioural, and cognitive approaches to teaching and learning), has been key to the development of SRSD.

Four initial foundations

Detailed descriptions of the evolution of SRSD over the past decades have been offered elsewhere (cf. Graham & Harris, 1989; Harris, 1982; Harris & Graham, 1992, 1999; Harris & Pressley, 1991). Here, we look at some of the most critical theoretical influences in the development of SRSD. Four theoretical and empirical sources provided the initial foundation for this model in the early 1980s. First, based on Meichenbaum's (1977) cognitive-behavioural intervention model, and its emphasis on Socratic dialogue as well as stages of intervention, Harris and Graham developed their initial stages of instruction and an emphasis on the role of dialogue/discussion in instruction. A number of basic principles from Meichenbaum's cognitive-behaviour modification approach were incorporated into our earliest version of SRSD (referred to as self-control strategy training in our first study, Harris & Graham, 1985): (1) emphasis on interactive learning between teacher and student, with responsibility for recruiting, applying, and monitoring strategies gradually placed on the student (much the same concept as scaffolding from the social-cognitive perspective or shaping and successive approximations from the behavioural perspective), (2) the use of sound instructional procedures including initial teacher direction and modelling, feedback, reinforcement, and individualization, (3) the inclusion of the student as an active collaborator, and (4) the modelling and development of self-statements designed to assist the student in comprehending the task, producing appropriate strategies, and using these strategies and verbalizations to mediate behaviour.

A second initial foundation, the work of Soviet theorists and researchers (including Vygotsky, Luria, & Sokolov) on the social origins of self-control and the development of the mind was very influential, and contributed further to the self-regulation and modelling components of the model (cf. Harris, 1982; Harris & Graham, 1992). Third, the work of Brown, Campione, and their colleagues on development of self-control, metacognition, and strategies instruction was also foundational (Brown, Campione, & Day, 1981). One critical aspect emphasized by Brown and her colleagues was 'informed instruction'; meaning that students should clearly understand what they are doing and why they are doing it, as this makes learning more meaningful and increases student motivation and commitment. Also important here was the emerging work on metacognition and learning being conducted by many researchers (see Harris, Alexander, & Graham, 2008). The fourth initial foundation for our approach was the work of Deshler, Schumaker, and their colleagues on the validation of acquisition steps for strategies among adolescents with learning disabilities (cf. Schumaker, Deshler, Alley, Warner, & Denton, 1982), steps that were also influenced by the work of Meichenbaum.

Behavioural research on self-regulation

Our early development of SRSD was also strongly influenced by early and important research on self-regulation conducted by behavioural researchers (Harris & Graham, 1985). These researchers identified four efficacious procedures: self-instruction, self-determined criteria, self-assessment, and self-reinforcement (Harris, 1982; O'Leary & Dubey, 1979; Rosenbaum & Drabman, 1979). Each of these self-regulation procedures were integrated into our strategies instruction model. Further, the work of Zimmerman and his colleagues on self-regulation was also a critical influence. Working from a social-cognitive perspective, they defined self-regulation as the 'process whereby students activate and sustain cognitions, behaviours and affects, which are systematically oriented towards attainment of their goals' (Schunk & Zimmerman, 1994, p. 309). Zimmerman (1989) also theorized that students are capable of self-regulating components of their learning behaviours, environment, and internal cognitive and affective processes. Schunk and Zimmerman (1997) formulated a model of the development of self-regulatory abilities, which has four levels of development: observation, imitation, self-control, and self-regulation. This model is consistent in many ways with Meichenbaum's and Brown's work.

Social-cognitive research on self-regulation and writing

In 1997, Zimmerman and Risemberg reviewed the models of writing developed by Hayes and Flower (1980) and by Bereiter and Scardamalia (1987). They argued that although these models included the task environment and self-regulatory strategies, they focused on the role of cognitive processes in students' writing *competence*, as opposed to writer *performance* and its self-regulated development. They further argued that 'explanations focusing on writing performance and its self-regulated development need to include the role of social, motivational, and behavioural processes as well as cognitive ones' (p. 75). Working from social-cognitive theory and self-regulation theory (Zimmerman, 1989), they proposed a model of writing composed of three fundamental forms of self-regulation: environmental, behavioural, and covert or personal. The authors argued that these triadic forms of self-regulation interact reciprocally via a cyclic feedback loop that allows writers to self-monitor and self-react to feedback about the effectiveness of specific self-regulatory techniques or processes.

Zimmerman and Risemberg (1997) argued that the self-regulation of writing involves a complex system of interdependent processes. Further, they placed particular emphasis on the construct of self-efficacy, as they proposed that these complex, interdependent processes are closely linked to an underlying sense of self-efficacy. A writer's sense of efficacy may be enhanced or diminished depending upon the perceived success of the self-regulatory strategies they put into play for controlling their actions, the writing environment, and their internal thoughts. Self-efficacy, in turn, influences intrinsic motivation for writing, the use of self-regulatory processes during writing, and eventual literary attainment. The work of Zimmerman and his colleagues, and that of other researchers on self-efficacy and attributions, has also strongly influenced the development of SRSD over the years. A critical and explicit goal in SRSD is the development of self-efficacy and attributions for effort and strategy use, as noted earlier.

Research on expertise

Another important influence on the development of SRSD over the past two decades has been research on the development of expertise. Research on the development of competence and expertise provided critical information for cognitive strategy instruction (Harris & Graham, 1992). As expertise develops, students exhibit a knowledge base that is increasingly coherent, principled, useful, and goal oriented (Alexander, 1997, 2003; Glaser, 1991). Not all learners progress to expertise; some progress only to competence, or remain at that stage for a long time. Examining the process of development to competence and potentially expertise has been important to strategies instruction designers. Writing researchers today continue to explore key characteristics distinguishing the expert from the novice writer, as well as individual differences in writing, and the implications of these characteristics for writing development (Galbraith, 1996; Galbraith & Torrance, 2004; Torrance, Thomas, & Robinson, 1999).

Research on strategies and strategies instruction in reading

Last, but certainly not least in any sense, all of our work on the development of SRSD for writing has been strongly influenced by research on strategies instruction in reading, especially that of Pressley and his colleagues. While initial models of strategies instruction varied in numerous ways, over time these models have converged to include typical components (Pressley & Harris, 2001, 2006). A critical factor in this recognition of core components was the articulation of the good information processor model and the good strategy user model (Harris, Alexander *et al.*, 2008; Pressley, Borkowski, & Schneider, 1987).

According to Pressley and his colleagues, the good information processor: knows a large number of strategies, and understands when, where, and why these strategies matter; is reflective and planful, selecting and monitoring strategies wisely; believes in the incremental development of abilities and the importance of effort; is intrinsically motivated, task oriented, and establishes mastery goals; accepts failure as a part of learning; has strong relevant knowledge and can access that knowledge rapidly; and has been supported in the development of these attributes by family, school, and society (Borkowski, Carr, Rellinger, & Pressley, 1990). The evolution of this model was based on the work on numerous researchers and theorists working from differing theories and viewpoints (cf. Pressley, 2005). Thus, it is not surprising that common components of strategies instruction have their bases in multiple areas of research from multiple theoretical perspectives, including research on development, behaviour, learning, and motivation (cf. Pressley & Hilden, 2006). Together, these components work to create change across affective, behavioural, and cognitive attributes of learners (Pressley & Harris, 2001; Pressley *et al.*, 2006).

Core components and characteristics of strategies instruction

Current components common to many approaches to strategies instruction, including the approach developed by Pressley and colleagues, include teacher modelling and explanations; powerful task strategies; support for working and long-term memory; teacher support (scaffolding) that is gradually faded until students develop independent use and ownership of the strategies; developing understanding of what is being learned, why, and where it can be used; and developing attributions for effort and strategy use and other means of enhancing motivation (Pressley & Harris, 2006; Pressley & Hilden, 2006; Pressley *et al.*, 1990). These components alone, however, are not adequate in creating effective strategies instruction. The nature of strategies instruction is as important as its components. Good strategies instruction is based on collaboration among teachers and students; emphasizes interactive learning that requires under-standing and meaningful processing; requires teachers to be enthusiastic and responsive to the instructional needs of learners varying in cognitive capacity, relevant knowledge, motivation, and other characteristics; and requires assessment of changes in affect, behaviour, cognition, and metacognition (Harris, Alexander *et al.*, 2008; Harris & Graham, 1992).

Unique characteristics of SRSD

At its inception in 1982, SRSD differed in several significant ways from other strategies instruction models (Harris & Graham, 1999; Harris, Reid, & Graham, 2004; Wong *et al.*, 2003). The majority of the early models of strategy instruction targeted normally achieving students, were based on one main theory, and development of self-regulation skills was implicitly embedded in intervention as opposed to being taught explicitly. SRSD, on the other hand, was initially developed for students with LD, was based on integrating findings from research based on multiple theories, and incorporated explicit instruction in and development of both writing and self-regulation strategies.

Explicitness

As we noted earlier, Harris and Graham began development of the SRSD approach to instruction with the underlying premise that students who face significant and often debilitating difficulties would benefit from an approach to instruction that deliberately and directly addressed their affective, behavioural, and cognitive characteristics, strengths, and needs (Harris, 1982). Further, they emphasized that these students often require more extensive, structured, and explicit instruction to develop skills, strategies (including academic, social, and self-regulation strategies), and understandings that their peers form more easily. Thus, explicit instruction in both writing and self-regulation strategies is an additional, critical feature of SRSD. The level of explicitness of instruction, however, should be adjusted to meet student needs (Harris & Graham, 1996). This perspective requires that the same academic and self-regulation strategies are not necessarily targeted for all students, and that instructional components and processes need to be individualized. As students' learning and behavioural challenges become more significant, strategy and self-regulation development becomes more complex and explicit, involving multiple learning tasks, components, and stages (Carroll, 1963; Sawyer *et al.*, 1992; Sexton *et al.*, 1998).

Explicit development of self-regulation

Many struggling learners and writers, including those with LD, experience difficulty with self-regulation, including the ability to activate and regulate strategic behaviour. Deficiencies in self-regulatory behaviours have considerable effects on students' emotional well-being, leading to low self-esteem and low intrinsic motivation (Garcia-Sanchez & Fidalgo-Redondo, 2006; Zimmerman, 1997). For these students, development of self-regulation skills is critical to their success in school. Informed by research on expertise in the writing domain as well as social cognitive theory and motivational theory, explicit development of self-regulation strategies was integrated throughout the stages of instruction in the SRSD model (Harris *et al.*, 2003; Harris *et al.*, 2004).

Explicit focus on motivation, attitudes, and beliefs

An additional way SRSD differed from other strategies instruction models was based on the premise that struggling learners and writers experience many affective, behavioural, and cognitive challenges (such as maladaptive attributions, low self-efficacy, low motivation and low engagement in academic tasks; Harris, 1982; Harris & Graham, 1996). Thus, SRSD was designed to directly addresses children's motivation, as well as their attitudes and beliefs about themselves as writers, by developing attributions for effort and strategy use, self-efficacy, and high levels of engagement. Instructional elements were developed that explicitly and consistently address goals for development in these areas.

Criterion-based learning

Finally, SRSD differed from other strategies instruction in that progression through the stages of instruction is criterion-based as opposed to time based. Students move through the instructional process at their own pace and do not proceed to later stages of instruction until they have met at least initial criteria for doing so. Just as importantly, instruction does not end until the student can use the strategy and self-regulation procedures efficiently, independently, and effectively. Criterion-based instruction is strongly supported by behavioural research and theory (cf. Worell & Stilwell, 1981) and by models of school learning (Carroll, 1963). This sets the stage for success in achieving desired outcomes for students who traditionally have been unsuccessful due partly to pace of instruction.

SRSD Instruction

Here, we present an overview of SRSD instruction, as space precludes a detailed presentation. Detailed descriptions of SRSD instruction are available to teachers, administrators, and parents, however.[1] We begin with a discussion of the characteristics of instruction critical to effective use of SRSD, then explain the process of instruction, and finally, address how maintenance and generalization are planned for and obtained.

Critical characteristics

There are five critical characteristics of SRSD instruction. First, as we have detailed, strategies, accompanying self-regulation procedures, and needed knowledge are explicitly taught. Second, children are viewed as active collaborators who work with the teacher and each other during instruction. Third, instruction is individualized so that the processes, skills, and knowledge targeted for instruction are tailored to children's needs and capabilities. Goals are adjusted to current performance for each student, with more capable writers addressing advanced goals. Instruction is further individualized through the use of individually tailored feedback and support. Fourth, as

---

[1] *For detailed descriptions of SRSD instruction, see Graham and Harris, 2005; Harris and Graham, 1996; Harris et al., 2003, 2008. Detailed lesson plans and support materials for instruction are provided in Harris et al. (2008). All the stages of instruction can be seen in both elementary and middle school classrooms in the video, 'Teaching students with learning disabilities in the regular classroom: using learning strategies' (ASCD, 2002). Finally, online interactive tutorials on SRSD are available at: http://iris.peabody.vanderbilt.edu. The tutorials include all stages of instruction and video from the ASCD video. From the IRIS homepage, select Resources, and then select Star Legacy Modules. For the first tutorial, click on 'Using Learning Strategies: Instruction to Enhance Learning'. For a tutorial on a persuasive writing strategy for elementary students, locate the header 'Differentiated Instruction', then click on the module titled 'Improving Writing Performance: A Strategy for Writing Expository Essays'. Finally, a website devoted to strategies instruction can be found at http://www.unl.edu/csi/.*

described earlier, instruction is criterion based rather than time based. Fifth, SRSD is an on-going process in which new strategies are introduced and previously taught strategies are upgraded. These characteristics are critical to the effectiveness of SRSD.

SRSD has been used successfully with entire classes, small groups, and in tutoring settings (Graham & Harris, 2003). Classroom teachers are as successful, or more successful, than research assistants in implementing SRSD (Graham & Harris, 2003; Harris *et al.*, 2006). Finally, lessons have typically run anywhere from 20 to 40 min (depending on grade level and class schedules) 3 to 5 days a week. In most of our work with teachers and students, instruction has taken less time than teachers anticipated. In the elementary grades, 8–12, 30–40 min lessons conducted over 3–5 weeks have typically been what students need to reach independent use of the writing and self-regulation strategies (further details by grade and genre can be found in Graham & Harris, 2003).

The process of instruction

Six basic stages of instruction are used to introduce and develop the writing and self-regulation strategies in the SRSD approach. These stages are outlined in Table 2. Throughout the stages, teachers and students collaborate on the acquisition, implementation, evaluation, and modification of these strategies. The stages are not meant to be followed in a 'cook-book' fashion. Rather, they provide a general format and guidelines. The stages can be reordered, combined, revisited, modified, or deleted to meet student and teacher needs. Further, the stages are meant to be recursive – if a concept or component is not mastered at a certain stage, students and teachers can revisit or continue that stage as they move on to others. Some stages may not be needed by all students. For example, some students may already have the background knowledge needed to use the writing strategy and self-regulation processes, and may skip this stage or act as a resource for other students who need this stage.

Generalization and maintenance

Procedures for promoting maintenance and generalization are integrated throughout the stages of instruction in the SRSD model. These include: identifying opportunities to use the writing and/or self-regulation strategies in other classes or settings, discussing attempts to use the strategies at other times, reminding students to use the strategies at appropriate times, analysing how these processes might need to be modified with other tasks and in new settings, and evaluating the success of these processes during and after instruction. It is helpful to involve others, including other teachers and parents, as they can prompt the use of the strategies at appropriate times in other settings. Booster sessions, where the strategies are reviewed and discussed and supported again if necessary, are very important for most of the students we have worked with in terms of maintaining the strategies.

SRSD: An illustration[2]

Sandy, a third grader with learning disabilities, was given the following question by her teacher: 'Should children your age be allowed to choose their own pet?' Sandy's class had

---

[2] *This illustration is adapted from Harris, Graham, and Adkins (2004).*

Table 2. SRSD stages of instruction

Develop and activate knowledge needed for writing and self-regulation

- Read works in the genre being addressed (personal narrative, persuasive essays, etc.) to develop declarative, procedural, and conditional knowledge, and important vocabulary (e.g. what is an *opinion?*; What are the parts of a persuasive essay, are they all here?; How do you think the author came up with this idea, What would you do?; What might the author have done to help herself come up with all of these ideas?; What might the author have done to organize the ideas?; What might the author do when frustrated?; and so on), appreciation of characteristics of effective writing (How did the writer grab your interest?), and other knowledge and understandings targeted for instruction. Continue development through the next two stages as needed until all key vocabulary, knowledge, and understandings are clear
- Discuss and explore both writing and self-regulation strategies to be learned; may begin development of self-regulation, introducing goal setting and self-monitoring

Discuss it

- Explore students' current writing and self-regulation abilities, attitudes and beliefs about writing, what they are saying to themselves as they write, and how these might help or hinder them as writers
- Graphing (self-monitoring) may be introduced, using prior compositions; this may assist with goal setting; graphing prior writing can be skipped if the student is likely to react negatively (performance during instruction is graphed)
- Further discuss strategies to be learned: purpose, benefits, how and when they can be used or might be inappropriate (generalization support)
- Establish students' commitment to learn strategy and act as collaborative partner; establish role of student effort and strategy use

Model it

- Teacher modelling and/or collaborative modelling of writing and self-regulation strategies, resulting in appropriate model compositions
- Self-instructions modelled can include problem definition, focusing attention and planning, self-evaluation and error correcting, coping and self-control, and self-reinforcement
- Analyse and discuss strategies and model's performance; make changes as needed
- Can model self-assessment and self-recording through graphing of model compositions
- Continue student development of self-regulation strategies across composition and other tasks and situations; discuss use here and in other settings (generalization support)

Memorize it

- Though typically begun in earlier stages, require and confirm memorization of strategies, mnemonic(s), and self-instructions as appropriate
- Continue to confirm and support memorization in following stages, make sure students have memorized the mnemonics and what they mean before independent performance

Support it

- Teachers and students use writing and self-regulation strategies collaboratively to achieve success in composing, using prompts such as strategy charts, self-instruction sheets, and graphic organizers (can initially use pictures with graphic organizers, then fade pictures in graphic organizers)
- Challenging initial goals for genre elements and characteristics of writing established collaboratively with individual students; criterion levels increased gradually until final goals met
- Prompts, guidance, and collaboration faded individually (graphic organizer replaced with student creating mnemonic on scratch paper) until the student can compose successfully alone
- Self-regulation components not yet introduced may begin (typically, goal setting, self-instructions, self-monitoring and self-reinforcement are all being used by this stage; additional forms of self-regulation, such as environmental control, use of imagery, and so on may be used as desirable)
- Discuss plans for maintenance, continue support of generalization

Independent performance

- Students able to use writing and self-regulation strategies independently; teachers monitor and support as necessary
- Fading of overt self-regulation may begin (graphing may be discontinued)
- Plans for maintenance and generalization continue to be discussed and implemented

---

Note. Adapted from Harris *et al.*, 2008.

been working on both developing a paragraph and writing an opinion essay since September; it was now January. Writing to persuade is an important skill in the state curriculum, and one assessed in the state writing competency test. Most of the students were doing well; they were able to write a paragraph of five or more sentences and clearly state their opinion, provide supporting details, and end with a concluding sentence. Sandy's teacher described her as 'not yet writing', and not especially fond of writing. In response to the question regarding choosing a pet, Sandy wrote the following:

> I like children my age should choose their own pet because they're old enough.

In consultation with the general and special education teachers, we determined that Sandy and several other third graders would profit from the SRSD approach to writing. Some of these students were LD, and some were considered at risk. All were writing one to two sentence opinion essays. Sandy and the other students worked in groups of two with their writing teacher (research assistants) in a quiet area for 20-min sessions, three times a week.

POW plus TREE

Sandy and her peers worked with us to learn *POW*: *P*ick an Idea, *O*rganize Notes, *W*rite and Say More. We established that *POW* is something you should do whenever you do any kind of writing, and that using *POW* 'gives power' to what you write. Then, instruction focused on learning *POW plus TREE* (*T*opic sentence, *R*easons – at least three, *E*xplain each reason further, and *E*nding, wrap it up right).

Stage 1: Develop background knowledge

Instruction began with a discussion of what the students already knew about opinion essays, including the purpose of opinion essayed and the elements that are commonly found in such an essay. Then, the teacher introduced *TREE* and stressed that good opinion essays make sense and have several parts. The teacher and students discussed why the living tree shown in the mnemonic chart they were given fits the parts: the topic sentence is like the trunk, as all the other parts are connected to it; the reasons and the explanations for your reasons are like the roots because they make the tree strong; and the ending (conclusion) is like the earth because it holds it all together (all materials mentioned can be found in Harris *et al.*, 2008). Together, they read several short model essays and identified these parts in each. The teacher and students filled out a graphic organizer for *TREE* for each essay they read together. Throughout this stage, important vocabulary, background knowledge, and declarative, procedural, and conditional knowledge the students needed were developed (see Table 2). The teacher began helping the students memorize the mnemonic. Finally, each time they met during this stage, the teachers and students discussed how they could 'transfer' what they were learning about *POW plus TREE* to other places and times when they wrote. Each time they met with the teacher, each student reported chances they had to transfer *POW plus TREE*. These discussions helped promote generalization.

Stage 2: Discuss it

Although a great deal of discussion obviously takes place during Stage 1 and in later stages, Stage 2 is called 'discuss it' because not only does the initial discussion of the strategy continue, but students are asked to evaluate and discuss their previous writing using what they have learned (Graham & Harris, 2003; Harris & Graham, 1996). During all stages of instruction, the teacher emphasized that learning *POW plus TREE* would take effort and commitment on the students' part, and that effort combined with these powerful strategies (or 'tricks') would result in being able to write good opinion essays. Each session during discuss it began with a quick review of the mnemonic (POW + TREE) to help memorize it and what it stands for. The teacher decided to continue reading and evaluating a couple more good opinion essays before she had the students evaluate their pre-test essay. As they read these model essays, she asked the students to brainstorm additional good reasons and explanations for reasons that the authors might have used.

Next, the teacher had each student get out their opinion essay about choosing a pet, and find out what parts they had. She stressed that it certainly was not a problem if they did not have all the parts when they wrote this essay – they had not learned this trick for writing opinion essays yet, and that is what they were here to learn together. Each student evaluated their essay, and students discussed what parts were commonly missing. The teacher also began discussion regarding what else writers do to make their essays powerful, including: give more than three reasons, use good vocabulary choice (what the students called use 'million dollar words'), catch the reader with an interesting first sentence, use an interesting ending sentence, and so on (these were modified to individual students' abilities). Examples of these were noted in the students' essays and in the model essays read. Then, each student was given a graph (a line of rockets with each rocket divided into five parts; this was used each time they wrote an opinion essay during instruction) and filled in the number of parts on the first rocket representing the number of parts he or she had in their pre-test essay. These students typically had one or two parts. Finally, the students and the teacher discussed the goal of working together: to write better opinion essays. Good opinion essays tell the readers what you believe, give you at least three reasons why, and have an ending sentence. They are fun for you to write, fun for others to read, make sense, and might convince the readers to agree with you! The students went on to Stage 3 when the teacher determined they had developed the necessary background knowledge, vocabulary, and understanding of what they were learning, and why they were learning it.

Stage 3: Model it

The teacher modelled how to use *POW plus TREE*, thinking out loud as she planned and wrote an essay. The students participated by helping her as she planned and made notes on the graphic organizer, and as she wrote her first draft. Together, they accepted and rejected possible ideas to support her premise and explanations for her reasons, keeping the reader in mind. They continued to modify their plan while writing the paper.

While planning and writing, the teacher used a variety of out loud self-instructions (see Table 2). She explained that saying these things to herself helped her work, and that sometimes she thought out loud and sometimes she said them in her head. Each student was given a sheet titled 'My self-statements' and asked to record one or more self-statements to say to help think of good ideas, to say while working, and to say to help check their work. Students were encouraged, but not forced, to use these self-statements throughout the next two stages of instruction, and their lists were left near them while they wrote.

Finally, the students evaluated this collaborative essay, and graphed the number of parts contained (the teacher, of course, had made sure that all five parts – premise, three reasons, and conclusion – were present) on their graphs. If the teacher decided students could profit from additional teacher-led or collaborative modelling, this was done.

Stage 4: Memorize it

While listed here as a stage, in fact memorizing the mnemonic and what it stands for had been going on since Stage 1. At this point, most students had the strategy memorized and were able to write the mnemonic on blank paper so they could make notes in the future using the mnemonic without a graphic organizer. Students who needed to do so engaged in more practice of the mnemonic and its meaning until it was memorized. As one student said, you cannot use what you cannot remember!

Stage 5: Support it

This stage is typically the longest. Research indicates, however, that students make the biggest jump in performance in this stage, and that support in using the strategy is necessary even after the explicit, collaborative modelling in Stage 3 (Harris & Graham, 1999). At first, the students worked together with the teacher's assistance to write an opinion essay, sharing ideas, crafting notes, and then writing a draft. The teacher re-modelled if necessary. At first, students kept out their mnemonic chart and list of self-statements wile they worked, and used the graphic organizer. Over time, the teacher provided less help and students began writing independently; pace was based on student performance.

For each essay written during *support it*, the student first set a goal to include all five essay parts. Each essay was evaluated and graphed by the student. Students were able to help each other throughout this stage as well as receive teacher help. They shared their essays with each other, providing feedback on both strengths and areas where improvements could be made in each other's arguments. Use of the mnemonic chart, list of self-statements, and graphic organizer was faded and then discontinued during this stage.

Stage 6: Independent performance

At this point, each student wrote 1–2 opinion essays without teacher or peer support. Students were encouraged to write the mnemonic and notes for each part on blank paper before writing. The teacher provided positive and constructive feedback as needed, and students continued to share their essays with each other. Graphing was continued for one or two essays, and then the students were told they could decide whether to continue graphing in the future. As in previous stages, the students shared opportunities and ideas for transfer of this strategy with each other and the teacher.

What to expect

Five weeks after she began instruction (13, 20-min sessions later), at the end of *independent performance*, Sandy wrote the following essay on her own, after planning on scratch paper:

Boys and Girls Soccer Team!

I believe boys and girls should not play soccer together. Boys could push the girls over for the ball because boys play rough sometimes. Girls might not kick too good on their team. Boys might be teasing the girls, because of that boys might get over excited. Boys really want to win the games. Boys might fight with each other because girls got mixed up with the goals. The girls might forget about the game. They went to the mall. Girls might wear some high heels because they forgot their sneakers at home. This is why girls should read my essay if you do not want to be bullied.

Sandy clearly has the concept of an opinion essay, and has made the strategies she learned her own. Her progress was typical among the students we taught. Obviously, there is more to be done and more to be learned, including how to revise this draft, but she now has the foundation for doing so.

Limitations and the research we need

Harris and Graham have emphasized from the beginning that SRSD should not be thought of as a panacea; promoting students' academic competence and literacy requires a complex integration of skills, strategies, processes, and attributes (Harris, 1982; Harris & Graham, 1996; Harris *et al.*, 2003). While SRSD makes an important contribution to teachers' instructional repertoires, it is not a complete writing curriculum. Further, there are a number of future research needs. Many questions remain to be answered regarding strategy instruction for all students; for example, further improvements in maintenance and generalization remain to be addressed.

As we noted previously, SRSD remains a dynamic and evolving model of strategies instruction, one that continues to be impacted by ongoing research and theory development. Currently, social-cognitive theory and research point to the value of peer support and peer involvement in instruction (cf. MacArthur, Schwartz, & Graham, 1991). This is an area of research requiring further attention in terms of SRSD – how can peer support best be incorporated successfully into SRSD, and does it create further improvements in performance? In two recent studies, we predicted that the addition of a peer support component to SRSD instruction could lead to incremental gains in writing, knowledge, and motivation (Graham, Harris, & Mason, 2005; see Graham, Harris, & Zito, 2005, for a discussion of both studies). These two initial studies indicated that peer support as part of SRSD resulted in some gains in immediate performance after instruction, as well as some gains in both maintenance and generalization (cf. Graham *et al.*, 2005). However, a great many questions remain to be addressed in terms of peer support. For example, these studies involved only struggling writers, and we did not examine if peer support is also effective with average and above average writers. Further, these initial studies of peer support as a component involved second graders, and we do not know how older students might respond to peer support as part of SRSD.

Social-cognitive theory further posits that learners often receive useful and persuasive information from teachers, parents, and peers (Schunk & Zimmerman, 1997). Such information can be received through modelling, a key component of SRSD. No research has addressed the effectiveness of peers as models in the SRSD approach; all research to date has involved the teacher as writing model. Further, writing anxiety is one student characteristic that might be addressed through SRSD, and is a characteristic we have observed in many students we have worked with. No research, however, has specifically addressed if, and how, SRSD impacts writing anxiety. Future research in SRSD might also address how SRSD can be further modified for students who experience severe writing anxiety.

In our opinion, one of the most intriguing questions is the long-term results of strategy instruction and development of self-regulation across the grades in writing and other domains. No such research has been conducted; the longest studies have involved teaching two writing strategies within a single school year (Graham, Harris, & Zito, 2005). Parents could be partners in such long-term intervention, and research is needed here. Researchers have also argued that a focus on how teachers become adept at, committed to, and supported in strategy instruction is needed, as is more work aimed at filtering this approach in supporting schools (Harris & Alexander; 1998; Pressley & Harris, 2006). As Levin and O'Donnell (1999) explained, teachers must become knowledgeable of research supported practices; then they must decide if their classroom and students are an appropriate match to the treatment and validating data; and finally, they must implement and evaluate the effects of the treatment with their own students.

We believe that the continued integration of knowledge gained from various theoretical perspectives, including constructivist theories such as social cognitive theory, result in continually improving models of strategies instruction.

Conclusion

Throughout this paper, we have communicated the importance of multiple theoretical and empirical works in the evolution and future of SRSD. This position might be referred to as theoretical pragmatism or theoretical pluralism. We believe that such a position remains important not only in the study of writing intervention, but in the study of writing itself. While many theories have contributed to the study of writing, including cognitive theory and social-cognitive theory, Prior (2006) noted that sociocultural theories 'represent the dominant paradigm for writing research today' (p. 54). Interestingly, however, as theories evolve, theorists respond to both critiques of their paradigm and to new ideas. Harris, Santangelo, and Graham (2008, in press) argued that developments in socio-cultural theory have occurred in the past few decades alongside developments in cognitive, information processing, social-cognitive theory, and others. Thus, over time it can become more difficult to ascertain critical differences between some theories, especially at an applied level.

The challenges faced by students with difficulties in learning and writing, and indeed by all of us today, are complex. When we treat competing viewpoints with thoughtfulness and respect, a powerful repertoire for teaching and learning can be developed. This does not negate the important contributions made by competing theories, and the importance of this competition in advancing our thinking and research (Dubin, 1978; Harris & Alexander, 1998; Harris & Graham, 1992; Harris *et al.*, 2003). As Dubin urged, let us work to 'give up constraining commitments to theories, methods, and apparatus' (p. 276). By studying hypotheses rather than substantiating theories, we can focus on 'finding out', with a 'willingness to ask *open* questions unhampered by the prior constraints of a particular view or method' (Dubin, 1978, p. 278). Let this indeed by the future of research and instruction in writing.

References

Alexander, P. (1997). Mapping the multidimensional nature of domain learning: The interplay of cognitive, motivational, and strategic forces. In M. Maehr & P. Pintrich (Eds.), *Advances in motivation and achievement* (Vol. 10, pp. 213–250). Greenwich, CT: JAI Press.

Alexander, P. (2003). The development of expertise: The journey from acclimation to proficiency. *Educational Researcher, 32*(8), 10–14.

Applebee, A., Langer, J., Jenkins, L., Mullis, I., & Foertsch, M. (1990). *Learning to write in our nations' schools*. Princeton, NJ: Educational Testing Service.

Applebee, A., Langer, J., & Mullis, I. (1986). *The writing report card: Writing achievement in American schools*. Princeton, NJ: Educational Testing Service.

Applebee, A., Langer, J., Mullis, I., Latham, A., & Gentile, C. (1994). *NAEP 1992: Writing report card*. Washington, DC: US Government Printing Office.

Association for Supervision and Curriculum Development (2002). *Teaching students with learning disabilities in the regular classroom: Using learning strategies* [videotape 2]. Retrieved March 1, 2009 from http://shop.ascd.org/productdisplay.cfm?productid=602084

Bereiter, C., Burtis, P., & Scardamalia, M. (1988). Cognitive operations in constructing main point in written composition. *Journal of Memory and Language, 27*, 261–278.

Bereiter, C., & Scardamalia, M. (1987). *The psychology of written composition*. Hillsdale, NJ: Erlbaum.

Brown, A. L., Campione, J. C., & Day, J. D. (1981). Learning to learn: On training students to learn from texts. *Educational Researcher, 10*, 14–21.

Borkowski, J. G., Carr, M., Rellinger, E. A., & Pressley, M. (1990). Self-regulated strategy use: Interdependence of metacognition, attributions, and self-esteem. In B. F. Jones (Ed.), *Dimensions of thinking: Reviewing the research* (pp. 53–92). Hillsdale, NJ: Erlbaum.

Carroll, J. B. (1963). A model of school learning. *Teachers College Record, 64*, 723–733.

Curry, K. A. (1997). *A comparison of the writing products of students with learning disabilities in inclusive and resource room settings using different writing instruction approaches*. Boca Raton, FL: Florida Atlantic University, Unpublished doctoral dissertation.

Dubin, R. (1978). *Theory building*. New York: The Free Press.

Englert, C. S., Raphael, T. E., & Anderson, L. M. (1992). Socially mediated instruction: Improving students' knowledge and talk about writing. *Elementary School Journal, 92*, 411–449.

Englert, C. S., Raphael, T. E., Anderson, L., Anthony, H., Stevens, D., & Fear, K. (1991). Making writing strategies and self-talk visible: Cognitive strategy instruction in writing in regular and special education classrooms. *American Educational Research Journal, 28*, 337–373.

Flower, L., & Hayes, J. (1980). The dynamics of composing: Making plans and juggling constraints. In L. Gregg & R. Steinberg (Eds.), *Cognitive processes in writing* (pp. 31–50). Hillsdale, NJ: Erlbaum.

Galbraith, D. (1996). Self-monitoring, discovery through writing and individual differences in drafting strategy. In G. Rijlaarsdam, H. van den Bergh, & M. Couzijn (Eds.), *Studies in writing, Vol. 1: Theories, models, and methodology in writing research* (pp. 121–144). Amsterdam: Amsterdam University Press.

Galbraith, D., & Torrance, M. (2004). Revision in the context of different drafting strategies. In L. Allal, L. Chanquoy, & P. Largy (Eds.), *Revision: Cognitive and instructional processes* (pp. 63–86). Dordrecht, The Netherlands: Kluwer Academic Publishers.

Garcia-Sanchez, J., & Fidalgo-Redondo, R. (2006). Effects of two types of self-regulatory instruction programs on students with learning disabilities in writing products, processes, and self-efficacy. *Learning Disability Quarterly, 29*, 181–211.

Glaser, R. (1991). Expertise and assessment. In M. Wittrock & E. Baker (Eds.), *Testing and cognition* (pp. 17–30). Englewood Cliffs, NJ: Prentice Hall.

Glaser, C., & Brunstein, J. (2007). Improving fourth-grade students' composition skills: Effects of strategy instruction and self-regulatory procedures. *Journal of Educational Psychology, 99*, 297–310.

Graham, S. (2006). Writing. In P. Alexander & P. Winne (Eds.), *Handbook of educational psychology* (pp. 457–478). Mahwah, NJ: Erlbaum.

Graham, S., & Harris, K. R. (1989). Improving learning disabled students' skills at composing essays: Self-instructional strategy training. *Exceptional Children, 56*, 201–216.

Graham, S., & Harris, K. R. (1994). The role and development of self-regulation in the writing process. In D. Schunk & B. Zimmerman (Eds.), *Self-regulation of learning and performance: Issues and educational applications* (pp. 203–228). New York: Erlbaum.

Graham, S., & Harris, K. R. (1996). Self-regulation and strategy instruction for students with writing and learning difficulties. In S. Ransdell & M. Levy (Eds.), *Science of writing: Theories, methods, individual differences, and applications* (pp. 347–360). New York: Erlbaum.

Graham, S., & Harris, K. R. (2000). The role of self-regulation and transcription skills in writing and writing development. *Educational Psychologist, 35*(1), 3–12.

Graham, S., & Harris, K. R. (2002). Prevention and intervention for struggling writers. In M. Shinn, G. Stoner, & H. Walker (Eds.), *Interventions for academic and behavior problems II: Preventive and remedial approaches* (pp. 589–610). Bethesda, MD: National Association of School Psychologists.

Graham, S., & Harris, K. R. (2003). Students with learning disabilities and the process of writing: A meta-analysis of SRSD studies. In H. L. Swanson, K. R. Harris, & S. Graham (Eds.), *Handbook of learning disabilities* (pp. 323–344). New York: Guilford Press.

Graham, S., & Harris, K. R. (2005). *Writing better: Effective strategies for teaching students with learning difficulties*. Baltimore, MD: Brookes.

Graham, S., & Harris, K. R. (2009). Evidence-based writing practices: Drawing recommendations from multiple sources. *British Journal of Educational Psychology Monograph Series II*(6), 97–114.

Graham, S., Harris, K. R., & Fink-Chorzempka, B. (2000). Is handwriting causally related to learning to write? *Journal of Educational Psychology, 92*, 620–633.

Graham, S., Harris, K. R., & Fink-Chorzempa, B. (2002). Contributions of spelling instruction to the spelling, writing, and reading of poor spellers. *Journal of Educational Psychology, 94*, 669–686.

Graham, S., Harris, K. R., & Mason, L. (2005). Improving the writing performance, knowledge, and motivation of struggling young writers: The effects of self-regulated strategy development. *Contemporary Educational Psychology, 30*, 207–241.

Graham, S., Harris, K. R., & Reid, R. (1992). Developing self-regulated learners. *Focus on Exceptional Children, 24*(6), 1–16.

Graham, S., Harris, K. R., & Zito, J. (2005). Promoting internal and external validity: A synergism of laboratory experiments and classroom based research. In G. Phye, D. H. Robinson, & J. Levin (Eds.), *Experimental methods for educational intervention* (pp. 235–265). San Diego, CA: Elvieser.

Graham, S., & Perin, D. (2007a). *Writing next: Effective strategies to improve writing of adolescent middle and high school*. Washington, DC: Alliance for Excellence in Education.

Graham, S., & Perrin, D. (2007b). A meta-analysis of writing instruction for adolescent students. *Journal of Educational Psychology, 99*, 445–476.

Graham, S., & Perrin, D. (in press). What we know, what we still need to know: Teaching adolescents to write. *Scientific Studies in Reading*.

Harris, K. R. (1982). Cognitive-behavior modification: Application with exceptional students. *Focus on Exceptional Children, 15*(2), 1–16.

Harris, K. R. (1986). The effects of cognitive-behavior modification on private speech and task performance during problem solving among learning disabled and normally achieving children. *Journal of Abnormal Child Psychology, 14*, 63–76.

Harris, K. R., & Alexander, P. A. (1998). Integrated, constructivist education: Challenge and reality. *Educational Psychology Review, 10*(2), 115–127.

Harris, K. R., Alexander, P., & Graham, S. (2008). Michael Pressley's contributions to the history and future of strategy research. *Educational Psychology, 43*(2), 86–96.

Harris, K. R., & Graham, S. (1985). Improving learning disabled students' composition skills: Self-control strategy training. *Learning Disability Quarterly, 8,* 27–36.

Harris, K. R., & Graham, S. (1992). Self-regulated strategy development: A part of the writing process. In M. Pressley, K. R. Harris, & J. Guthrie (Eds.), *Promoting academic competence and literacy in school* (pp. 277–309). New York: Academic Press.

Harris, K. R., & Graham, S. (1996). *Making the writing process work: Strategies for composition and self-regulation.* Cambridge, MA: Brookline Books.

Harris, K. R., & Graham, S. (1999). Programmatic intervention research: Illustrations from the evolution of self-regulated strategy development. *Learning Disability Quarterly, 22,* 251–262.

Harris, K. R., Graham, S., & Adkins, M. (2004). *The effects of teacher-led SRSD instruction on the writing performance of struggling writers.* Presentation at Pacific Coast Research Conference, CA, February 2004.

Harris, K. R., Graham, S., Brindle, M., & Sandmel, K. (in press). Metacognition and children's writing. In D. J. Hacker, J. Dunlosky, & A. C. Graesser (Eds.), *Handbook of metacognition in education.* Mahwah, NJ: Erlbaum.

Harris, K. R., Graham, S., & Mason, L. (2003). Self-regulated strategy development in the classroom: Part of a balanced approach to writing instruction for students with disabilities. *Focus on Exceptional Children, 35,* 1–16.

Harris, K. R., Graham, S., & Mason, L. (2006). Improving the writing, knowledge, and motivation of struggling young writers: Effects of self-regulated strategy development with and without peer support. *American Educational Research Journal, 43,* 295–340.

Harris, K. R., Graham, S., Mason, L., & Friedlander, B. (2008). *Powerful writing strategies for all students.* Baltimore, MD: Brookes.

Harris, K. R., & Pressley, M. (1991). The nature of cognitive strategy instruction: Interactive strategy construction. *Exceptional Children, 57,* 392–405.

Harris, K. R., Reid, R., & Graham, S. (2004). Self-regulation among students with LD and ADHD. In B. Wong (Ed.), *Learning about learning disabilities* (3rd ed., pp. 167–195). Orlando, FL: Academic Press.

Harris, K. R., Santangelo, T., & Graham, S. (2008). Self-regulated strategy development in writing: An argument for the importance of new learning environments. *Instructional Sciences, 36,* 395–408.

Harris, K. R., Santangelo, T., & Graham, S. (in press). Metacognition and strategy instruction in writing. In H. S. Waters & W. Schneider (Eds.), *Metacognition, strategy use and instruction.* New York: Guildford.

Harris, K. R., Schmidt, T., & Graham, S. (1998). Every child can write: Strategies for composition and self-regulation in the writing process. In K. R. Harris, S. Graham, & D. Deshler (Eds.), *Advances in teaching and learning. Vol. 2: Teaching every child every day: Learning in diverse schools and classrooms* (pp. 131–167). Cambridge, MD: Brookline Books.

Hayes, J. (1996). A new framework for understanding cognition and affect in writing. In M. Levy & S. Ransdell (Eds.), *The science of writing: Theories, methods, individual differences, and applications* (pp. 1–27). Mahwah, NJ: Erlbaum.

Hayes, J., & Flower, L. (1980). Identifying the organization of writing processes. In L. Gregg & E. Steinberg (Eds.), *Cognitive processes in writing* (pp. 3–30). Hillsdale, NJ: Erlbaum.

Hayes, J. R. (2006). New directions in writing theory. In C. MacArthur, S. Graham, & J. Fitzgerald (Eds.), *Handbook of writing research* (pp. 28–40). New York: Guilford Press.

Isnard, N., & Piolat, A. (1994). The effects of different types of planning on the writing of argumentative text. In G. Eigler & T. Jechle (Eds.), *Writing: Current trends in European research* (pp. 121–132). Freiburg: Hochschul Verlag GmbH.

Kellogg, R. T. (1994). *The psychology of writing.* Oxford: Oxford University Press.

Levin, J., & O'Donnell, A. (1999). What to do about educational research's credibility gaps? *Issues in Education: Contributions from Educational Psychology, 5,* 177–229.

MacArthur, C., Schwartz, S., & Graham, S. (1991). Effects of a reciprocal peer revision strategy in special education classrooms. *Learning Disability Research and Practice, 6,* 201–210.

McCutchen, D. (2006). Cognitive factors in the development of children's writing. In C. MacArthur, S. Graham, & J. Fitzgerald (Eds.), *Handbook of writing research* (pp. 115–130). New York: Guilford Press.

Mason, L. H. (2004). Explicit self-regulated strategy development versus reciprocal questioning: Effects on expository reading comprehension among struggling readers. *Journal of Educational Psychology, 96*, 283–296.

Meichenbaum, D. (1977). *Cognitive behavior modification: An integrative approach.* New York: Plenum.

O'Leary, S. G., & Dubey, D. R. (1979). Applications of self-control procedures for children: A review. *Journal of Applied Behavior Analysis, 12*, 449–465.

Pressley, M. (2005). Oh, the places an educational psychologist can go!...and how young educational psychologists can prepare for the trip (apologies to Dr. Seuss). *Educational Psychology, 40*, 137–153.

Pressley, M., Borkowski, J. G., & Schneider, W. (1987). Cognitive strategies: Good strategies users coordinate meta-cognition and knowledge. In R. Vasta & G. Whitehurst (Eds.), *Annals of child development* (Vol. 4, pp. 89–129). Greenwich, CT: JAI Press.

Pressley, M., Graham, S., & Harris, K. R. (2006). The state of educational intervention research. *British Journal of Educational Psychology, 76*, 1–19.

Pressley, M., & Harris, K. R. (2001). Teaching cognitive strategies for reading, writing, and problem solving. In A. L. Costa (Ed.), *Developing minds: A resource book for teaching thinking* (3rd ed., pp. 265–286). Alexandria, VA: Association for Supervision and Curriculum Development.

Pressley, M., & Harris, K. R. (2006). Cognitive strategies instruction: From basic research to classroom instruction. In P. A. Alexander & P. Winne (Eds.), *Handbook of educational psychology* (2nd ed., pp. 265–286). New York: MacMillan.

Pressley, M., & Hilden, K. R. (2006) Cognitive strategies: Production deficiencies and successful strategy instruction everywhere. In D. Kuhn & R. Siegler (Eds.) (W. Damon R. Lerner, Series Editors), *Handbook of child psychology, Vol. 2: Cognition, perception, and language* (6th ed., 511–556). Hoboken NJ: Wiley & Sons

Pressley, M., Woloshyn, V., Lysynchuk, L. M., Martin, V., Wood, E., & Willoughby, T. (1990). A primer of research on cognitive strategy instruction: The important issues and how to address them. *Educational Psychology Review, 2*, 1–58.

Prior, P. (2006). A sociocultural theory of writing. In C. MacArthur, S. Graham, & J. Fitzgerald (Eds.), *Handbook of writing research* (pp. 54–66). New York: Guilford.

Rogers, L. & Graham, S. (2007). *A meta-analysis of single-subject design writing research.* Manuscript in preparation.

Rosenbaum, M. S., & Drabman, R. S. (1979). Self-control training in the classroom: A review and critique. *Journal of Applied Behavior Analysis, 12*, 467–485.

Sawyer, R., Graham, S., & Harris, K. R. (1992). Direct teaching, strategy instruction, and strategy instruction with explicit self-regulation: Effects on the composition skills and self-efficacy of students with learning disabilities. *Journal of Educational Psychology, 84*, 340–352.

Scardamalia, M., & Bereiter, C. (1986). Written composition. In M. Wittrock (Ed.), *Handbook of research on teaching* (3rd ed., pp. 778–803). New York: MacMillan.

Schumaker, J. B., Deshler, D. D., Alley, G. R., Warner, M. M., & Denton, P. H. (1982). Multipass: A learning strategy for improving reading comprehension. *Learning Disability Quarterly, 5*, 295–304.

Schunk, D. H., & Zimmerman, B. J. (1994). *Self-regulation of learning and performance: Issues and educational applications.* Hillsdale, NJ: Erlbaum.

Schunk, D. H., & Zimmerman, B. J. (1997). Social origins of self-regulatory competence. *Educational Psychologist, 32*(4), 195–208.

Sexton, M., Harris, K. R., & Graham, S. (1998). Self-regulated strategy development and the writing process: Effects on essay writing and attributions. *Exceptional Children, 64*(3), 295–311.

Swedlow, J. (1999). The power of writing. *National Geographic, 196*, 110–132.

Torrance, M., Thomas, G. V., & Robinson, E. J. (1999). Individual differences in the writing behavior of undergraduate students. *British Journal of Educational Psychology, 69*, 189-199.

Wong, B., Harris, K. R., Graham, S., & Butler, D. (2003). Cognitive strategies instruction research in learning disabilities. In L. Swanson, K. R. Harris, & S. Graham (Eds.), *Handbook of research on learning disabilities* (pp. 323-344). New York: Guilford Press.

Worell, J., & Stilwell, (1981). *Psychology for teachers and students*. New York: McGraw-Hill.

Zimmerman, B. (1989). A social cognitive view of self-regulated learning. *Journal of Educational Psychology, 81*, 329-339.

Zimmerman, B., & Reisemberg, R. (1997). Becoming a self-regulated writer: A social cognitive perspective. *Contemporary Educational Psychology, 22*, 73-101.

Zimmerman, B. J. (1997). Dimensions of academic self-regulation: A conceptual framework for education. In D. H. Schunk & B. J. Zimmerman (Eds.), *Self-regulation of learning and performance: Issues and educational applications* (pp. 3-21). Hillsdale, NJ: Erlbaum.

Teaching and Learning Writing, 137–157
BJEP Monograph Series II, 6
© 2009 The British Psychological Society

The
British
Psychological
Society

www.bpsjournals.co.uk

Development and standardization of a new handwriting speed test: The Detailed Assessment of Speed of Handwriting

Anna L. Barnett[1]*, Sheila E. Henderson[2], Beverly Scheib[2] and Joerg Schulz[3]

[1]Department of Psychology, Oxford Brookes University, Oxford, UK
[2]School of Psychology and Human Development, Institute of Education, University of London, London, UK
[3]Department of Psychology, University of Hertfordshire, Hatfield, UK

Background. Handwriting remains an important skill throughout a student's school career and beyond. Only when the basic elements of this skill can be performed 'automatically' and quickly, can sufficient processing capacity be allocated to higher level components of writing such as composition. Although problems with handwriting are common and can lead to academic underachievement, few tools are available to measure handwriting quality or speed.

Aim. The aim of this paper is to describe the development and UK standardization of a comprehensive test of handwriting speed, the Detailed Assessment of Speed of Handwriting.

Methods. A stratified sample of 546 children between the ages of 9 and 16 performed five tasks: copying under 'best' and 'fast' instructions, writing the alphabet, free writing for 10 min, and a non-language based task involving drawing intersecting lines within concentric circles.

Conclusions. Our data suggest that standard scores on the first four tasks plus a composite score of speed of writing may be used to provide objective evidence of 'slowness' of handwriting. In addition, the profile of scores across tasks along with standard scores on the fifth task, provide practitioners working in health and educational settings with supplementary information useful for describing the needs of those with handwriting difficulties in more detail. Preliminary data showing adequate reliability and validity of this new instrument are also reported.

Despite the increasing use of computers in everyday life, handwriting remains an important skill for recording information, expressing one's thoughts on paper and

Correspondence should be addressed to Dr Anna L. Barnett, Department of Psychology, Oxford Brookes University, Headington Campus, Gipsy Lane, Oxford OX3 0BP, UK (e-mail: abarnett@brookes.ac.uk).

DOI:10.1348/000709909X421937

communicating ideas to others. In most schools, pupils spend much of the day performing tasks involving writing and regular assessment is based on handwritten work (Dennis & Swinth, 2001; McHale & Cermak, 1992). As they progress from primary, through secondary, to higher education, the writing demands placed upon the student increases rather than decreases. In most professional settings too, handwriting skills are important. A confident, legible, and fast hand is therefore a prerequisite for satisfactory progress through formal education and beyond.

The skill of handwriting does not develop spontaneously and has to be taught for some time before a fast, fluent hand is acquired. Early in the teaching process, the focus tends to be on the formation, and hence legibility, of letters and words (Dornan & Taylor, 2005). Later, speed of production becomes a crucial factor as survival in secondary school requires the ability to take notes quickly, write to dictation at a speed which is externally imposed, and write continuously for extended periods of time – as in exams which may last several hours. Finally, the writer needs to develop the skill to the point where speed and ease of reading/legibility can be controlled in a flexible manner. Only then can appropriate adaptations to different task demands be made, such as the neatness required for a public wall display, the speed required in a time-limited exam or the compressed scribbling that will suffice as a personal record of a homework assignment.

In primary schools in the UK, there is considerable variation in the priority assigned to handwriting as a skill to be acquired (Barnett, Stainthorp, Henderson, & Scheib, 2006). Consequently, the way it is taught, and the standards achieved vary too. In some schools, the teaching of handwriting is excellent and few pupils are reported to have difficulty. In others, very little time is spent on formal teaching and the final standard achieved leaves many pupils unable to cope with the demands of a busy secondary school curriculum. Since recent research shows a clear link between the physical ability to write rapidly and achievement in the broader aspects of writing, schools not paying sufficient attention to the skill are failing their pupils. For example, Connelly and Hurst (2001) and Graham, Berninger, Abbott, Abbott, and Whitaker (1997) have shown that if the perceptual-motor aspects of handwriting have not evolved to a level requiring little attention, then written output will be reduced, not only in terms of quantity but also in quality. In other words, it is only when handwriting is as near to 'automatic' as possible that sufficient processing capacity can be allocated to higher level components of writing, involving creating ideas, planning and reviewing. A finding consistent with the work of Connelly and Hurst (2001) is that of Tucha, Tucha, Walitza, Kaunzinger, and Lange (2007), who have shown that an overemphasis on teaching for neatness in handwriting is detrimental to the development of fluent and fast production.

In surveys conducted over the last three decades, estimates of the number of primary schoolchildren experiencing serious difficulties with handwriting have consistently hovered around 12% (Barnett *et al.*, 2006; Hartnell, 1994; Rubin & Henderson, 1982). For some of these children, poor handwriting seems to be an isolated problem, with no other area of their development and learning causing major concern. We may speculate that for these children, difficulties may have arisen as a result of insufficient or inappropriate teaching and/or lack of appropriate practice opportunities. For others, however, their handwriting difficulties are just one component of a broader spectrum of learning problems. For example, difficulties with handwriting have been reported as common among children with dyslexia (Phelps & Stempel, 1991), specific language impairment (Dockrell, Lindsay, Connelly, & Mackie, 2007), attention deficit hyperactivity disorder (Tucha & Lange, 2005), developmental coordination disorder

(Geuze, 2005; Mandich, Miller, Polatajko, & Missiuna, 2003), and Asperger syndrome (Henderson & Green, 2001). Whatever the origins and precise nature of the problem, difficulty in handwriting has been shown to result in under-achievement in children, generally (e.g. Briggs, 1970; Simner, Leedham, & Thommassen, 1996). Moreover, poor handwriting is not easy to hide in a classroom situation as a child's fellow pupils can see the problem as well as the teacher. It is hardly surprising, therefore that difficulties in this area have also been linked to poor self-esteem and relationships with peers (Phelps, Stempel, & Speck, 1985).

The continued reliance on handwriting as an important mode of communication across the life-span coupled with the negative impacts of difficulties in this area strongly suggest a need for an objective means of assessing the various aspects of handwriting over time. In primary school, for example, it is important to identify any child with a difficulty as early as possible so that help can be provided before problems become entrenched. Although secondary school teachers do not expect to have to deal with handwriting at this stage in a child's school career, the surveys mentioned above suggest that their expectations are often not met. Screening of all pupils on entry to secondary school would help to identify those who have failed to reach an adequate standard. Immediate intervention at this point in time might ensure that no child would approach later public examinations unable to demonstrate their full potential. A second reason for quantifying a student's level of handwriting performance and comparing this with the performance of other students of the same age stems from the need to formally determine eligibility for support, outside that provided within the classroom setting. For example, in the UK, such information would be important when applying for access arrangements in examinations (Qualifications and Curriculum Authority, QCA, 2003) or for financial support (e.g. for the purchase of a computer or other recording device). A third reason for using an objective measure of handwriting can be linked to recent emphasis on the need to demonstrate that any intervention for children with special needs works (Sackett, Straus, Richardson, Rosenberg, & Haynes, 2000).

Rosenblum, Weiss, and Parush (2003) provide a comprehensive review of existing tests of handwriting. Although some of these meet basic psychometric requirements for acceptability, many do not (Barnett & Henderson, 2005). This is particularly true of tests of legibility or overall quality of the written product. There are several reasons for this. One derives from the fact that handwriting is a taught skill. Thus the level of attainment reached by any one child will depend partly on the quality and quantity of teaching they have received. Another reason derives from the fact that many different alphabet styles are taught in English speaking countries. Within these, some have a national handwriting style used by all children. When this is the case, it is possible to develop a test in which prototypic exemplars can be applied universally for all children. For example, in the USA the evaluation tool of children's' handwriting (ETCH, Amundson, 1995) is based on the D'Nealian, a looped cursive style taught throughout much of the USA. In other countries, such as the UK, each school is free to choose its own writing style and these may vary from a very upright 'ball and stick' type with only some joins to a fully-joined looped cursive (Barnett *et al.*, 2006). These qualitative differences, which may seem minor, make it difficult to develop scoring systems which can be applied easily to samples from different schools, using different styles and often result in low inter-rater reliability.

In contrast to measuring legibility and/or the quality of a piece of handwriting, it is relatively straightforward to obtain an objective and reliable estimate of the *speed* of writing performance and several tests of speed of handwriting do exist (e.g. Killen,

Dempsey, & O'Mahony, 2008; Wallen, Bonney, & Lennox, 1996). However, all of these tests rely on the use of only one task and none have adequate UK norms. In view of the importance of speed of production noted above, the objective of the current project, therefore, was to produce an 'ecologically valid' test of the speed at which students could produce handwriting with up-to-date UK norms. We named this test the Detailed Assessment of Speed of Handwriting (DASH).

Handwriting speed can be measured simply by recording the amount of writing produced in a given time, or by recording the time taken to produce a given amount of writing. In either case, the measurement units are relatively clear and easy to work with. Behind this simplicity, however, important choices have to be made regarding the details of the writing task, which will have an impact both on how the task is performed and how performance should be interpreted. Our primary objective for the DASH was to develop a series of tasks, which tapped as many different aspects of handwriting *speed* as possible. These tasks had to be amenable to objective and reliable scoring, which would in turn provide a solid foundation for standardization. We also set ourselves the target of keeping the overall time limit to 30 min, to allow the DASH to be manageable within a school timetable.

In what follows, the evolution of the DASH is described in two phases. Phase 1 describes the development of the instrument. Phase 2 describes the generation of norms and selected aspects of reliability and validity.

Phase 1: Development of the instrument

In this section, the rationale for each of the five tasks contained in the DASH is outlined, along with any pilot work relevant to its selection and refinement. More general pilot work is reported in the test manual (Barnett, Henderson, Scheib, & Schulz, 2007).

Free Writing

In order to meet our criterion of 'ecological' validity, we began by considering the advantages and disadvantages of a Free Writing task. Perhaps, the strongest reason for including such a task is that it is a multifaceted activity which most children beyond the age of 6 or 7 are required to perform in school on a regular basis. In addition, as students get older, success in an examination setting becomes more and more dependent on the ability to generate a piece of writing from scratch, at speed. It is perhaps predictable, therefore, that those responsible for deciding whether a child's difficulties are serious enough to warrant help in the classroom and/or in examinations (Backhouse, 2007) use a Free Writing task in their assessment. Of the various tests in existence, however, none provide adequate UK norms (e.g. Allcock, 2001; Connor, 1995; Dutton, 1991; Roaf, 1998; Waine, 2001).

Although the ecological validity argument is a strong one, there is an equally strong argument against using a Free Writing task as a measure of speed of production, especially if it is the *only* measure used. A Free Writing task is a complex and intellectually demanding task requiring competence in a number of motor, cognitive, and metacognitive processes, all to be performed simultaneously (Torrance & Galbraith, 2006). For example, ideas must be generated and developed into an organized and cohesive unit, working memory must be employed to maintain the storyline, and the spelling and punctuating of the resultant text must be worked out. At the same time, planning, and executing the movements required to form the letters and words must be undertaken, and the letters and words on the page arranged in a specified way. Clearly, the measure of *speed* of production obtained from such a task is difficult to interpret as so many of the factors just mentioned influence the total time taken.

Having weighed up the advantages and disadvantages, we decided that a Free Writing task should be included as one of the five tasks in the DASH in order to gauge the impact of a speed constituent on compositional performance. We were attracted to the topic 'My Life' as our own experience over the years had suggested that children were rarely at a loss for something to write about. To be absolutely sure of this choice, however, a pilot study was conducted in which the DASH task was compared with another commonly used Free Writing task, that of writing about 'My Favourite Person'.

A total of 51 children between the ages of 10 and 11 participated in the study. All were in year 6 in the same school and were tested in their own classrooms, writing with their usual pen on lined paper. They completed two 10-min writing tasks, separated by a week. Comparison of the number of words produced on these two topics revealed that significantly more words were produced under the title 'My Life' ($t = 2.14$, $p < .05$), thus confirming the view that our chosen topic adequately stimulated ideas for writing. Once the topic had been settled, we then experimented with the way in which the task was introduced to children and found that production of a 'spider diagram' displaying a range of facets of 'My Life' helped generate even more ideas to write about.

Ten minutes was chosen as the time limit for this task, as this seemed long enough to allow the older children to generate a fair amount of text and short enough not to overwhelm younger children unused to extended periods of writing. Another important consideration was the length of time recommended by the UK Joint Council for Qualifications (JCQ, 2007), the body responsible for overseeing the arrangements made for children who need extra help to gain access to the national curriculum and manage national qualification examinations. At the time we were developing the DASH, JCQ recommended a time limit of 10 min, with the required score being the number of words written per minute. Consistent with these guidelines, the Free Writing task in the DASH is performed for a total of 10 min with the main raw score being the mean number of words per minute, calculated from the whole 10-min period.

As noted above, the amount of writing produced in a 10-min time frame does not only depend on the speed at which letters and words can be formed but also depends on various 'non-motor' factors. More competent writers will, for example be able to plan what to write and decide how to spell words *while* they are writing, whereas others will stop writing to concentrate on these aspects of the task. In order to obtain some information on the continuity of writing throughout the 10-min period, we experimented with the use of time markers equally spaced throughout the task. We found that the children had no difficulty with this procedure and it allowed us to interpret the data more accurately. For example, by plotting a child's profile over the five 2-min periods, a distinction can be made between one who writes slowly throughout the 10-min period from another who writes a lot for a couple of minutes then simply runs out of ideas.

Sentence copying

As an alternative to a Free Writing task, it is often argued that a copying task offers the 'cleanest' measure of a child's ability to write legibly, at an acceptable speed. There is no need for creativity, spelling is not a problem, and memory demands are minimized as long as the sentence to be copied is always present. The popularity of this view is reflected in the fact that copying is probably the most commonly used task in published studies of children's handwriting. However, in the existing literature, the material employed varies from test to test and from study to study. For example, the phrase 'cats and dogs' was used by Ziviani and Watson-Will (1998), the sentence 'the quick brown fox jumps over the lazy dog' by Wallen *et al.* (1996) and a paragraph of running text by, e.g. Blöte and Hamstra-Bletz (1991); Graham, Berninger and Weintraub (1998); Rubin and Henderson (1982). Variation is also found in the way the material is presented and the total writing time, with some authors requiring the child to write for 1 min, others 3 min, and others longer still. One criticism of 'brief' copying tasks asserts that a few minutes is unrepresentative of most classroom writing tasks. Wallen *et al.* (1996), for example, urge users of their test to consider the possibility that a child's test score might *overestimate* their ability to sustain more demanding writing tasks.

Both teachers and therapists working with children with difficulties note that some are actually incapable of altering the speed of their handwriting, whereas others can do so but at great cost to legibility. A criticism of existing tests of handwriting speed is that they usually do not include a measure of the child's 'normal' writing speed, which can be compared to their writing under 'speed' instructions. To address this issue in the DASH, we decided to include two tasks with identical content and time constraints. In the first, the child would be required to write in their 'best' handwriting, then later, 'as fast as possible but legibly', for the same length of time. Whereas the first provides us with a baseline estimate of what the child is capable of doing when trying their best, the second allows us to judge the extent to which the child can follow a 'speed' instruction. The DASH provides norms for these tasks separately, as well as information on the difference between them.

Once a writing task has been chosen and the length of writing time established, the next consideration must be the task instructions. As noted above, an important factor in understanding a problem with speed of production is the question of flexibility. Is the writer capable of altering the speed at which they produce letters and/or words or not? In our view, none of the existing instruments yield an answer to this question, often because the instructions have the potential to create conflict in the mind of the child. For example, in their test, Wallen *et al.* (1996) ask the child to 'Write as *quickly* but as *neatly* as you can until I tell you to stop'. While we concede that it is essential to convey to the children that they must not write so fast that the product becomes illegible, the extent to which individuals will interpret the balance between the twin criteria of *speed* and *neatness* will vary considerably from child to child and will also depend on the tone of voice being used to enunciate each criterion. The problem of this 'speed-accuracy trade off' is not easy to solve. It is one which recurs in all sorts of contexts and is one which experimental psychologists have been studying for well over a 100 years (see Schmidt & Wrisberg, 2000, for a review).

Everyone in the field is familiar with the sentence we chose for our copying task. 'The quick brown fox jumps over the lazy dog' has been used in many previous research studies mainly because it contains every letter of the alphabet. We chose a 2-min period for both versions of this repetitive copying task (best and fast), each yielding a score indicating the mean number of words written per minute. This allows enough time to obtain a sufficient writing sample from the slowest (often youngest) writers but is short enough to avoid the problem of boredom or fatigue. The inclusion of a half-way time mark allows for a further breakdown of performance if necessary. It took time to refine the verbatim instructions for the two variants of this task ('best' vs. 'fast' writing), our main concern being to ensure that the contrast between the two conditions was brought out clearly, while at the same time encouraging the child to hold on to the idea that legibility was desired in both cases. Successive attempts at using different instructions led us to the most reliable method of administration and therefore adequate reliability.

Writing the alphabet

Although free writing and copying are very different in the demands they place upon a child, both require the ability to generate letters of the alphabet. To assess this subskill, we decided to include a version of the task used in a number of recent studies (e.g. Berninger, 2001; Berninger *et al.*, 1997; Connelly, Campbell, MacLean, & Barnes, 2006) i.e. writing the alphabet in lower case. Not only does this task offer an insight into how fast the child can generate a sequence of letters which is over-learned (at least in most cases), it is also a task that has been shown to be a good predictor of both compositional fluency and quality (Graham *et al.*, 1997). Unlike the 15-s version used by Berninger (2001), we do not have strict rules for writing style and letter formation. The DASH version of this task is extended to 1 min, providing a score of the number of correctly sequenced lower case letters written per minute. When the test is being administered individually, this task also allows the observer to determine how well the child knows the movement sequences required to form each letter accurately.

Since variants of this task have been extensively used in previous research with demonstrable reliability and validity, there was no need to change its administration. However, because our interest lay more in the motor output component of the task, changes were made to previously employed scoring systems. For example, in contrast to some systems which apply stringent criteria to the judgment of lower and upper case, we give the child the benefit of the doubt in cases where the letter form is identical (e.g. upper and lower case p).

Graphic Speed

Forming even the simplest of letters such as a 'c' or an 'l' consistently requires good control of a pencil or pen, so that a smooth line is produced in the right direction and orientation. The fact that children with writing difficulties find it much more difficult to achieve such consistency has been demonstrated in several studies (Smits-Engelsman & van Galen, 1997; Smits-Engelsman, Niemeijer, & van Galen, 2001; Wann & Kardirkamanathan; 1991). In light of these findings we sought to include a test in the DASH, which provided a measure of how quickly children could produce some very basic movements in an accurate and consistent fashion. In order to avoid any negative effects associated with learning to write, we decided to remove any visual reference to actual letter forms and produce a test which was fun for the children. There are many paper-and-pencil tests in existence, which require the child to trace round or copy shapes (Beery, Buktenica, & Beery, 2004) but in most of these there are no time limits and the shapes to be copied often increase in complexity, reaching a level beyond that required to form the letters of the English language. After experimenting with various tasks which required the child to make both straight and curved lines in a controlled manner, we settled on a variant which requires the child to make a series of crossed lines which intersect within an inner circle and finish within the boundaries of an outer circle. This task yielded a score indicating the number of correctly produced symbols in a 1-min period. By using a task which is easy to explain and constrains the movements to be made, we managed to achieve acceptable inter-rater reliability of .85.

A number of studies have been undertaken which set out to determine whether tests of 'basic' graphic skills can be used to *predict* later handwriting ability. While most of these report positive correlations between test scores and ratings of handwriting ability (Daly, Kelley, & Krauss, 2003; Tseng & Chow, 2000), this is not an invariant finding (Barnett, 1994; Berninger *et al.*, 1992; Maeland & Karlsdottir, 1991) and the amount of variance accounted for is often rather modest. In our case, we do not intend to use our graphic speed test as a predictor of handwriting ability. Instead, we see it as a rough indicator of whether the child has enough pencil control to produce letter shapes consistently over time.

When exploring the potential uses of the DASH, it was clear that some professionals would use the test almost exclusively with individual children, while others would find it beneficial to administer the test to an entire class. As a result, we decided to try to produce a test which could be administered either in a one-to-one setting or as a group activity. Since the Free Writing task seemed to be the one which would be most susceptible to a change in testing circumstances, we explored this issue on this task alone. Fifty-one children from three classes of year 5 children (aged 9–10 years) took part in the study. All completed the Free Writing task individually and in a class of 19–20 children. In order to control for an effect of order of testing, half of the children were tested first individually, then as a group, the other half were tested in the reverse order. A repeated measures analysis of variance on these data showed that there was no effect of group versus individual testing and no effect of order of testing ($F < 1.0$ in both cases). This finding clearly demonstrates that there is no effect of setting on children's performance on the task. Since this outcome has been confirmed informally on other tasks, we suggest that users of the DASH as a whole can be confident that results obtained in an individual setting will be equivalent to those obtained in a group setting and vice-versa.

In sum, the DASH includes five tasks which, taken together, should allow teachers and other professionals working with children to obtain a comprehensive picture of a child's ability to write at speed under different circumstances. Our next step was to gather normative data on these tasks, to determine whether they might yield a meaningful composite score, then to examine the psychometric properties of the test.

Phase 2: The generation of UK norms

The norms for the DASH were gathered as part of a larger project, focusing on the assessment of motor performance in children. This involved the re-standardization of the Movement Assessment Battery for Children, an already established test (Movement ABC, Henderson & Sugden, 1992), as well as the standardization of the DASH. Since the performance test within the Movement ABC (Movement ABC 2; Henderson, Sugden, & Barnett, 2007) is designed for use with children aged 3–16 years and the DASH for children aged 9–16, the sampling procedure adopted had to encompass the whole age range. Once the whole sample had been identified, we then checked that our subsample of 9- to 16-year-olds adequately represented the population.

The sampling procedure

For the project as a whole, a stratified sampling plan was developed to ensure that representative proportions of children from each demographic group in the UK would be included. Data gathered from the 2001 census provided the basis for this stratification. The sampling plan involved a cell structure that identified appropriate numbers of children for each cell, defined in terms of age, gender, geographic region, race/ethnic group, and parental education.

The 2001 census divides the UK into 12 geographic regions (see Table 4). The number of children required for each cell of the sample was calculated in accordance with the proportions of the UK population of under 17-year-olds living in each region. Areas of different population density within each region (rural, suburban, and urban) were chosen on the basis of the general density characteristics of that region. Within the overall cell structure, children were sought who were the closest in demographic characteristics to each cell in terms of gender and for age from 9 years to 16 years 11 months inclusive.

For race/ethnic group, each child was categorized by his or her parents. For sampling purposes, four categories were employed: white, black (including African, Caribbean, and black other), Asian (including Indian, Pakistani, and Bangladeshi), and other (also including Chinese, mixed race, and other). Within each geographic region and for each age group, the intended ratios for ethnic groups were based on the race/ethnicity proportions for persons under the age of 16 in the UK population.

In the UK, data on educational level are particularly unstable across age owing to the very significant changes made in the examination systems over the past 30 years. For this study, therefore, sampling was based only on data from the population aged between 25 and 45 years. Information on educational level was obtained from parental consent forms, where questions were phrased as they appear in the 2001 census. Where the father was living with the child, the average educational level of both parents was used; otherwise the mother's educational level was used.

In sum, a matrix of the 12 geographic regions by 5 parental educational levels for each combination of gender, age, and race/ethnicity formed the basis of the sampling plan. Expected cell frequencies were adjusted to the nearest whole number. Invitations to participate in the project were made by letter and telephone to state schools chosen to be representative of geographic region, social class, population density (rural, suburban and urban) and race/ethnic composition. Within each region several schools were sampled to include children of all appropriate ages and to represent the rural/suburban/urban mix of the region. In all, 34 primary/middle and 22 secondary schools participated in the study.

Parental consent forms and instructions for distributing these for whole classes of children were mailed to participating schools. The consent form requested the child's date of birth, gender, race/ethnicity, and use of English as well as the parents' educational qualifications. Children were tested only if they could speak and understand English. Children receiving special needs support in the school were *not* excluded from testing.

The returned parental consent forms contained the demographic information needed to select children for testing within the sampling plan. The lists of identified children within a school were distributed to examiners, along with a list of possible substitutes in the event of non-availability. Each child was assigned to an examiner, usually an occupational therapist, physiotherapist, or psychologist, who had experience in the use of individually administered tests. Examiners were trained in the administration of the DASH and testing was carried out between November 2005 and July 2006.

Representativeness of the sample

The sample size for the DASH was 546, made up of 254 boys (46.5%) and 292 girls (53.5%). Tables 1–4 show (a) the number of children at each age year (b) the distribution by parental educational level (c) the breakdown by race/ethnic group and (d) the breakdown by geographic region. In Tables 2–4, the number of children included in the DASH standardization sample is shown alongside the expected number for that variable. For each of these stratification variables, Chi square 'goodness of fit' tests were conducted to determine whether the distributions of our sample differed from that expected on the basis of the UK 2001 Census data. On only one variable, geographic region did the sample proportions differ significantly from the proportions specified by the census data ($\chi^2 = 113.19, p < .001$). There were slightly fewer children in Scotland and Northern Ireland than expected and slightly more in the north of England.

Table 1. Number of boys and girls in each age year in the standardization sample

Age (years)	Boys	Girls	Total
9	30	38	68
10	43	41	84
11	33	42	75
12	37	38	75
13	35	47	82
14	28	27	55
15	14	30	44
16	34	29	63
Total	254	292	546

Table 2. Parental educational level: Characteristics of the sample and predicted figures based on the 2001 census

Parental educational level	Sample		2001 census	
	N	%	N	%
0	120	21.9	90	16.4
1	97	17.8	122	22.3
2	149	27.3	143	26.2
3	41	7.5	48	8.8
4	139	25.5	143	26.2
Total	546		546	

Notes. The 2001 census data for parental levels of qualification are based on those for UK adults between the ages of 25 and 45. Educational level data are based on the highest level of qualification and is classified as follows: Level 0: no academic, vocational or professional qualifications; Level 1: one or more 'O'-levels, CSEs or GCSEs (each at any grade), NVQ Level 1, foundation GNVQ; Level 2: five or more 'O'-levels, five or more CSEs (grade 1), five or more GCSEs (grades A–C), school certificate, one or more 'A'-levels or 'AS'-levels, NVQ Level 2, Intermediate GNVQ or equivalents; Level 3: two or more 'A'-levels, Four or more 'AS'-levels, Higher School Certificate, NVQ Level 3, Advance GNVQ or equivalents; Level 4: First Degree, Higher Degree, NVQ levels 4–5, HNC, HND, and/or recognized professional qualification.

Table 3. Race/ethnic group: Characteristics of the standardization sample and predicted figures based on the 2001 census

Race/ethnic group	Sample		2001 census	
	N	%	N	%
White	488	89.4	479	87.6
Black	18	3.3	15	2.8
Asian	16	2.9	31	5.7
Other	24	4.4	21	3.9
Total	546		546	

Notes. The targets are based on the percentage of children under 17 years old who belong to each group according to the 2001 census. The percentage of ethnic minority children in this age group is larger (12.4%) than for the whole population (7.88%).

Table 4. Geographic region. Characteristics of the standardization sample and predicted figures based on the 2001 census

UK region	Sample		Census	
	N	%	N	%
North-east	57	10.4	25	4.6
North-west	86	15.8	54	9.9
Yorkshire and Humberside	56	10.3	65	11.9
East Midlands	47	8.6	46	8.5
West Midlands	53	9.7	50	9.2
East of England	16	2.9	34	6.2
London	31	5.7	55	10.1
South-east	114	20.9	92	16.9
South-west	33	6.0	33	6.0
Wales	26	4.8	22	4.1
Scotland	18	3.3	51	9.3
Northern Ireland	9	1.6	18	3.3
Total	546	100.0	546	100.0

Administration of the DASH tasks

As far as order of administration of the five tasks in the DASH was concerned, it was imperative that the copying in 'best' handwriting came first, as this ensured that the child would receive the appropriate instructions without any awareness of the speed instructions, which would come later. In contrast, it was felt that the Free Writing task should be the last task, so that any fatigue effects that might occur could not have a knock-on effect on the shorter tasks. Pilot work also showed that the positioning of the Graphic Speed task between the initial writing tasks and the lengthier Free Writing task injected a lighter note, and made the children more relaxed prior to undertaking the longest task. Once these constraints had been taken account of the following order emerged as most manageable: (1) Copy Best (2) Alphabet Writing (3) Copy Fast (4) Graphic Speed, and (5) Free Writing. Feedback from testers involved in the pilot work helped us to develop comprehensive guidelines, which enhanced the reliability of the scoring protocol for each task.

Scoring of the DASH tasks

The calculation of standard scores for each task

The distribution of raw scores at each age group was used to derive standard scores for each task, using a mean of 10 and standard deviation of 3 as our metric. This conversion was accomplished by preparing cumulative frequency distributions of raw scores for each age group, normalizing these distributions, and deriving appropriate scaled scores for each task. These standard scores are presented in the test manual.

Derivation of a total DASH standard score

Although the profile of a child's performance on the different tasks of the DASH is informative, a total score which can be used in a summary statement seemed to us essential. Several steps were taken to determine the suitability of computing a total DASH score. Firstly, correlations between the five tasks were examined (see Table 5). This analysis revealed that four were substantially intercorrelated but the fifth, the *Graphic Speed* task had rather low correlations, with values as low as 0.20 in some age groups. Secondly, a principal component analysis was conducted to investigate the factor structure of the five DASH tasks at each age group. In each case, only one strong component emerged, explaining between 57 and 69% of the total variance. Once again, the graphic speed test stood out from the other four tasks, with factor loadings ranging from 0.32 to 0.75 with five under 0.60. Factor loadings on the four remaining tasks were high across all age groups (ranging from .74 to .94), suggesting that they can be regarded as a homogenous set of tasks which can usefully be combined to produce a meaningful total score.

Table 5. Ranges of Pearson correlation coefficients between the DASH tasks

	Copy Best	Copy Fast	Alphabet Writing	Free Writing
Copy Fast	.60–.80			
Alphabet Writing	.53–.67	.62–.75		
Free Writing	.42–.61	.50–.81	.46–.64	
Graphic Speed	.21–.60	.19–.57	.05–.60	.25–.51

The total DASH score was therefore calculated as the sum of the rounded normalized standard scores for the following tasks: Copy Best, Alphabet Writing, Copy Fast, and Free Writing. The total scores have a mean of 40 and a standard deviation (*SD*) of 10. To facilitate interpretation, these total scores were then transformed into a total standard score, which has a normal distribution with a mean of 100 and a *SD* of 15. Percentile ranks for the Total Standard Score are provided in the test manual.

Supplementary information

The DASH total standard score provides the assessor with a stable overall measure of handwriting speed. The standard scores from the component tasks then allow the user to plot a profile of performance which describes the consistency (or inconsistency) of the child's performance across four tasks with different requirements. In addition to these scores, the DASH provides three sources of supplementary information that should be useful to the teacher or therapist working with individual children.

The first supplementary score provides information on the child's ability to increase the tempo of his performance under speed instructions. Here, we have taken the difference between the child's score when asked to write 'in their best writing' and when asked to write quickly in the copying task. Raw scores from the Copy Best and Copy Fast tasks were used to compute a 'Copy Speed Difference' score. Frequency distributions for the difference score in each age group were examined to identify the difference score best representing the 15th percentile. These are provided in the test manual and may be used as cut-off scores indicating a poor response to the speed instruction. For example, if the Copy Speed Difference score for a 12-year-old child is less than three words, this indicates that they may have some difficulty in speeding up. This score is most meaningful if a child has a poor standard score for the Copy Best and/or Copy Fast task.

The second type of supplementary information comes in the form of a profile of a child's performance over the five time periods, which make up the 10 min Free Writing task. This provides valuable information on the child's ability to write continuously and therefore the extent to which the total amount produced can be interpreted as their optimum speed of performance.

The third source of supplementary information is the standard score derived from the *Graphic Speed* task, which was designed to measure the speed at which children could produce simple movements accurately and consistently. Although the analyses reported above suggest that this task taps a different set of skills to the other DASH tasks, it may be very informative when testing children with suspected movement difficulties. In this case, when performance is poor on the main writing tasks it can be helpful to know whether or not this is associated with more general motor control difficulties on the Graphic Speed task.

Psychometric properties of the DASH

Investigation of the reliability and validity of a test is a multifaceted, ongoing process, which should add continuously to what is known about the psychometric properties of the instrument and the uses to which it has been put. Preliminary findings on the reliability and validity of the DASH are presented in the test manual and here we summarize some of the main findings.

As a measure of reliability, we began by calculating the internal consistency of the test using the rounded normalized standard scores. The values for Cronbach's alpha for the total scores ranged from .83 to .89, indicating a high degree of homogeneity of the four main tasks and therefore excellent reliabilities for all eight age groups. These reliability coefficients allowed us to calculate a standard error of measurement value for each age group and for the total sample.

Inter-rater agreement on the DASH was examined by comparing independent ratings of scripts from our normative sample. The intra-class correlations (ICC) were all greater than 0.99 except for the Graphic Speed task (ICC = 0.85). Test–retest reliability was examined in two separate studies, one with children aged 9–10 years and the other with 14- to 15-year-olds. The children were tested twice at an interval of 1–2 weeks. The test–retest correlations from both studies ranged from .50 to .92. The reliability coefficients for the copying tasks were the lowest, although these were above .70 for the older age group. Test–retest reliability was also sufficiently good for the total DASH, with values above .80.

At the same time as investigating the reliability of the DASH, we were able to obtain some preliminary data on its validity. When a test is designed to be used across a wide age range, a basic aspect of validity is the sensitivity of the test scores to changes in age (see Figures 1–3). Figure 1 shows the developmental trends in average performance for 9- to 16-year-old children for the Copy Best and Copy Fast task. This indicates that children appear to have reached their maximum performance level on the Copy Best task at around 15–16 years, whereas on the Copy Fast task there might still be further improvement in subsequent years.

The developmental trends for the Alphabet and Free Writing task are displayed in Figures 2 and 3, respectively. The performance trend for the Alphabet task across the age groups reveals an unusual jump from 12 to 13 years, likely to be the result of a sampling error. Otherwise, the trend shows a continuous improvement in performance which is less pronounced for the older age groups. The shape of the developmental trend in performance for the Free Writing task (see Figure 3) is also nonlinear so there appears to be potential for further growth as the maximum performance level has not yet been reached.

The year on year gain in performance was investigated using ANOVA, and the results indicated significant mean differences between the age groups for all four tasks; Copy Best, $F(7, 538) = 42.06$, $p < .001$, $\eta^2 = .35$, Copy Fast, $F(7, 538) = 46.4$, $p < .001$, $\eta^2 = .42$, Alphabet Writing, $F(7, 538) = 27.46$, $p < .001$, $\eta^2 = .26$, and Free Writing, $F(7, 538) = 56.51$, $p < .001$, $\eta^2 = .42$. The amount of variance explained by the factor 'age groups' (i.e. η^2) suggests that the developmental trends in performance for each task are rather strong. When the Sum of Squares for the factor 'age groups' was broken down into a linear and nonlinear trend component, significant deviations from a linear trend of the means were found for Copy Best, $p = .003$, $\eta^2 = .024$, Copy Fast, $p = .001$, $\eta^2 = .025$, Free Writing, $p = .009$, $\eta^2 = .019$, but not for the Alphabet task, $p = .17$.

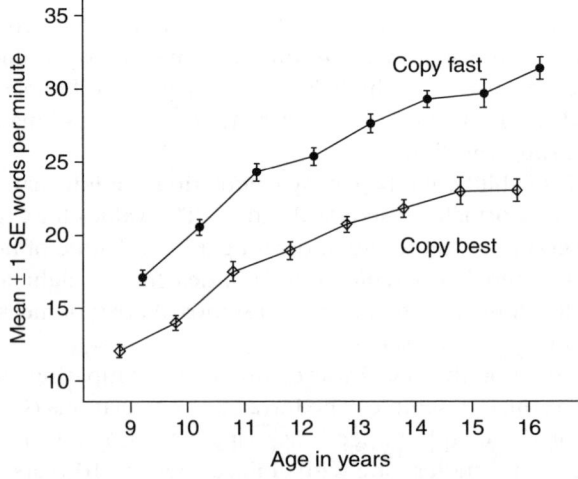

Figure 1. Developmental trends in performance (means + 1 *SE*) for the Copy Best and Copy Fast tasks.

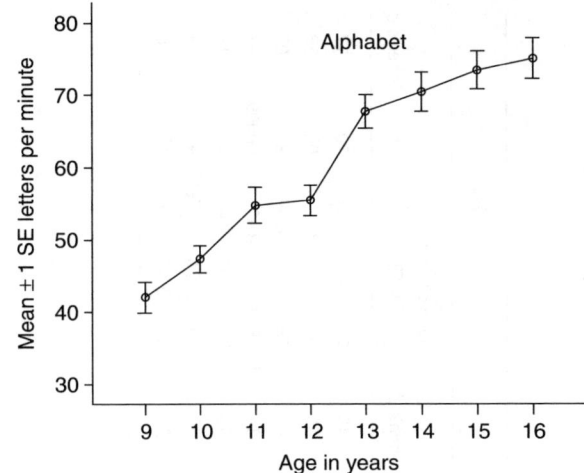

Figure 2. Developmental trends in performance (means + 1 *SE*) for the Alphabet Writing task.

Table 6 shows the results of *post hoc* analyses of the mean difference in performance between adjacent age groups. To prevent inflation of the alpha error due to multiple testing, the critical *p*-value for each *post hoc* comparison was set at $p = .007$ (Bonferroni adjustment). From these tests, it emerged that for the four core DASH tasks significant year on year gains in performance tended to be confined to the younger age groups. For the older age groups, any effects were small and not statistically significant (> 13 years). This is in accordance with the notion of a general growth curve pattern of performance towards a natural upper limit.

Analyses of variance revealed significant main effects for gender on each of the four main DASH tasks, with girls writing faster than boys in all cases. *F* values ranged from 12.04 ($p < .001$) for the Copy Best task to 41.88 ($p < .0001$) for Free Writing. Corresponding effect sizes (Cohen's *d*) ranged from .25 to .42. There was also a significant main effect of gender for the DASH total score ($F(1, 537) = 27.10$,

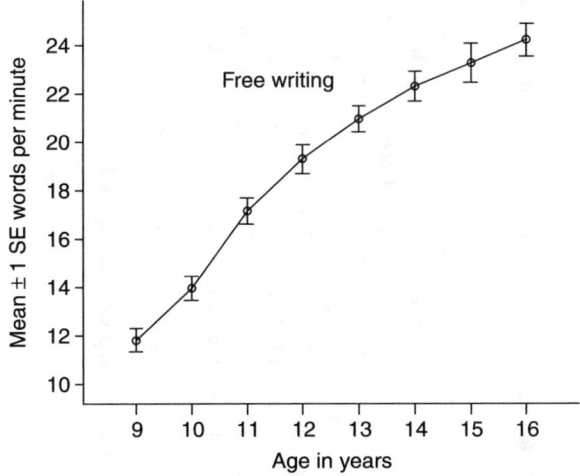

Figure 3. Developmental trends in performance (means + 1 *SE*) for the Free Writing task.

Table 6. Results of the average increase in performance year on year for the DASH tasks

Age groups	Copy Best			Copy Fast			Free Writing			Alphabet		
	Mean difference (95-CI)	p	Cohen's d	Mean difference (95-CI)	p	Cohen's d	Mean difference (95-CI)	p	Cohen's d	Mean difference (95-CI)	p	Cohen's d
9–10	1.93 (0.23–3.58)	.02	.39	3.44 (1.74 – 5.13)	.00007	.65	2.16 (0.61 – 3.72)	.006	.45	5.28 (0.98 – 11.53)	.10	.27
10–11	3.51 (1.9–5.11)	.00002	.69	3.78 (2.12 – 5.43)	.000008	.71	3.17 (1.66 – 4.69)	.00004	.66	7.44 (1.35 – 13.53)	.02	.38
11–12	1.42 (−0.23–3.07)	.09	.29	1.07 (−0.63 – 2.77)	.22	.20	2.15 (−0.60 – 3.70)	.007	.45	0.68 (−5.58 – 6.94)	.83	.03
12–13	1.79 (0.17 – 3.40)	.03	.35	2.25 (0.59 – 3.91)	.008	.42	1.65 (0.13 – 3.18)	.03	.34	12.29 (6.17 – 18.42)	.00009	.63
13–14	1.07 (−0.68–2.83)	.23	.21	1.65 (−0.17 – 3.46)	.08	.31	1.36 (−0.30 – 3.02)	.11	.28	2.72 (−3.96 – 9.41)	.42	.14
14–15	1.19 (−0.86 – 3.23)	.25	.23	0.42 (−1.69 – 2.52)	.70	.08	0.96 (−0.97 – 2.88)	.33	.20	3.00 (−4.76 – 10.76)	.45	.14
15–16	0.06 (−1.9–2.04)	.95	.02	1.69 (−0.35 – 3.73)	.11	.32	0.96 (−0.91 – 2.83)	.32	.20	1.63 (−5.91 – 9.16)	.67	.08

Note. The critical *p*-value is *p* = .007.

$p < .0001$), with a Cohen's d of .51. There were no significant age by gender interactions for any of the tasks.

As noted above, factor analysis provided us with strong evidence of the validity of the total score at all ages. In all age groups, only one substantial factor emerged from the four main DASH tasks, explaining between 68 and 75% of the total variance. The size of the factor loadings was high, clearly justifying the calculation of a total DASH score as the sum of the four task scores.

Data on the discriminative validity of the DASH was gathered in two separate studies. The first showed statistically significant differences ($t > 2$, $df = 22$, $p < .05$) between a group of 11- to 13-year-old children with special educational needs and an age-matched group from the normative sample on all except one of the DASH tasks (Copy Best). The second study showed statistically significant differences on the Free Writing task ($t = 5.29$, $df = 79$, $p < .001$) between a group of students with and without dyslexia (Tait, 2007). Concurrent validity of the DASH has also been examined by comparing performance on the Free Writing task with the writing task used by Allcock (2001). In a group of 15 students with special educational needs the correlation between the two was 0.63 ($p < .05$).

Conclusion

Many professionals in education and in health are called upon to assess children's handwriting, yet the number of psychometrically sound instruments available to them is relatively few. The main objective of the present project was to develop a reliable and valid test of handwriting *speed* that could be used flexibly in a variety of settings, with a broad range of pupils.

When developing a new test, both theoretical and practical issues must be considered in tandem. From a theoretical viewpoint, it is important to start with a clear idea of the construct(s) to be measured then decide how these constructs should be operationalized. Having made these decisions, practical considerations regarding equipment, task presentation, length of the tasks, etc. need to be addressed. Also crucial at this stage, is the purpose(s) of the assessment and the constraints these might place on content.

Over the last 20 years, our understanding of the processes involved in writing has advanced considerably. In parallel, there have been remarkable advances in our understanding of how we control our movements. Unfortunately, however, the merging of these two bodies of knowledge into a comprehensive theory of *writing* which takes adequate account of the production end (i.e. the handwriting end) of the process is yet to come. In the absence of such a theory, our rationale for the DASH leant heavily upon logical analysis of what should and should not be included, supplemented by our own clinical experience and the advice of expert teachers. As noted earlier, teachers were concerned that the writing activities to be included should be 'realistic' and similar to tasks typically performed in the classroom. Their suggestions ranged from simple copying tasks, through dictation, to free writing under different stimulus conditions. Some teachers working with children with difficulties wanted further differentiation of tasks, such as near and far copying, while others wanted to manipulate memory load by comparing copying text with writing the same material to dictation. On the whole, we found their suggestions reassuringly consistent with our own thinking. Once certain practical criteria had been applied, it was not difficult, therefore, to find a set of tasks which not only represented the full range of writing tasks undertaken by children of different ages, but also had some basis in previous research.

The five tasks included in the DASH were considered suitable for children from the age of 9 years onwards. By this time, children in the UK have been in school for at least 4 years and will have had quite varied and extensive writing experience. For most children younger than this, the cognitive demands of the DASH tasks may be disproportionate and the results are therefore difficult to interpret. Our normative data demonstrates that all five DASH tasks are suitable for students at least up to the age of 16 years and that they are sensitive to developmental changes across the age range. Further exploratory work also suggests that the tasks are appropriate for older students in a university setting (Tait, 2007) and at the time of writing we are embarking on a project to extend the norms upwards, to the age of 25 years.

With regard to gender our findings were consistent with previous research on a range of writing tasks. This suggests that there are true gender differences in handwriting, rather than a specific bias in the DASH (Berninger, Graham, Weintraub, & Shafer, 1998; Wallen *et al.*, 1996). Although, it is sometimes suggested that separate test norms should be provided for boys and girls, in our opinion, there would be no justification for this. In terms of writing performance at school (including class work and examinations), one would not want to treat boys and girls who were classified as 'slow writers' differently. The demands placed upon them are the same so it would not be appropriate to introduce a distinction for assessment purposes.

The finding that performance on the DASH was no different in an individual and a group setting suggested that the test was equally suitable for both and prompted us to develop guidelines for group administration. If used for screening, the DASH provides a relatively short group test that can be used to select children whose writing is so poor that they would be unable to cope with the day-to-day demands of school. If used as an individual test, the DASH allows for careful observation of the child face-to-face. Such observation should include not only the product of the child's efforts but also the *way* this product was achieved. These aspects of performance are not formally assessed in the DASH but we provide guidelines for recording such information in the manual (relating, for example, to posture, positioning, and pen grip).

In contrast to some other handwriting tests, the primary focus of the DASH is on speed of handwriting, rather than specifically on aspects of handwriting quality or letter formation. However, we do recognize that handwriting must be legible as well as fast in order to provide the writer with a tool for communication. It is important to note therefore that our measure of speed is based on letters and words that can be deciphered by the reader. Totally illegible letters/words are not included in the score but beyond this, there is no attempt to quantify the degree of 'neatness' or 'legibility' of the writing. However, on the DASH record form we provide prompts which may be used for guidance in describing the quality of handwriting (for example, the shape, size, and slant of letters). These, along with the profile of the child's performance across the five tasks, can help to identify aspects of the writing which may interfere with fluency or legibility. Such information may be useful in deciding how best to help children develop their handwriting skill.

Although more data from the DASH is needed on specific user and client groups, we feel that we have produced an instrument with sufficiently robust psychometric properties to allow its use in the UK immediately. It may be used in primary and secondary school settings to help identify students with slow handwriting, describe their level of performance and to monitor changes over time. Data from the DASH may be helpful when applying for resources for those with handwriting difficulties and also in planning the details of intervention programmes designed to improve handwriting skills. There are various approaches to intervention for students with handwriting difficulties. Sometimes this will involve a movement programme specific to the skill of handwriting (e.g. see Christensen, 2005). At other times, an alternative mode of communication involving information technology (such as word processing or speech recognition) will be considered more appropriate (see MacArthur, 2009).

Acknowledgements

We are grateful to Pearson (formerly Harcourt) Assessment, Action Medical Research, and the Freemason's Grand Charity for funding this work and to Professor John Rust, Professor Susan Golombok, and Dr. Emma Lycett for their expert assistance in sample selection. We thank all the children who participated in this study, our many testers (listed in the DASH manual) and Jessica Falconer and Paula Halsall, who provided useful validity data.

References

Allcock, P. (2001). The understated difficulties of slow handwriting. *Handwriting Today, 1*, 56–60.

Amundson, S. J. (1995). *Evaluation tool of children's handwriting (ETCH)*. Homer, AK: O.T. Kids.

Backhouse, G. (2007). *Dyslexia: Assessing the need for access arrangements during examinations* (3rd ed.). Evesham, UK: Patoss.

Barnett, A. (1994). Graphic skills of clumsy children. *Handwriting Review, 8*, 104–112.

Barnett, A., & Henderson, S. E. (2005). Assessment of handwriting in children with developmental coordination disorder. In D. Sugden & M. Chambers (Eds.), *Children with developmental coordination disorder* (pp. 168–188). London: Whurr Publishers Ltd.

Barnett, A., Henderson, S. E., Scheib, B., & Schultz, J. (2007). *Detailed Assessment of Speed of Handwriting (DASH)*. London: Pearson Assessment.

Barnett, A., Stainthorp, R., Henderson, S., & Scheib, B. (2006). *Handwriting policy and practice in English primary schools*. An exploratory study, London: Institute of Education.

Beery, K. E., Buktenica, N. A., & Beery, N. A. (2004). *The Beery-Buktenica developmental test of visual motor integration* (5th ed.). Los Angeles, CA: Western Psychological Services.

Berninger, V. W. (2001). *Process assessment of the learning (PAL). Test Battery for Reading and writing*. San Antonio, TX: The Psychological Corporation.

Berninger, V. W., Graham, S., Weintraub, N., & Shafer, W. (1998). The development of handwriting speed and legibility in grades 1 through 9. *Journal of Educational Research, 92*, 42–52.

Berninger, V., Vaughan, K., Abbott, R., Abbott, S., Brooks, A., Rogan, L., *et al.* (1997). Treatment of handwriting fluency problems in beginning writing: Transfer from handwriting to composition. *Journal of Educational Psychology, 89*, 652–666.

Berninger, V. W., Yates, C., Cartwright, A., Rutberg, J., Remy, E., & Abbott, R. (1992). Lower-level developmental skills in beginning writing. *Reading and Writing: An Interdisciplinary Journal, 4*, 257–280.

Blöte, A., & Hamstra-Bletz, L. (1991). A longitudinal study on the structure of handwriting. *Perceptual and Motor Skills, 72*, 983–994.

Briggs, D. (1970). The influence of handwriting on assessment. *Educational Research, 13*, 50–55.

Christensen, C. A. (2005). The role of orthographic-motor integration in the production of creative and well-structured written text for students in secondary school. *Educational Psychology, 25*, 441–453.

Connelly, V., Campbell, S., MacLean, M., & Barnes, J. (2006). Contribution of lower-order letter and word fluency skills to written composition of college students with and without dyslexia. *Developmental Neuropsychology, 291,* 175–196.

Connelly, V., & Hurst, G. (2001). The influence of handwriting fluency on writing quality in later primary and early secondary education. *Handwriting Review, 2,* 50–56.

Connor, M. (1995). Handwriting performance and GCSE concessions. *Handwriting Review, 9,* 7–21.

Daly, C. J., Kelley, G. T., & Krauss, A. (2003). Relationship between visual-motor integration and handwriting skills of children in kindergarten: A modified replication study. *American Journal of Occupational Therapy, 57,* 459–462.

Dennis, J. L., & Swinth, Y. (2001). Pencil grasp and children's handwriting legibility during different-length writing tasks. *American Journal of Occupational Therapy, 55,* 175–183.

Dockrell, J., Lindsay, G., Connelly, V., & Mackie, C. (2007). Constraints in the development of writing skills in children with specific language impairments. *Exceptional Children, 73,* 147–164.

Dornan, G., & Taylor, J. (2005). *Which handwriting scheme? A review of currently available publications* (2nd ed.). London: National Handwriting Association.

Dutton, K. P. (1991). Writing under examination conditions: Establishing a baseline. *Handwriting Review, 2,* 80–101.

Geuze, R. H. (2005). Motor impairment in DCD and activities of daily living. In D. Sugden & M. Chambers (Eds.), *Children with developmental coordination disorder* (pp. 19–46). London: Whurr Publishers Ltd.

Graham, S., Berninger, V., Abbott, R., Abbott, S., & Whitaker, D. (1997). Role of mechanics in composing of elementary school students: A new methodological approach. *Journal of Educational Psychology, 89,* 170–182.

Graham, S., Berninger, V., & Weintraub, N. (1998). The relationship between handwriting style and speed and legibility. *Journal of Educational Research, 5,* 290–296.

Hartnell, N. (1994). The teaching of handwriting in primary schools – a current update. *Handwriting Review,* 47–52.

Henderson, S. E., & Green, D. (2001). Handwriting problems in children with Asperger's syndrome. *Handwriting Review, 2,* 65–79.

Henderson, S. E., & Sugden, D. A. (1992). *Movement assessment battery for children.* London: The Psychological Corporation.

Henderson, S. E., Sugden, D. A., & Barnett, A. L. (2007). *Movement assessment battery for children* (2nd ed.). Examiner's Manual, London: Pearson Assessment.

Joint Council for Qualifications (2007). *Regulations and guidance relating to candidates who are eligible for adjustments in examinations GCSE, GCE, GNVQ, AEA, entry level, basic skills & key skills. Access arrangements and special consideration.* London: JCQ.

Killen, H., Dempsey, M., & O'Mahony, P. (2008). *The Irish adaptation of the handwriting speed test.* Dublin: Association of Occupational Therapists of Ireland.

MacArthur, C. A. (2009). Technology and struggling writers: A review of research, *British Journal of Educational Psychology Monograph Series II(6),* 161–177.

Maeland, A. F., & Karlsdottir, R. (1991). Development of reading, spelling and writing skills from third to sixth grade in normal and dysgraphic school children. In J. Wann, A. M. Wing, & N. Sovik (Eds.), *Development of graphic skills* (pp. 179–184). London: Academic Press.

Mandich, A., Miller, L. T., Polatajko, H. J., & Missiuna, C. (2003). A cognitive perspective on handwriting: Cognitive orientation to daily occupational performance (CO-OP). *Handwriting Review, 2,* 41–47.

McHale, K., & Cermak, S. (1992). Fine motor activities in elementary school: Preliminary findings and provisional implications for children with fine motor problems. *American Journal of Occupational Therapy, 46,* 898–903.

Phelps, J., & Stempel, L. (1991). The identification of dyslexia handwriting through graphoanalysis. In J. Wann, A. M. Wing, & N. Sovik (Eds.), *Development of graphic skills* (pp. 191–204). New York: Academic Press.

Phelps, J., Stempel, L., & Speck, G. (1985). The children's handwriting scales: A new diagnostic tool. *Journal of Educational Research, 79*, 46–50.

Qualifications and Curriculum Authority (2003). *Assessment and reporting arrangements. Key stage 3*. London: QCA.

Roaf, C. (1998). Slow hand: A secondary school survey of handwriting speed and legibility. *Support for Learning, 13*, 39–42.

Rosenblum, S., Weiss, P. L., & Parush, S. (2003). Product and process evaluation of handwriting difficulties. *Educational Psychology Review, 15*, 41–81.

Rubin, N., & Henderson, S. E. (1982). Two sides of the same coin: Variations in teaching methods and failure to learn to write. *Special Education: Forward Trends. Research Supplement, 9*, 17–24.

Sackett, D., Straus, S., Richardson, W., Rosenberg, W., & Haynes, R. (2000). *Evidence-based medicine: How to practice and teach evidence based medicine*. London: Churchill Livingstone.

Schmidt, R. A., & Wrisberg, C. A. (2000). *Motor learning and performance*. Champaign, IL: Human Kinetics.

Simner, M. L., Leedham, C. G., & Thomassen, A. J. W. M. (1996). *Handwriting and drawing research. Basic and applied issues*. Amsterdam: IOS Press.

Smits-Engelsman, B. C. M., & van Galen, G. P. (1997). Dysgraphia in children: Lasting psychomotor deficiency or transient developmental delay? *Journal of Experimental Child Psychology, 67*, 164–184.

Smits-Engelsman, B. C. M., Niemeijer, A., & van Galen, G. P. (2001). Fine motor deficiency in children diagnosed as DCD based on poor grapho-motor ability. *Human Movement Science, 20*, 161–182.

Tait, E. (2007). *The assessment of handwriting speed in university students*. Oxford Brookes University, unpublished manuscript.

Torrance, M., & Galbraith, D. (2006). The processing demands of writing. In C. A. MacArthur, S. Graham, & J. Fitzgerald (Eds.), *Handbook of writing research* (pp. 67–82). New York: Guilford Press.

Tseng, M. H., & Chow, S. M. K. (2000). Perceptual-motor function of school-age children with slow handwriting speed. *American Journal of Occupational Therapy, 54*, 83–88.

Tucha, O., & Lange, K. W. (2005). The effect of conscious control on handwriting in children with attention deficit hyperactivity disorder. *Journal of Attention Disorders, 9*, 323–332.

Tucha, L., Tucha, O., Walitza, S., Kaunzinger, I., & Lange, K. W. (2007). Movement execution during neat handwriting. *Handwriting Review, 6*, 44–48.

Waine, L. (2001). Writing speed: What constitutes 'slow'? An investigation to determine the average writing speed of year 10 pupils. In R. Rose & I. Grosvenor (Eds.), *Doing research in special education. Ideas into practice* (pp. 75–87). London: David Fulton Publishers.

Wallen, M., Bonney, M.-A., & Lennox, L. (1996). *The handwriting speed test*. Adelaide: Helios.

Wann, J. P., & Kardirkamanathan, M. (1991). Variability in children's handwriting: Computer diagnosis of writing difficulties. In J. Wann, A. M. Wing, & N. Sovik (Eds.), *Development of graphic skills: Research perspectives and educational implications* (pp. 224–236). London: Academic Press.

Ziviani, J., & Watson-Will, A. (1998). Writing speed and legibility of 7–14-year-old school students using modern cursive script. *Australian Occupational Therapy Journal, 45*, 59–64.

Teaching and Learning Writing, 159–175
BJEP Monograph Series II, 6
© 2009 The British Psychological Society

The British Psychological Society

www.bpsjournals.co.uk

Technology and struggling writers: A review of research

Charles A. MacArthur*

University of Delaware, Newark, New Jersey, USA

Background. Technology applications have the potential to support struggling writers by easing the physical processes involved in writing, helping to manage planning and revising processes, and supporting social interaction and communication.

Aims. This paper aims to illustrate the potential of technology to support struggling writers across a wide range of ages and writing ability.

Arguments. This article reviews research on word processing; assistive technology tools that aid with transcription, such as, spelling checkers, word prediction, and speech recognition; tools that support planning, such as, outlining, prompting, and concept mapping software; and automated essay evaluation.

Conclusions. Closing comments focus on the need for better research on tools to support traditional writing outcomes and for research on the benefits and challenges of new information and communication technologies.

> We arn go to cllams crsmtree fuar. My mom iz meat me a Halloween castom. I ma deing a cll boy. I ma going to gammazizt [Anthony, a 9-year-old boy with dyslexia, transcribed from a handwritten journal entry].

Anthony (a pseudonym) had trouble with both reading and writing. You may experience some of the same difficulty his teacher had in reading his journal entry about his trip to a Christmas tree farm, his cowboy costume, and his gymnastics class. Word prediction software with speech synthesis helped him to write independently in his journal and also to read the teacher's response.

> Students should be able to work. But, the student and his fammly should lay down some ground rules. The parant should alway be included in the disision because they have already lived in that sicuation and for the most part know what is going on. Also, a job is good if there is a money problem and the student is not heping them to servive. Third, it has ben found that colloge student do better with a job than ones just doing colage. People might disagree with this and say

* Correspondence should be addressed to Charles A. MacArthur, School of Education, University of Delaware, 017B Willard Hall, Newark, NJ DE 19716, USA (e-mail: macarthu@udel.edu).

DOI:10.1348/000709909X422954

> what about grades but, it is this writers opinan that a parrant and sudent should sit down and discus that and come to terms with each oter [Marcia, a secondary school student with a learning disability (LD)].

Marcia (pseudonym), who was probably college bound, read with good comprehension, though slowly, but struggled to meet school demands for writing reports and essays. The combination of a planning strategy and speech recognition software enabled her to write longer and better quality papers.

These two cases illustrate the potential of technology to support struggling writers across a wide range of ages and writing ability. In this paper, I focus on struggling writers and how technology can support their performance and learning. The paper begins with a review of research on the most common and most studied application, word processing. It then considers tools that may help students avoid problems in transcription skills of spelling and handwriting and produce text more fluently and accurately, including speech synthesis, word prediction, and speech recognition. Next, I address tools to support planning and revising processes, such as outlining, prompting, and concept mapping software. The next section focuses on automated essay scoring (AES) systems and their potential use in instruction. In a final section, I reflect briefly on ways in which new information and communication technologies may change the skills required to be considered fully literate. New technologies afford both potential benefits and new challenges for struggling writers. In concluding comments, I consider the kinds of research that are needed to help the field make better use of technology to support writing and writing instruction for struggling writers.

At the outset, I would like to discuss a few general issues that affect decisions about which tools are helpful to writers and that can inform decisions about instruction. First, tools in general are designed to help people do tasks with greater proficiency or ease. However, tools also impose new burdens and challenges; they may require training or impose new cognitive challenges. For example, word processing removes concerns with handwriting, but requires typing, which may slow text production and take attention away from the content of writing, unless the student has developed fluent typing skills. Dictating to a tape-recorder removes concerns about the mechanics of writing, but imposes a new burden on working memory because the user cannot see the text already written. Search tools on the Internet greatly expand the amount of information available to use in our writing, but impose tremendous challenges for critical evaluation of information. Whether a new tool will increase or decrease the overall cognitive burden depends on the skills of an individual student and the quality of training. Furthermore, the demands of writing tasks in a given social context and the motivation and cognitive ability of a student determine how much burden is acceptable. Part of the role of research on technological tools is to understand these new burdens and challenges and to improve the tools or design instruction to deal with them.

Second, the value and effects of writing tools, especially for struggling writers, depend very much on how the tools are integrated with instruction. For example, word processors make revising much easier, and proficient writers may use this capability to revise more extensively, differently, and perhaps more effectively. However, for developing writers with limited knowledge of how to evaluate and revise, simply using a word processor will have little effect on their revising processes or results. We have found that students with learning disabilities (LDs) do not revise more or more effectively when using a word processor than when writing by hand (MacArthur & Graham, 1987). However, word processing can remove physical and motivational barriers to revising and make it far easier to teach students to revise effectively (Graham & MacArthur, 1988).

Third, technology changes rapidly, creating challenges in planning and delivering instruction and also in conducting research on its effects. Given the challenges of budgeting and staff development, schools will always be somewhat behind the times in access to technology. Research will never be able to investigate all the applications that are developed. Researchers should attempt to plan studies to get at the underlying design issues, both for the technology and for instruction, rather than focusing on limitations of current tools. For example, in studying the effects of speech recognition software, we included a composing condition in which students dictated to a typist who produced a simultaneous copy in order to examine the effects of dictation without the limitations of current speech recognition software (MacArthur & Cavalier, 2004).

Word processing

Word processors are flexible writing tools that have potential to support the cognitive and social processes involved in writing in many ways. The most often-mentioned capability is the ease of revising, which may encourage writers to revise more and which supports instruction in writing as a recursive process involving cycles of planning, drafting, and revising. For struggling writers, the editing capabilities offer the opportunity to produce texts that are neat and free of errors. Although typing is a new skill that must be learned, it is a major help for students with handwriting problems. Word processors can also support the social processes involved in writing by enhancing opportunities for publication and collaboration. The visibility of the screen and the use of typing facilitate collaborative writing. Students can work together at the computer with a clear, legible view of the developing text without individual handwriting to show who wrote which sentences. Word processing greatly facilitates publication in multiple forms, both print and electronic. Of course, word processing is also an essential component of all other forms of computer support of writing.

A substantial number of studies have investigated the effects of using word processors in combination with writing instruction. Studies have compared writing instruction with versus without word processing across a wide range of ages from elementary school to college. Several meta-analyses have found moderate positive effects on length and quality of writing with larger effects for lower-achieving writers. Bangert-Drowns (1993) reported small to moderate positive effect sizes (ESs) for length (.36) and quality (.27). However, the small ES for quality is better viewed as a moderate ES (.49) for 9 studies of remedial instruction for struggling writers and a near-zero ES (.06) for 11 studies with average writers. Goldberg, Russell, and Cook (2003) found somewhat larger ESs for length (.50) and quality (.41). A recent meta-analysis of 19 studies including those reviewed by the earlier analyses but limited to grades 4–12 (age 9–17) (Graham & Perin, 2007) found an ES of .51 for writers in general but a larger ES of .70 for low achieving writers (overall ES = .55).

An important practical issue regarding use of word processing is typing. Unless students have received typing instruction, the attention required by typing and the slower rate of production may negatively affect the length and quality of writing. Handwriting fluency is correlated with writing quality (Graham, Berninger, Abott, Abott, & Whitaker, 1997), and there is evidence that typing fluency likewise affects quality. Studies with Australian secondary students (Christensen, 2004) and with British primary students (Connelly, Gee, & Walsh, 2007) have found significant correlations between typing speed and quality of typed compositions. In addition, Connelly *et al.* (2007) found that students' typing was slower than their handwriting, and their typed compositions were significantly lower in quality than handwritten ones. In the USA, Russell and his colleagues (Russell, 1999; Russell & Haney, 1997) have done a series of studies comparing handwriting and word processing on writing tests and have consistently found effects of typing skill. For example, Russell (1999) found that the effect of word processing depended on typing skill; it had a positive effect on essay quality for secondary students with above average typing speed $(20 + wpm)$ $(ES = +0.5)$ but a negative effect for students with below average typing $(ES = -0.4)$. These findings suggest that students need to learn to type with relative fluency if they are to make effective use of word processing.

Research on the effects of word processing on revising is mixed. In their meta-analysis, Goldberg *et al.* (2003) found six studies that investigated effects on revising; although the results could not be aggregated because they used different measures, all six studies reported that students who used word processing did more revising. It is not clear, however, how effectively they revise. Cochran-Smith, in her 1991 review of word processing in elementary classes, found more surface revision. MacArthur and Graham (1987) asked students with LDs to draft and revise compositions with handwriting and word processing without any special instruction. They found no differences in the amounts and types of revision; the only difference was that word processing led to more revisions *during* the first draft and handwriting led to more *between* drafts. Most revisions were surface revisions that had no impact on writing quality. Word processing makes revising easier, but of course, it does not teach students how to evaluate and revise effectively.

Word processing in combination with instruction in revising can be effective in helping struggling writers learn to revise in ways that improve the quality of their writing. MacArthur and his colleagues explored this possibility in three related studies. The first study evaluated a revising strategy for individual students (Graham & MacArthur, 1988). The other two studies investigated peer-revising strategies with instruction provided by research assistants (Stoddard & MacArthur, 1993) and by teachers in classrooms (MacArthur, Schwartz, & Graham, 1991). In all three studies, instruction resulted in increases in the amount and quality of revisions and in improvements in the quality of the final drafts. The results demonstrate that specially designed instruction can help students take advantage of the power of word processing to improve revision. The results do not demonstrate that the word processor is essential to the instruction, but my experience helping teachers implement revising instruction without word processing indicates that there is substantial student resistance to frequent revision when recopying is needed.

Spelling checkers, to no one's surprise, have proven helpful to students who have difficulty with spelling. Middle school students with LD (ages 12–14) corrected 37% of their spelling errors with a spell checker compared to 9% unaided in one study (MacArthur, Graham, Haynes, & De La Paz, 1996). College students with LD (McNaughton, Hughes, & Clark, 1997) fixed 60% of their errors using a spelling checker compared to 11% with handwriting. What are more instructionally relevant than the overall effect are the limitations of spelling checkers. The most prominent limitation is that they fail to detect errors that are some other word, including homonyms (e.g. 'bred' for 'bread') and other errors (e.g. 'were' for 'where'). The spelling checker misses my typo 'form' for 'from'. This limitation explained about half of the uncorrected errors in the MacArthur *et al.*'s (1996) study. Students need to learn how common this problem is and learn to look for these types of errors when proofreading. The other common limitation is that, even when it does flag errors, the spelling checker does not always include the correct word in its list of suggestions, especially when words are badly misspelled. Students can be taught to try alternate, perhaps phonetic, spellings when the desired word does not appear. Other problems, that were less common in the MacArthur *et al.* study, include the checker flagging proper nouns and slang as errors, and students not recognizing the correct word in the list of suggestions.

Some word processors designed for use by students have special features to overcome these problems. A homonym checker flags all common homonyms. Adjustable size dictionaries can help avoid some of the problem with missing errors that are other real words. Some systems include speech synthesis to pronounce words in the suggestion list. Some of these tools may be helpful for young students or those with severe spelling problems.

An important practical issue is access. If students are to gain the full benefit from word processing, it is important that they have sufficient access to complete the entire composing process from first draft to publication on the word processor. Drafting with pencil and paper and then typing on the word processor is difficult for students without touch-typing skills. Potential solutions include computer labs devoted to writing or sets of inexpensive laptops designed just for word processing.

Word processors with spelling checkers can offer significant help to struggling writers in translating their words into text fluently and accurately. In the next few sections, I consider three tools that go beyond word processing to offer further support in transcription – speech synthesis, word prediction, and speech recognition.

Transcription support: Speech synthesis, word prediction, and speech recognition

Speech synthesis

Speech synthesis, or text-to-speech, software converts text into speech. It is the key component of screen reading programs designed to support reading for individuals with visual or reading disabilities. It is also included in several word processing programs designed for young children or students with literacy problems. The rationale for using speech synthesis for writing support is that individuals with poor reading skills may more readily detect errors in their writing by listening to the text read to them than by reading. Reading skill is clearly a component of effective revising ability (Hayes, 2004). They may notice errors in grammar or pick up some of those 'other real word' spelling errors that the spelling checker missed.

Unfortunately, relatively little research has investigated whether speech synthesis can support editing. In an early study (Borgh & Dickson, 1992), elementary students without disabilities used a word processor with editing prompts; for half of the students, the word processor included speech synthesis. No differences were found in amount of revision or on the length and quality of papers. In a study of college students with LD (Raskind & Higgins, 1995), students detected more errors with speech synthesis than without, although the difference was not large (35% vs. 25% detection), and data on actual correction of errors was not reported. Also, error detection was lower than might be expected with a spelling checker.

Thus, research does not provide much guidance in this area, though it seems that the effects of speech synthesis on editing are modest. It can, however, provide meaningful support for fluent reading and comprehension (for a review, see MacArthur, Ferretti, Okolo, & Cavalier, 2001). In writing, it may be used in combination with other programs. For example, one might use it after running the spelling checker to help identify additional errors, or after using speech recognition software to find errors in dictation. It is also worth noting that the quality of the speech synthesis may make an important difference; newer software generally has more comprehensible speech.

Word prediction

Word prediction software 'predicts' what word the user intends to type based on the initial letters, syntax, common word pairs, and individual user history, with more sophisticated programs using more predictive cues. Predictions are presented in a list for the user to select. For example, if I type 'My f', the software might predict 'friend', 'family', and 'first'. If I had typed 'My best f', it might pick up the common phrase 'best friend' and put 'friend' first in the list of predictions, or recognize that a noun was needed and not include 'first' in the list. It was initially developed for individuals with physical and communication disabilities to reduce the number of keystrokes needed to communicate. However, it has also been marketed and studied for individuals with spelling problems. Even poor spellers can often correctly spell the first few letters of a word. Recent software even includes flexible spelling that works like a spelling checker to include possible phonetic spellings; for example, 'fo' might produce 'phone' in the list of choices.

Newell *et al.* (1992) reported a series of case studies of word prediction use by 17 students with a range of disabilities, including cerebral palsy, visual and hearing impairments, developmental delay, and language and LDs. Of the six students that had mild to moderate language and LDs, five showed improvements in accuracy of spelling, quantity of writing, and motivation.

The example at the beginning of this article of Anthony's journal entry is taken from a series of studies I did on word prediction with upper elementary school students with LD and severe spelling problems (MacArthur, 1998, 1999). Both studies used small numbers of students in a multiple baseline or alternating treatments design. Students wrote in dialogue journals back and forth to their teachers. Across the two studies, six of the eight students showed dramatic differences in the spelling and legibility of their writing between word prediction and handwriting or word processing. During baseline, their writing ranged from 55 to 85% legible words (i.e. readable in isolation) and 42 to 75% correctly spelled words. With word prediction, all six students increased their percentage of both legible and correctly spelled words to above 90%. A more recent study (Handley-Moore, Deitz, Billingsley, & Coggins, 2003) with similar students found similar effects; two of three students made substantial improvements in legibility and spelling.

In addition to supporting the overall effects of word prediction, these studies shed light on important design issues such as dictionary size, prediction algorithms, and complexity of the interface. If the dictionary is too small, it will not have the needed vocabulary; if it is too large, there may be too many suggestions and the user may have to type more letters before getting an accurate prediction. More sophisticated prediction algorithms that use syntax and words and phrases used frequently by individual users make a difference. The match between the dictionary size and the demands of the writing task is also important. Two strategies have been used to manage the problem of dictionary size. The first is to offer dictionaries of different sizes for the user to choose. The second is to offer a relatively small basic dictionary, plus topical dictionaries that can be chosen depending on the writing topic. Important issues in interface design include how many choices to offer, speech synthesis support for selection, and phonetic spelling options. The best software offers multiple options for the users to tailor it to their needs.

Overall, word prediction offers substantial support to students with severe spelling problems. As with any tool, there are new burdens as well. Students need to attend to the list of suggestions and make choices, which can slow text production. For students who make relatively few errors, it is probably better to follow the common recommendation to ignore spelling during drafting and use a spelling checker later. Students who have physical disabilities or fine motor problems that make typing difficult might also benefit. A final intriguing but unstudied possibility is that the topical dictionaries might be used in combination with instruction to improve students' vocabulary by supporting their use of new words in writing.

Speech recognition

For the purpose of avoiding the difficulties and time required by transcription, dictation would seem ideal. Dictation is common in many business environments as a way to speed production of routine memos and letters, and some famous authors have depended on dictation. Winston Churchill, who supported his life-style for many years through extensive writing, produced most of his work by dictating in the wee hours of the morning to a team of two secretaries who typed up his work for later revision (Manchester, 1988). For students with LD and other struggling writers, dictation generally enables them to produce longer and better compositions than they could produce with handwriting (Graham, 1990; MacArthur & Graham, 1987; Reece & Cummings, 1996).

Speech recognition software makes dictation possible without the support of another person. It has one advantage over regular dictation to a tape-recorder or secretary – the user can see the text as it is written. This permits writers to review the text that was just written as they plan the next phrase, sentence, or paragraph. Reece and Cummings (1996), in an elegant series of studies, demonstrated the advantage of being able to see the text. They compared handwriting, normal dictation to a tape-recorder, and a simulated speech recognition system – actually a typist producing text on a screen visible to the writer. For average writers, seeing the text on the screen resulted in better text than normal dictation. However, the advantage disappeared when students were instructed to pre-plan their essays, indicating that the visible text was most important for on-line planning. For poor writers, both dictation conditions were superior to handwriting regardless of planning, indicating that the burden of transcription was interfering with their writing.

Current speech recognition systems do not, however, work as well as this simulated system. First, despite improvements over the past decade, accuracy is still limited. Reviews have reported accuracy for trained adults ranging from 90 to 98% (Alwang, 1998). I typically get about 97% accuracy, and most errors are in small words and word endings that are articulated carefully in normal speech. MacArthur and Cavalier (2004), working with students, ages 15–16, found an average accuracy of 87% after about 2 h of training. Second, new cognitive burdens and attentional demands are imposed. Users must articulate carefully, dictate punctuation and formatting, and monitor the accuracy of the text. Third, they need to learn new editing methods. The system never produces misspelled words, so students need to learn to look for incorrect words. Most speech recognition software includes a playback feature and/or speech synthesis to help users identify discrepancies between the dictated and recognized text.

A few studies have investigated speech recognition with writers with LD. (There are also some studies of adults using speech recognition on work tasks [e.g. Leijten, 2007].) The earliest study (Higgins & Raskind, 1995) was with college students with LD, who face demands to produce substantial amounts of text with high accuracy. Students composed essays via dictation to a human, dictation using speech recognition, or unassisted (i.e. word processing or handwriting at the student's choice). Quality ratings were higher with speech recognition than in the unassisted condition. Quinlan (2004) trained middle-school students (ages 11–14) with and without problems in writing fluency to use speech recognition to a criterion of 80% accuracy when reading a passage. Students then wrote brief narrative papers within a 10-min time limit using handwriting and speech recognition. The writers with fluency problems, but not the average writers, produced longer texts with fewer errors using speech recognition. However, quality did not differ significantly.

MacArthur and Cavalier (2004) studied speech recognition as a potential test accommodation for students with LD. Secondary students (ages 14–15) with and without LD received 6 h of training in speech recognition and a simple planning routine for writing persuasive essays similar to those used on high-stakes tests. They composed essays in three conditions: handwriting, dictation to a person, and speech recognition. Students with LD made fewer errors using speech recognition than handwriting. More important, they produced essays of higher quality with speech recognition than handwriting, and even better essays when dictating to a person. No differences in quality were found for students without LD. The results support the use of speech recognition and dictation in general as a test accommodation because these supports helped students with LD to circumvent their disability but gave no advantage to average writers.

Further research is needed to explore the potential of speech recognition. Research has not investigated the effects of long-term use of speech recognition that would provide users time to adapt to its special demands. The practical implications of using speech recognition also deserve study. It is difficult to use in a school setting because it requires a relatively quiet environment, and it is probably socially unacceptable to dictate in public.

Support for planning and revising

A variety of computer tools are available that are designed to help writers plan and revise. In this section, I will discuss two categories of programs: first, prompting programs support writers by asking them a series of questions or presenting reminders to engage in various processes during planning, drafting, and/or revising. Prompting programs were among the earliest types of writing software. One of the earliest studies of word processing on microcomputers, as they were called then, looked at the effects of a programme that provided generic prompts to support revision (Daiute, 1986). Second, concept-mapping (CM) software permits writers to draw concept maps, or graphic organizers or semantic webs, on the computer where they are more flexible than paper organizers. Some concept mapping software (e.g. Inspiration) will automatically generate an outline from the map.

Prompting programs

Theoretical and empirical support for prompting methods can be found in research on procedural facilitation (Bereiter & Scardamalia, 1987). For example, providing students with generic prompts to evaluate individual sentences or to consider overall organization has been found to enhance revision and overall quality of writing (Bereiter & Scardamalia, 1987; De La Paz, Swanson, & Graham, 1998; Graham, 1990). As an additional example, giving students goal-setting prompts to consider audience has been found to enhance planning and increase overall quality (Ferretti, MacArthur, & Dowdy, 2000; Midgette, Haria, & MacArthur, 2008).

However, the research on computer-provided prompts has been mixed. The writing partner (Zellermayer, Salomon, Globerson, & Givon, 1991), a relatively sophisticated example of prompting software, provided metacognitive prompts based on cognitive models of writing during planning, drafting, and revising stages. The prompts were interactive in that later questions were based on students' answers to earlier questions. A study with secondary school students produced mixed results. Students were randomly assigned to one of three groups: writing partner with solicited guidance (SG) or with unsolicited guidance (USG), or regular word processing control (C). The only difference between the two experimental groups was that the USG group saw the *drafting* prompts at random intervals without asking for them, whereas the SG group checked the prompts when they wished. Planning and revising support were identical, and both groups accessed the prompts equally often. Pre- and post-test essays were written by hand without support in order to test for transfer. Students in the USG group earned higher quality ratings both on essays written with support and on handwritten post-test essays than the other two groups, which did not differ from each other. The reason for the difference between the SG and USG groups was not clear. Unfortunately, no further research was conducted with this tool to replicate or extend the findings.

In other research, Reynolds and Bonk (Bonk & Reynolds, 1992; Reynolds & Bonk, 1996) studied a programme that provided revising prompts with middle school students (ages 11–14) and college students. With middle school students (Bonk & Reynolds, 1992), they found no effect on revision or quality on essays written with programme support or on transfer essays. Using the same programme with college students (Reynolds & Bonk, 1996), they found increases in revision and writing quality on essays written with programme support; no transfer essays were written. One possible explanation, other than the age of the students, is that the college students had just received 9 weeks of instruction in revision as a generative and evaluative process, so that the prompts may have functioned to remind them to use what they had learned.

Only one study of prompting software was conducted with struggling writers, specifically students with LD (Englert, Wu, & Zhao, 2005). The on-line system prompted students to generate a title, topic sentences, details, and a conclusion for a personal narrative. Personal narratives written with support were better organized and contained more relevant content. The study did not test for transfer to papers written without support.

The rationale for prompting programs is reasonable and supported by research on non-computer procedural facilitation. The mixed results indicate that the approach is promising but that effects depend on specific instructional design features. My own perspective is that prompting programs should be used in combination with instruction on strategies such that the prompts are reminding students to use processes they have already learned. This view is consistent with the general principle that the effects of technology on writing depend on how it is integrated with instruction.

Concept mapping

Concept maps are visual representations of relationships among different ideas using nodes and links. Concept maps and other kinds of graphic organizers are widely used in content area and writing instruction. A recent meta-analysis of 55 studies (Nesbit & Adesope, 2006) found the use of concept maps to be associated with increased knowledge of content in the areas of science, psychology, statistics, and nursing. Graphic organizers representing common text structures have been used effectively in many planning strategies (Graham, 2006). Thus, there is good reason to expect that CM software might help writers to generate and organize ideas.

Electronic concept maps offer greater flexibility than paper-and-pencil versions. First, electronic maps are easily revised and expanded. New ideas can be inserted and ideas can be grouped into different categories easily. Electronic maps can be expanded beyond the reasonable limits of paper maps. In addition, electronic maps can be displayed with details hidden to view the organization of the higher-level topics. Second, electronic maps can be automatically converted into outlines. One of the challenges of using concept maps in writing is developing a linear written product from a map with multiple links. Conversion of the map to an outline provides a linear organization; the sequence of that organization can then be altered as needed. Third, the contents of the map or outline can be directly transferred to a rough draft in a word processor.

Few studies have explored the use of CM software. Anderson-Inman and Horney (1998) have conducted a number of descriptive and qualitative studies of concept mapping as a tool to support reading and studying, though not specifically for writing. Sturm and Rankin-Erickson (2002) investigated the effects of concept mapping on the writing of middle school students with LD. Students received instruction in mapping with paper-and-pencil and electronic mapping and then wrote essays under three conditions: no mapping, hand mapping, and computer mapping. Length and quality of essays increased from pre- to post-test, but no differences were found among the three conditions at post-test.

My colleagues and I (Klein, MacArthur, & Najera, 2007) have just completed an experimental study of concept mapping with fifth-grade students (age 10). We used Inspiration software with a template we created for compare-contrast writing. Students were randomly assigned to three groups. All groups received instruction in the characteristics of compare-contrast writing and practice in planning and writing two essays. The CM group was taught to use a template for compare-contrast writing to generate a map, which they printed and used while writing the essay on a word processor. The CM plus transfer group used the template to generate a map, converted the map to an outline, wrote complete topic and detail sentences in the outline mode, and transferred the outline to a word processor where they cleaned up the format and sentences and added further detail. The control group (C) learned to brainstorm ideas on the word processor and then wrote the essay. Both an essay written with concept-map support and a transfer essay written via handwriting without mapping support were scored for text structure elements of compare-contrast writing (e.g. comparisons, topic sentences with categories) and for overall quality. Preliminary analysis shows that students in both CM groups received higher text structure scores than the control on the supported post-test. Differences in overall quality were in the predicted direction but not statistically significant. No transfer effects were found, which is not surprising given the brevity of the instruction.

Further research is needed to explore the effectiveness of concept mapping software and to develop effective instructional routines for using it. A variety of important instructional issues need to be addressed. One issue is how to design templates for concept maps. Another is how to make use of the capability of automatically generating outlines or rough drafts from concept maps. Overall, an important issue is how much and what type of instruction is needed to help students with LD make effective use of concept mapping. A larger issue is the connection between reading and writing. Particularly in the case of expository writing forms such as compare-contrast, it makes sense to teach reading and writing together. We studied compare-contrast writing in isolation in order to have experimental control, but in a real classroom, students would write compare-contrast essays based on their reading with the purpose of enhancing their content knowledge. CM software might support reading comprehension and the process of gathering information to use in writing.

Automated essay scoring

AES systems are able to reliably score the overall quality of essays; some also provide reliable analytic scores of separate traits and evaluate content. An extensive body of research demonstrates that AES systems are as reliable as human raters (for a review, see Shermis, Burstein, & Leacock, 2006). My focus in this article is on recently developed instructional programs that use AES to give students feedback on their writing and make recommendations for revision. The rationale for using AES in instructional programs is straightforward. Teacher feedback has a positive impact on the revising and writing of students (Beach & Friedrich, 2006). However, giving feedback on writing is a time-consuming task for teachers, which limits the amount and immediacy of feedback that students receive. Systems using AES can provide nearly instant feedback as often as students request it. In addition, systems can store student writing and evaluations and produce reports for teachers on student progress, which can be used to inform instruction.

Very little research has been conducted to date on programs that provide automated feedback. Two studies have examined classroom use of programs. Grimes and Warshauer (2006) conducted a case study of nine language arts teachers in five secondary schools using two different programs. Teachers and administrators had positive opinions about the impact of the programs on motivation and on revision. However, they did not use them much. Even in the schools with laptops for every student, students wrote on average only 2.38 papers on the system in a full year. Furthermore, teachers seldom scheduled time for revision. Only 28% of papers were revised at all, and most revisions were minor changes in mechanics. Students also liked the programs even though only half of them thought the scores were accurate; they liked the rapid feedback and the low-stakes nature of the scores. Attali (2004) analyzed about 33,000 essays submitted to one company's system over a year. Of these, only 29% were revised. Of the revised essays, final drafts compared to initial drafts improved in quality, length, and errors. The results indicate rather limited use of the system for revision, but provide some support that using it is helpful to students, at least for papers that were revised.

Three studies with sixth- and eighth-grade students (ages 11–13) have investigated the effects of a programme to support learning to write summaries, *Summary Street*

(Franzke, Kintsch, Caccamise, Johnson, & Dooley, 2005; Steinhardt, 2001; Wade-Stein & Kintsch, 2004). Learning to write summaries is a valuable skill that can enhance reading comprehension and writing (Graham & Perin, 2007). *Summary Street* uses latent semantic analysis to evaluate the semantic content of writing and how well it matches criterion texts. The programme evaluates student summaries and provides feedback on how well the summaries cover each section of a text, whether they meet length requirements, and which sentences might be redundant or irrelevant. *Summary Street* was compared to writing on a word processor that only gave feedback on length and spelling. In all three studies, students' summaries were judged higher in quality and content coverage. Franzke *et al.* (2005) found that the gains transferred to better performance on items from a high-stakes reading comprehension test that required writing summaries but not to other types of comprehension items.

The use of AES in instruction to provide formative feedback to students is a promising area of development. More research is needed on the effects of the systems and on what schools and teachers need to do to take advantage of their potential.

New directions

The research reviewed in this article has focused primarily on the use of technology to support the development of traditional writing skills. Word processing, word prediction, speech recognition, concept mapping tools, and automated feedback may be of great help to struggling writers in producing written compositions. Researchers can design studies to investigate whether these tools and appropriate instruction result in better writing. However, technology has a broader impact on literacy in the development of new environments for writing and new forms of written communication, which may be more important in the long run but which are more complex to study.

Some scholars argue that technology will transform the nature of literacy and literacy practices (see the volume by Reinking, McKenna, Labbo, & Kieffer, 1998). New electronic forms of text differ from traditional printed text in several ways that affect both the social and cognitive processes involved in literacy (MacArthur, 2006). First, electronic texts integrate multiple media, including graphics, sound, and video, in ways that transform how meaning is represented. Second, the non-linear nature of hypertext means that authors must anticipate the needs of readers who will read only parts of the text or read parts in different orders and who will need direction in navigating the text. The organizational demands are different. Third, the Internet provides access to an enormous amount of information, which requires the development of skills in information search, critical evaluation, and citation of sources (Coiro & Dobler, 2007). The process of gathering information for writing is dramatically changed. Finally, and perhaps most important, the Internet has introduced dramatically new social contexts for writing, such as blogs, zines, personal web pages, simulated worlds, and social networking sites. In the classroom, classroom Internet projects offer access to audiences beyond the teacher and classmates.

A growing body of qualitative research has investigated the use multimedia composing software or Internet communication technology, though few studies have focused on struggling writers. I mention just a few examples. Garner and Gillingham (1996) studied the classrooms of six teachers who were pioneers in use of the Internet for intercultural communication projects. The teachers changed their teaching methods to devote more effort to inquiry projects that drew on student interests and authentic problems. The projects enhanced motivation for writing and encouraged children to attempt to understand cultural differences and consider audience needs. Karchmer (2001) studied 13 teachers who made extensive use of the Internet. The elementary teachers regularly published their students' writing on class web pages, in collaborative projects with other schools, or at on-line writing sites. The secondary teachers used the Internet more for access to information than for publication of student work. Erickson and Lehrer (1998) studied the use of hypermedia composing software for collaborative inquiry projects in middle school (ages 12–14) social studies classes. They described the development of composing skills, including research skills, planning and management, audience consideration, organization, presentation, and evaluation.

Few studies involved struggling writers. Ferretti and Okolo (1996) studied multimedia inquiry projects in social studies in elementary classrooms (ages 9–11) team taught by special and general education teachers. In two studies, they found that students' knowledge of historical events increased and that students with LD learned as much as their non-disabled peers.

New technologies for literacy afford both potential benefits and new challenges for struggling writers. The incorporation of multiple media may be especially appropriate for struggling writers because it offers multiple ways for them to learn and demonstrate their knowledge rather than relying solely on reading and writing. The opportunity to write for diverse audiences and in a variety of informal modes may be especially motivating for students who struggle with school writing. At the same time, new skills will be required for students to access information from the Internet and learn to integrate multiple media in compositions. For example, the simple process of scanning Internet documents to determine their relevance may be challenging for students with weak reading fluency.

Concluding comments

In closing, I would like to offer a few reflections on the state of research and the state of practice. On one hand, practice has not kept up with research; the few reliable findings of research have not widely affected classroom practice. For example, a substantial amount of research indicates that word processing in combination with instruction has a moderate positive impact on students' writing, especially for struggling writers. Research also indicates that typing skill is important to realize the benefits of word processing. Yet, relatively few schools provide sufficient access to technology for students to use word processing throughout the writing process from drafting to publication, and many schools do not provide adequate typing instruction. In the USA, many states do not permit the use of word processing on high-stakes tests, despite research showing that students who are familiar with word processing and type well are disadvantaged by having to write by hand.

On the other hand, the research base is very limited, and the quality of the existing research is uneven. The only conclusion with extensive research support is that word processing can enhance writing instruction, especially for weak writers. Smaller numbers of studies support the use of assistive technology, such as word prediction and speech recognition, with students with transcription difficulties, but the research does not yet tell us which students will benefit or how these applications will work in typical school settings. The research on software to support planning and revising shows promise, but the findings are either mixed or limited, and little research has focused on struggling writers. Research on using AES to provide repeated feedback to students is just beginning. Considerable research has investigated the impact of hypermedia on reading but less has addressed the problems and potentials of composing hypermedia. Research on using the Internet in literacy instruction has included both reading and writing activities, but most of the work to date consists of case studies of innovative teachers.

Part of the problem is that research has difficulty keeping up with the development of new applications, even those designed for use in schools, much less those used in the wider society. In some areas, such as the use of the Internet for cross-classroom projects, much of what we know as a field has come from case studies of pioneering teachers (Garner & Gillingham, 1996; Karchmer, 2001). In other areas, commercial developers have led the way, producing promising but as yet untested applications like the use of AES to provide feedback to students. Non-school applications like e-mail, text messaging, and social networking sites may have even greater impact on students' literacy development. Researchers need to be selective in making decisions about the types of research that will be most productive in improving education.

One promising research trend is the increasing use of design studies to develop effective educational approaches in classroom settings (Kelly, 2003). Design studies avoid global questions about the effects of particular technologies in favour of questions about how to design methods that integrate technology with instruction in ways that function effectively and efficiently in real classrooms. The emphasis is on instructional design, both of the technological tools and of the details of instruction and classroom interaction. Typically, several rounds of implementation are conducted while collecting a wide range of evidence, including teacher and student perspectives, classroom interaction, and learning outcomes. Researchers, developers, and teachers work as partners to develop integrated instructional approaches. Transfer to other classrooms is facilitated by the rich examples of implementation from the design studies. Professional development can be focused on implementation of the integrated package of technology and instruction.

Although technology has great promise as a support for struggling writers, relatively little research has been completed. More research is needed, both design research to refine instructional methods and rigorous effectiveness research to justify the substantial investments required to use technology in the schools. In the meantime, teachers need to make the best decisions they can, based on tentative research and their own experience, and they need to assess whether instruction is working in their setting. Given the important role that teachers have taken in using technology in classrooms, researchers should work together with practitioners to advance our understanding.

References

Alwang, G. (1998, October 20). Speech recognition: Finding its voice. *PC Magazine* Online, retrieved from http://www.zdnet.com/pcmag/features/speech98/index.html

Anderson-Inman, L., & Horney, M. A. (1998). Transforming text for at-risk readers. In D. Reinking, M. C. McKenna, L. D. Labbo, & R. D. Kieffer (Eds.), *Handbook of literacy and technology* (pp. 15–44). Mahwah, NJ: Erlbaum.

Attali, Y. (2004). *Exploring the feedback and revision features of criterion.* Paper presented at the National Council on Measurement in Education (NCME), San Diego, CA, USA, April 12–16, 2004.

Bangert-Drowns, R. L. (1993). The word processor as an instructional tool: A meta-analysis of word processing in writing instruction. *Review of Educational Research, 63*(1), 69–93.

Beach, R., & Friedrich, T. (2006). Response to writing. In C. A. MacArthur, S. Graham, & J. Fitzgerald (Eds.), *Handbook of writing research* (pp. 222-234). New York: Guilford.

Bereiter, C., & Scardamalia, M. (1987). *The psychology of written composition*. Hillsdale, NJ: Erlbaum.

Bonk, C. J., & Reynolds, T. H. (1992). Early adolescent composing within a generative-evaluative computerized prompting framework. *Computer in Human Behavior, 8*, 39-62.

Borgh, K., & Dickson, W. P. (1992). The effects on children's writing of adding speech synthesis to a word processor. *Journal of Research on Computing in Education, 24*(4), 533-544.

Christensen, C. A. (2004). Relationship between orthographic-motor integration and computer use for the production of creative and well structured written text. *British Journal of Educational Psychology, 74*(4), 551-565.

Cochran-Smith, M. (1991). Word processing and writing in elementary classrooms: A critical review of related literature. *Review of Educational Research, 61*, 107-155.

Coiro, J., & Dobler, E. (2007). Exploring the online reading comprehension strategies used by sixth-grade skilled readers to search for and locate information on the Internet. *Reading Research Quarterly, 42*, 214-257.

Connelly, V., Gee, D., & Walsh, E. (2007). A comparison of keyboarded and handwritten compositions and the relationship with transcription speed. *British Journal of Educational Psychology, 77*, 479-492.

Daiute, C. A. (1986). Physical and cognitive factors in revising: Insights from studies with computers. *Research in the Teaching of English, 20*, 141-159.

De La Paz, S., Swanson, P. N., & Graham, S. (1998). The contribution of executive control to the revising of students with writing and learning difficulties. *Journal of Educational Psychology, 90*, 448-460.

Englert, C. S., Wu, X., & Zhao, Y. (2005). Cognitive tools for writing: Scaffolding the performance of students through technology. *Learning Disabilities Research and Practice, 20*, 184-198.

Erickson, J., & Lehrer, R. (1998). The evolution of critical standards as students design hypermedia documents. *Journal of the Learning Sciences, 7*, 351-386.

Ferretti, R. P., MacArthur, C. A., & Dowdy, N. S. (2000). The effects of elaborated goals on the argumentative writing of students with learning disabilities and their normally achieving peers. *Journal of Educational Psychology, 92*, 694-702.

Ferretti, R. P., & Okolo, C. M. (1996). Authenticity in learning: Multimedia design projects in the social studies for students with disabilities. *Journal of Learning Disabilities, 29*, 450-460.

Franzke, M., Kintsch, E., Caccamise, D., Johnson, M., & Dooley, S. (2005). Summary Street: Computer support for comprehension and writing. *Journal of Educational Computing Research, 33*, 53-80.

Garner, R., & Gillingham, M. G. (1996). *Internet communication in six classrooms: Conversations across time, space, and culture*. Mahwah, NJ: Erlbaum.

Goldberg, A., Russell, M., & Cook, A. (2003). The effect of computers on student writing: A metaanalysis of studies from 1992 to 2002. *Journal of Technology, Learning, and Assessment, 2*(1), 1-51.

Graham, S. (1990). The role of production factors in learning disabled students' compositions. *Journal of Educational Psychology, 82*, 781-791.

Graham, S. (2006). Strategy instruction and the teaching of writing: A meta-analysis. In C. A. MacArthur, S. Graham, & J. Fitzgerald (Eds.), *Handbook of writing research* (pp. 187-207). New York: Guilford.

Graham, S., Berninger, V. W., Abbott, R. D., Abbott, S. P., & Whitaker, D. (1997). Role of mechanics in composing of elementary school students: A new methodological approach. *Journal of Educational Psychology, 89*, 170-182.

Graham, S., & MacArthur, C. (1988). Improving learning disabled students' skills at revising essays produced on a word processor: Self-instructional strategy training. *Journal of Special Education, 22*, 133-152.

Graham, S., & Perin, D. (2007). *Writing next: Effective strategies to improve writing of adolescents in middle and high schools.* New York: Carnegie Corp.

Grimes, D., & Warschauer, M. (2006). *Automated scoring in the classroom.* Paper presented at the American Educational Research Association, San Francisco, CA, USA, April 7-11, 2006.

Handley-More, D., Deitz, J., Billingsley, F. F., & Coggins, T. E. (2003). Facilitating written work using computer word processing and word prediction. *American Journal of Occupational Therapy, 57,* 139-151.

Hayes, J. (2004). What triggers revision? In L. Allal, L. Chanqouy, & P. Largy (Eds.), *Revision: Cognitive and instructional processes* (Vol. 13, pp. 9-20). Boston, MA: Kluwer.

Higgins, E. L., & Raskind, M. H. (1995). Compensatory effectiveness of speech recognition on the written composition performance of postsecondary students with learning disabilities. *Learning Disability Quarterly, 18,* 159-174.

Karchmer, R. (2001). The journey ahead: Thirteen teachers report how the Internet influences literacy and literacy instruction in their k-12 classrooms. *Reading Research Quarterly, 36,* 442-466.

Kelly, A. E. (Ed.), (2003). Research as design. Introduction to theme issue: The role of design in educational research. *Educational Researcher, 32*(1), 3-4.

Klein, R., MacArthur, C. A., & Najera, K. (2007). *The effects of concept mapping software on middle school students' writing* (Unpublished manuscript).

Leijten, M. (2007). *Writing and speech recognition.* Utrecht: LOT, Netherlands Graduate School of Linguistics.

MacArthur, C. A. (1998). Word processing with speech synthesis and word prediction: Effects on the dialogue journal writing of students with learning disabilities. *Learning Disability Quarterly, 21,* 1-16.

MacArthur, C. A. (1999). Word prediction for students with severe spelling problems. *Learning Disability Quarterly, 22,* 158-172.

MacArthur, C. A. (2006). The effects of new technologies on writing and writing processes. In C. A. MacArthur, S. Graham, & J. Fitzgerald (Eds.), *Handbook of writing research* (pp. 248-262). New York: Guilford.

MacArthur, C. A., & Cavalier, A. (2004). Dictation and speech recognition technology as accommodations in large-scale assessments for students with learning disabilities. *Exceptional Children, 71,* 43-58.

MacArthur, C. A., Ferretti, R. P., Okolo, C. M., & Cavalier, A. R. (2001). Technology applications for students with literacy problems: A critical review. *Elementary School Journal, 101,* 273-301.

MacArthur, C., & Graham, S. (1987). Learning disabled students' composing under three methods of text production: Handwriting, word processing, and dictation. *Journal of Special Education, 21,* 22-42.

MacArthur, C. A., Graham, S., Haynes, J. A., & De La Paz, S. (1996). Spelling checkers and students with learning disabilities: Performance comparisons and impact on spelling. *Journal of Special Education, 30,* 35-57.

MacArthur, C. A., Schwartz, S. S., & Graham, S. (1991). Effects of a reciprocal peer revision strategy in special education classrooms. *Learning Disabilities Research and Practice, 6,* 201-210.

Manchester, W. (1988). *The last lion: Winston Spencer Churchill, alone 1932-1940.* New York: Brown & Co.

McKenna, M. C. (2006). Introduction: Trends and trajectories of literacy and technology in the new millennium. In M. C. McKenna, L. D. Labbo, R. D. Kieffer, & D. Reinking (Eds.), *International handbook of literacy and technology* (Vol. 2, pp. xi-xviii). Mahwah, NJ: Erlbaum.

McNaughton, D., Hughes, C., & Clark, K. (1997). The effect of five proofreading conditions on the spelling performance of college students with learning disabilities. *Journal of Learning Disabilities, 30,* 643-651.

Midgette, E., Haria, P., & MacArthur, C. A. (2008). The effects of content and audience awareness goals for revision on the persuasive essays of fifth- and eighth-grade students. *Reading and Writing: An International Journal, 21*, 131–151.

Nesbit, J. C., & Adesope, O. O. (2006). Learning with concept and knowledge maps: A meta-analysis. *Review of Educational Research, 76*, 413–448.

Newell, A. F., Arnott, J., Booth, L., Beattie, W., Brophy, B., & Ricketts, I. W. (1992). Effect of 'PAL' word prediction system on the quality and quantity of text generation. *Augmentative and Alternative Communication, 8*, 304–311.

Quinlan, T. (2004). Speech recognition technology and students with writing difficulties: Improving fluency. *Journal of Educational Psychology, 96*, 337–346.

Raskind, M. H., & Higgins, E. (1995). Effects of speech synthesis on the proofreading efficiency of postsecondary students with learning disabilities. *Learning Disability Quarterly, 18*, 141–158.

Reece, J. E., & Cummings, G. (1996). Evaluating speech-based composition methods: Planning, dictation, and the listening word processor. In C. M. Levy & S. Ransdell (Eds.), *The Science of writing* (pp. 361–380). Mahwah, NJ: Erlbaum.

Reinking, D., McKenna, M. C., Labbo, L. D., & Kieffer, R. D. (Eds.), (1998). *Handbook of literacy and technology*. Mahwah, NJ: Erlbaum.

Reynolds, T. H., & Bonk, C. J. (1996). Facilitating college writers' revisions within a generative-evaluative computerized prompting framework. *Computers and Composition, 13*(1), 93–108.

Russell, M. (1999). Testing writing on computers: A follow-up study comparing performance on computer and on paper. *Educational Policy Analysis Archives, 7*(20). from http://epaa.asu.edu/epaa/v7n20/

Russell, M., & Haney, W. (1997). Testing writing on computers: An experiment comparing student performance on tests conducted via computer and via paper-and-pencil. *Education Policy Analysis Archives, 5*(3). Retrieved from http://epaa.asu.edu/epaa/v5n3.html

Shermis, M., Burstein, J., & Leacock, C. (2006). Applications of computers in assessment and analysis of. In C. A. MacArthur, S. Graham, & J. Fitzgerald (Eds.), *Handbook of writing research* (pp. 403–416). New York: Guilford.

Steinhart, D. (2001). Summary Street: An intelligent tutoring system for improving student writing through the use of latent semantic analysis. Unpublished dissertation, Institute of Cognitive Science, University of Colorado, Boulder.

Stoddard, B., & MacArthur, C. A. (1993). A peer editor strategy: Guiding learning disabled students in response and revision. *Research in the Teaching of English, 27*, 76–103.

Sturm, J. M., & Rankin-Erickson, J. L. (2002). Effects of hand-drawn and computer-generated concept mapping on the expository writing of students with learning disabilities. *Learning Disabilities Research and Practice, 17*, 124–139.

Wade-Stein, D., & Kintsch, E. (2004). Summary Street: Interactive computer support for writing. *Cognition and Instruction, 22*, 333–362.

Zellermayer, M., Salomon, G., Globerson, T., & Givon, H. (1991). Enhancing writing-related metacognitions through a computerized writing partner. *American Educational Research Journal, 28*, 373–391.

NEW IN JANUARY 2010

British Journal of Educational Psychology

The
British
Psychological
Society

MONOGRAPH SERIES II:

Psychological Aspects of Education – Current Trends

NUMBER 7 – Understanding number development and difficulties

EDITED BY: *Richard Cowan, Matthew Saxton and Andrew Tolmie*

CONTENTS:

For more information, please see www.bps.org.uk/bjepmonographs

British Journal of Psychology

The
British
Psychological
Society

Special Issue – Celebrating a Century of Psychological Research

Five articles written by legendary figures and originally published in the *British Journal of Psychology*, reprinted alongside commentaries by contemporary world leaders.

Watson (1920) – *Is thought subvocal speech?*

With commentaries by Mark E. Bouton (University of Vermont) and Geoffrey Hall (University of York)

Bartlett (1925) – *The relationship between thinking and feeling*

With commentaries by Tim Dalgleish (University of Cambridge) and Brian Parkinson (University of Oxford)

Piaget (1928) – *Children's understanding of causality*

With commentaries by Michael J. Chandler (University of British Columbia) and Paul L. Harris (Harvard University)

Cattell (1946) – *The structure and measurement of personality and individual differences*

With commentaries by Philip L. Ackerman (Georgia Institute of Technology) and William Revelle (Northwestern University)

Gibson (1958) – *The theory of direct perception*

With commentaries by Brian Rogers (University of Oxford) and William H. Warren (Brown University)

Available to purchase at the one-off price of £25!

For more information please visit *www.bpsjournals.co.uk/journals/bjp*

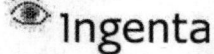